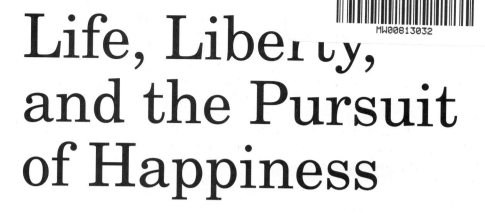

Life, Liberty, and the Pursuit of Happiness

DOCUMENTS IN AMERICAN HISTORY, VOLUME I: TO 1877

FIRST EDITION

Edited by
P. Scott Corbett
Oxnard College

Ronald C. Naugle
Nebraska Wesleyan University

Boston   Burr Ridge, IL   Dubuque, IA   Madison, WI   New York
San Francisco   St. Louis   Bangkok   Bogotá   Caracas   Kuala Lumpur
Lisbon   London   Madrid   Mexico City   Milan   Montreal   New Delhi
Santiago   Seoul   Singapore   Sydney   Taipei   Toronto

McGraw Hill Higher Education

LIFE, LIBERTY, AND THE PURSUIT OF HAPPINESS: DOCUMENTS IN AMERICAN HISTORY, VOLUME I: To 1877

Published by McGraw-Hill, a business unit of The McGraw-Hill Companies, Inc., 1221 Avenue of the Americas, New York, NY, 10020. Copyright © 2004 by The McGraw-Hill Companies, Inc. All rights reserved. No part of this publication may be reproduced or distributed in any form or by any means, or stored in a database or retrieval system, without the prior written consent of The McGraw-Hill Companies, Inc., including, but not limited to, in any network or other electronic storage or transmission, or broadcast for distance learning.

Some ancillaries, including electronic and print components, may not be available to customers outside the United States.

This book is printed on acid-free paper.

1 2 3 4 5 6 7 8 9 0 FGR/FGR 0 9 8 7 6 5 4 3

ISBN 0–07–283999–6

Publisher: *Lyn Uhl*
Senior sponsoring editor: *Steve Drummond*
Developmental editor: *Kimberly McGrath*
Marketing manager: *Katherine Bates*
Senior project manager: *Jean Hamilton*
Production supervisor: *Carol A. Bielski*
Associate designer: *George J. Kokkonas*
Permissions editor: *Connie Dowcett*
Cover design: *George J. Kokkonas*
Typeface: *10/12 Palatino*
Compositor: *GAC Indianapolis*
Printer: *Quebecor World Fairfield Inc.*

Library of Congress Control Number: 2003106815

www.mhhe.com

DEDICATION

Our families encouraged and supported us in many ways;
We dedicate this collection of primary works to them.

Tracy Cui Yi Corbett
who many years ago inspired a seeker for meaning to give up smoking
and content himself with a long life as a historian.

Robert P. Corbett, Christopher Daniels Corbett and
Daniel Cui Corbett
three individuals, two generations and one family
living history, studying history and making history.

Gretchen Rohn Naugle
who long ago took the boy out of the carnival
but left the carnival in the boy.

Meredith Susannah Rohn Naugle
a metallurgical engineer who learned from her unconventional parents
she could achieve anything she set her mind to.

CONTENTS

12 *Of Power and Pillars* 112

13 *Lone and Assembled Stars*   124

14 *Purity*   133

15 *Bleeding Kansas*   146

INTRODUCTION

The range of documents appropriate for the study of American history is exceptionally rich. In assembling this volume, we have again been impressed both by the degree to which documents provide a deeper understanding of the times and context within which they were produced, and by how they connect with both preceding and succeeding events. The experience has reinforced our conviction that documentary study is an invaluable means to understand the American past. Yet, the study of primary documents for this purpose raises substantive issues ranging from historical interpretation to pedagogy. Where to begin and what to include become the most important questions.

We begin with what we believe many Americans already know and/or think they understand about the major events and themes of our nation's history. It is, after all, the recognition of names, events, and issues related to the past and the perception of knowledge and understanding of those elements that underlies American behavior and provides a foundation for American identity. Identifying a thematic framework for selecting documents that furnish insight into the American past became the first task. "Life, liberty, and the pursuit of happiness" quickly emerged as such a touchstone. It is a phrase omnipresent in the minds of Americans during the course of the recent past and one that has become a litany for what America was, is, and still aims to be. It has served frequently as a prism, even *the* prism to understand and interpret events and issues that have affected the entire course of the American republican experiment.

"Life, liberty, and the pursuit of happiness" also serves for many Americans as the bedrock of inalienable rights that channels the energies of citizens and their government into performing duties and shouldering responsibilities. Yet, for all that Americans pack into the phrase, the document from which it is derived, the Declaration of Independence, had its own unique and particular purpose grounded in a specific time and place. By going to the source, the document itself, it becomes clear that the Declaration of Independence did not create a mechanism or instrument of government, as many commonly assume. Rather than create freedoms and establish the role of government for Americans, the phrase "life, liberty, and the pursuit of happiness" in the Declaration was a rhetorical device to justify revolution and inspire people to dedicate their "lives," fortunes and "sacred honor" to achieving an independent and self-sustaining government that would then and only then secure those rights. Nor did the Declaration of Independence create an independent United States of

America; it merely served notice of the intention of the colonial revolutionaries to lead their neighbors and countrymen to that end.

As the central organizing theme for this collection of documents, "life, liberty, and the pursuit of happiness" provided the context for both selecting documents and for relating them to the unfolding events of American history. Some variation of the theme has certainly propelled people to this continent well before independence and every day since. In that process the theme has acquired a malleability that has enabled it to be reshaped at various times by various players in the nation's historical drama.

Various communities and subcommunities on the North American stage have defined "life, liberty, and the pursuit of happiness" differently or had different expectations of how it should be applied or used to guide behavior and policy. Native Americans, African Americans, women, various religious bodies or sects, and certain classes have all seized upon the phrase as ammunition for their battles and struggles to have those terms meaningfully articulated and implemented according to their specific visions and desires. Going to the source to understand the fabric of American history must therefore include consideration of the perspectives of such groups as they struggled to alter or preserve their American landscape.

Finally, it has become obvious over the years that the typical classroom contains persons who differ in how they learn, what they find interesting, and in how they formulate and articulate their knowledge. Work on multiple learning styles pioneered by Howard Gardner in numerous experiments over the past thirty or so years has identified nine multiple intelligences including verbal/ linguistic, math/logical, visual/spatial, musical/rhythmic, bodily/kinesthetic, naturalist, interpersonal, intrapersonal, and existential. Accordingly though the selections in this book and the organization of the chapters will not strictly adhere to a format requiring equal representation of each of the nine intelligences. We have tried to include documents and other primary sources that might appeal to the broader range of intelligences that exist within today's classrooms. In some cases a single prompt may serve to release the energies and the inspiration of more than one of the intelligences. For example, the photographs from the Vietnam era (Chapter 30) might connect with anyone's visual/spatial intelligence, but they might also resonate with the interpersonal or the existential intelligences of students as they suggest, in more powerful ways, fundamental issues regarding human relations and the consequence of power.

The importance of learning what primary sources are and how their content becomes the choice historians make in formulating narratives and interpretations about the past may not seem self-evident these days. With so many historians laboring long and hard to create readable and stimulating accounts of the past, we may be lured into forgetting the importance of deriving some of our knowledge of our past from the original concepts and ideas grounded in their own time and place. It has been observed repeatedly over the years that the crucial rationale for the study of the nation's past is the need for citizens to become knowledgeable enough to utilize and shepherd their own freedoms and claims to the Declaration's inalienable rights of life, liberty, and the pursuit of happiness. Critical thinking, the desire and ability to go beyond the pat and convenient understandings placed before us, is an essential tool in effectively sustaining our democratic government and society. The importance of knowing something from firsthand experience and therefore being immune to attempts to delude or to shake that knowledge through subsequent interpretation and explanation of events was on General Dwight D. Eisenhower's mind in the spring of 1945. On April 12, 1945, Eisenhower, along with Generals George S. Patton and Omar Bradley, toured the death camp at Ohrdruf, a minor sub-camp of Buchenwald. "The things I saw beggar description," said Eisenhower on first viewing the death camps. "I made the visit deliberately, in order to be in a position to give firsthand evidence of these things if ever, in the future, there develops a tendency to charge these allegations merely to propaganda." We hope these volumes and the study of the documents they include will enable readers to develop the knowledge and skills that will deepen their appreciation, strengthen their understanding of and reinforce their commitment to the claims of the "self-evident truths" of life, liberty, and the pursuit of happiness.

To some degree the work that has gone into these two volumes represents the best of our combined experience and careers in studying and teaching history at various institutions and among different cultures across the United States and in other parts of the world. Sometimes the greatest insights into American history are derived from teaching it to non-Americans who ask questions and are puzzled about issues that would never arise in a classroom in Nebraska or California.

We are grateful for the time and effort our professors and mentors at the University of Kansas, in particular Norman Yetman, Walter Sedelow, Daniel Bays (now at Calvin College), David Katzman, and Theodore A. Wilson, invested in us and the good education we received there from them and others. We hope we have succeeded in passing the torch to the generations of students that have populated our classrooms.

As we have gathered, evaluated, and assembled the documents for these volumes, we have been blessed with the support of various people and institutions. We thank Nebraska Wesleyan University, which has long supported creative scholarship and innovative teaching. We are also grateful to Oxnard College, which has provided a home and secure base of operation as well, and to Tomas Salinas of the history department, who has been a valued friend and colleague.

In assembling these documents, a few individuals have assisted us in ways that were valued and appreciated. We owe a special debt of gratitude to Nebraska Wesleyan University Librarian, John Montag, skilled bibliographer, historian, and teaching colleague, who helped us identify and locate many of the documents we chose to include. At California State University, Northridge, two library assistants, Esperanza Bedolla and Milton Folk, were kind and cheerful in retrieving the documents and books we sought.

We are also grateful for the support and encouragement we have received from the people at McGraw-Hill. Steven Drummond, long-time friend and advocate for history throughout his distinguished career in the publishing industry, has remained firmly behind this project and continues to be a role model, mentor, and friend. Connie Dowcett's cheery disposition and tireless effort in handling much of the editing and permissions duties will always be appreciated and cherished, as will the grace and intelligence Kimberly McGrath lent to the project from beginning to end.

P. Scott Corbett
Camarillo, California

Ronald C. Naugle
Lincoln, Nebraska

1

Toward Distant Horizons

In the not too distant past, Americans were taught that their history began with the European discovery of lands in the Western Hemisphere. Even today, all too many Americans still learn or believe that the origin of American civilization can be traced to European mariners in search of a western trade route to Asia, who instead stumbled onto previously unknown lands in what quickly became known as the Americas. The ensuing conflict among nations for control of this newfound land resulted in British dominance on the North American continent, to be overthrown by their own subjects bent on independence, liberty, and their own peculiar definition of equality and the pursuit of happiness. Thus was born the United States.

While brief and tidy, such an explanation, of course, overlooks the fact that other, non-European peoples had already discovered the continent and made it their home for centuries. How, when, and from where Native Americans came to America is being sorted out by anthropologists, archeologists, and historians yet today. While many tenaciously hang on to the belief that Asians crossed over a frozen Bering Strait ice bridge some twelve thousand years ago, others profess the belief that peoples, propelled by southern trade winds, reached the South American continent on crude rafts centuries earlier. Regardless of the merits of either explanation, one fact is true. When Europeans became aware of the existence of this new world and were able to travel back and forth from Europe, immense changes began to take place in the world. The Americas changed, Europe changed, and Africa and Asia were caught in a historical vortex in ways that shaped the world today.

The first selection in this chapter addresses the appearance of Vikings in the Americas well before Portugal and Spain sent out a generation of mariners and adventurers to survey the world and claim empires. Though the Vikings did not proceed to incorporate North America into their political and cultural world, their early encounters with North America illustrate themes that will prevail for hundreds of years. Some of those themes include a wonderment at what is new, different, and unknown. They also include confrontation and conflict between "insiders" or residents and "outsiders" or invaders, and perhaps more importantly, similarities in the pattern that develops as individuals, political systems, and cultures become the first outsiders to encounter an environment unknown to the world from which they came and attempt to capitalize on it as the "first to arrive."

The next document suggests that Christopher Columbus had very specific ideas about how he was going to personally benefit from his energy and efforts. He negotiated a contract with Isabella and Ferdinand that attempted to define everyone's role, responsibilities, and potential gain from his voyages. Aware of Europe's previous encounters with Asia, Columbus must have anticipated the result of his own explorations of the same region. As the next document illustrates, however, he could not have anticipated what he actually encountered because he was going not to Asia, but to what for him was a new world.

Spanish motivations for launching their American enterprises have often been characterized by the slogan "For God, Glory, and Gold." Explorers capitalized on the glory in a practical manner by publishing accounts of discovery and adventure in the Americas. Of course, those who published the most or got their names before the public, claiming fame as the premier explorer and adventurer in the new world, stood to profit most from the sale of such accounts and receive additional credit as well. This was the case, perhaps, with Amerigo Vespucci, who appeared to receive considerable attention as one such American adventurer.

The successes of Portugal and Spain inspired other maritime nations as well, as evidenced in the passage describing a portion of Sir Francis Drake's circumnavigation of the world and his interlude along the coast of present-day California. Though his experiences are several centuries after those of Thorvald and almost a hundred years after Columbus, the mechanisms of first encounters remained similar.

Finally, there is the question: Why would people leave Europe to brave the perilous voyage and precariousness of life in the Americas? Of course, life was not necessarily happier, more stable, or safer in Europe during the time of the "Age of Discovery." To have been a French Huguenot living in Vassy in 1562 could easily have proved fatal. Indeed, religious conflict during the Thirty Years War (1618–1648) significantly depopulated the heart of Europe. Aside from religious strife, there were class conflicts and disease, even plagues, that might have convinced any number of people, such as those listed in the final table, that going to Peru or Mexico was no more risky than staying in Spain.

DOCUMENT 1.1

Thorvald Goes to Wineland

Now Thorvald, with the advice of his brother, Leif, prepared to make this voyage with thirty men. They put their ship in order, and sailed out to sea; and there is no account of their voyage before their arrival at Leifs-booths in Wineland. They laid up their ship there, and remained there quietly during the winter, supplying themselves with food by fishing. In the spring, however, Thorvald said that they should put their ship in order, and that a few men should take the after-boat, and proceed along the western coast, and explore [the region] thereabouts during the summer. They found it a fair, well-wooded country. It was but a short distance from the woods to the sea, and [there were] white sands, as well as great numbers of islands and shallows. They found neither dwelling of man nor lair of beast; but in one of the westerly islands they found a wooden building for the shelter of grain. They found no other trace of human handiwork; and they turned back, and arrived at Leifs-booths in the autumn. The following summer Thorvald set out toward the east with the ship, and along the northern coast. They were met by a high wind off a certain promontory, and were driven ashore there, and damaged the keel of their ship, and were compelled to remain there for a long time and repair the injury to their vessel. Then said Thorvald to his companions, "I propose that we raise the keel upon this cape, and call it 'Keelness'"; and so they did. Then they sailed away to the eastward off the land and into the mouth of the adjoining firth and to a headland, which projected into the sea there, and which was entirely covered with woods. They found an anchorage for their ship, and put out the gangway to the land; and Thorvald and all of his companions went ashore. "It is a fair region here," said he; "and here I should like to make my home." They then returned to the ship, and discovered on the sands, in beyond the headland, three mounds: they went up to these, and saw that they were three skin canoes with three men under each. They thereupon divided their party, and succeeded in seizing all of the men but one, who escaped with his canoe. They killed the eight men, and then ascended the headland again, and looked about them, and discovered within the firth certain hillocks, which they concluded must be habitations. They were then so overpowered with sleep that they could not keep awake, and all fell into a [heavy] slumber from which they were awakened by the sound of a cry uttered above them; and the words of the cry were these: "Awake, Thorvald, thou and all thy company, if thou wouldst save thy life; and board thy ship with all thy men, and sail with all speed from the

Source: American historical documents, 1000–1904: With introductions and notes. New York: P.F. Collier, c1910. The Harvard Classics v. 43. at http://www.fordham.edu/halsall/mod/1000Vinland.html.

land!" A countless number of skin canoes then advanced toward them from the inner part of the firth, whereupon Thorvald exclaimed, "We must put out the war-boards on both sides of the ship, and defend ourselves to the best of our ability, but offer little attack." This they did; and the Skrellings, after they had shot at them for a time, fled precipitately, each as best he could. Thorvald then inquired of his men whether any of them had been wounded, and they informed him that no one of them had received a wound. "I have been wounded in my armpit," says he. "An arrow flew in between the gunwale and the shield, below my arm. Here is the shaft, and it will bring me to my end. I counsel you now to retrace your way with the utmost speed. But me ye shall convey to that headland which seemed to me to offer so pleasant a dwelling-place: thus it may be fulfilled that the truth sprang to my lips when I expressed the wish to abide there for a time. Ye shall bury me there, and place a cross at my head, and another at my feet, and call it Crossness forever after." At that time Christianity had obtained in Greenland: Eric the Red died, however, before [the introduction of] Christianity.

Thorvald died; and, when they had carried out his injunctions, they took their departure, and rejoined their companions, and they told each other of the experiences which had befallen them. They remained there during the winter, and gathered grapes and wood with which to freight the ship. In the following spring they returned to Greenland, and arrived with their ship in Ericsfirth, where they were able to recount great tidings to Leif.

DOCUMENT 1.2

Articles of Agreement, April 17, 1492

First, that Your Highnesses as actual Sovereigns of the said Ocean Seas from henceforth appoint the said Christopher Columbus their Admiral in all those Islands and Mainlands which by his labor and industry shall be discovered or acquired in the said Ocean Seas during his life and, after his death, his heirs and successors from one to the other perpetually with all the Rights and Privileges pertaining to that Office and just as Don Alonso Enríques, our High Admiral of Castile and his predecessors in the said office, held it in their jurisdictions.

It so pleases Their Highnesses. JOHAN DE COLOMA.

Further, that Your Highnesses appoint the said Don Christopher their Viceroy and Governor-General in all the said Islands and Mainlands which, as has been said, he may discover or acquire in the said Seas, and that for the Government of each and every one of them he may name three persons for each Office and that Your Highnesses may take and choose the one most suitable to your service, and thus the lands which Our Lord allows him to discover and acquire in the service of Your Highnesses will be better governed.

Source: Samuel Eliot Morrison, ed. and trans., *Journals and Other Documents on the Life and Voyages of Christopher Columbus* (New York: Heritage Press, 1963), pp. 27–28.

Item, that of all Merchandise whatsoever, whether Pearls, Precious Stones, Gold, Silver, Spiceries, and other Things and Merchandise of whatever kind, name, or description that may be, which may be bought, bartered, found, acquired, or obtained within the limits of the said Admiralty, Your Highnesses grant from henceforth to the said Don Christopher and decree that he take and keep for himself the tenth part of the whole after all expenses have been deducted, so that of all that remains free and clear he may have and take the tenth part for himself, and dispose of it as he pleases; the other nine parts remaining for Your Highnesses.

Further, that, if on account of the goods that he brings from the said Islands and Lands which, as has been said, may be acquired or discovered; or if [on account] of goods obtained in exchange for these from other merchants here, any suit arise in the place in which the said trade and transaction shall occur and take place; and if by the superiority of his office of Admiral it appertains to him to take jurisdiction over the said suit, it pleases Your Highnesses that he or his representative and no other magistrate take jurisdiction of the said suit and thus it is provided from henceforth.

DOCUMENT 1.3

Sunday, October 21, 1492

At ten o'clock I arrived here at the Cape of the Islet and anchored, and so did the caravels; and after having eaten I went ashore, where there was no other village but a single house, in which I found nobody, so that I believe that they had fled through fear, because they had left all their household gear. I allowed nothing to be touched, but set out with the captains and people to see the island. If the others already seen are very beautiful and green and fertile, this is much more so, and the large groves are very green. Here are some great lagoons, and around them, on the banks, the verdure is marvellous; and round about there is a marvellous amount of woodland, the grass like in April in Andalusia, and the singing of the little birds such that it would seem that man would never wish to leave here; and the flocks of parrots obscured the sun, and big and little birds of all sorts, and so different from ours that it is marvellous. Furthermore—it has trees of a thousand kinds, and all have their kinds of fruit, and all so fragrant that it is marvellous; and I had the greatest chagrin in the world not to recognize them, for I am well assured that they are all things of value; and I bring specimens of them and also of the plants. And thus walking around one of the lagoons I saw a reptile which we killed, and I bring the skin to Your Highnesses. It, as soon as we saw it, slid into the lagoon, and we followed it within, because it wasn't very deep, until we killed it with lances. It is 7 palms long, I believe there are many like it in these islands. Here I came upon aloes, and tomorrow I have decided to take aboard 10 quintals of it, for they tell me it is worth much.

Source: Samuel Eliot Morrison, ed. and trans., *Journals and Other Documents on the Life and Voyages of Christopher Columbus* (New York: Heritage Press, 1963), pp. 77–78.

Also while going in search of very good water, we came upon a village near here, half a league from my anchorage, and the people thereof, when they heard us, all fled and left their houses, and hid their clothing and whatever they had in the woods. I allowed not a thing to be touched, not even the value of a pin. Presently there came to us some of their men, and one came right up to us. I gave him some hawk's bells and glass beads, and he rested very content and very happy; and in order to strengthen the friendship and ask them for something I asked him to get water; and they, after I had gone on board the ship, came down to the beach with their calabashes filled and rejoiced in giving it to me, and I ordered them to be given another string of little glass beads, and they said that tomorrow they would come here. I sought here to fill up all the containers on the ships with water; and finally, if time permits, I shall leave to circumnavigate this island until I may have speech with this king and see if I can obtain from him the gold that I heard he has, and afterwards to depart for another much larger island which I believe must be Japan, according to the description of these Indians whom I carry, and which they call *Colba*, in which they say that there are ships and sailors both many and great and beyond this is another island which they call *Bofio*, which also they say is very big and the others which are between we shall see as we pass, and according as I shall find a collection of gold or spicery, I shall decide what I have to do. But in any case I am determined to go to the mainland and to the city of *Quisay* and to present Your Highnesses' letters to the Grand Khan, and to beg a reply and come home with it.

DOCUMENT 1.4

Literature of Discovery

Published Reports of Early Explorers

Explorer or Exploration	Number of Editions or Issues	Period Covered	Average per Year
Columbus	22	1493–1522	0.73
Vespucci	60	ca. 1502–1529 (?)	2.14
Cortes	18	1522–1532	1.64
Others[a]	30	1504–1530	1.11

[a]This includes accounts from Arias, Cabral, Diaz, Grijalva, Magellan, Valesquez, material on the discovery of Brazil not attributed to any specific author, and the composite history of Peter Martyr.

Source: Table prepared from material in Michael J. B. Allen and Robert L. Benson, eds., *First Images of America: The Impact of the New World on the Old*, vol. 2 (Berkeley: University of California Press, 1976), pp. 538, 550.

DOCUMENT 1.5

Sir Francis Drake on the California Coast, 1579

The 3 day following, viz., the 21, our ship having received a leake at sea, was brought to anchor neerer the shoare, that, her goods being landed, she might be repaired; but for that we were to prevent any danger that might chance against our safety, our Generall first of all landed his men, with all necessary provision, to build tents and make a fort for the defence of our selves and goods: and that wee might under the shelter of it with more safety (what ever should befall) end our businesse; which when the people of the countrey perceived us doing, as men set on fire to war in defence of their countrie, in great hast and companies, with such weapons as they had, they came downe unto us, and yet with no hostile meaning or intent to hurt us: standing, when they drew neere, as men ravished in their mindes, with the sight of such things as they never had seene or heard of before that time: their errand being rather with submission and feare to worship us as Gods, then to have any warre with us as with mortall men. Which thing, as it did partly shew itselfe at that instant, so did it more and more manifest itself afterwards, during the whole time of our abode amongst them. At this time, being willed by signes to lay from them their bowes and arrowes, they did as they were directed, and so did all the rest, as they came more and more by companies unto them, growing in a little while to a great number, both of men and women.

To the intent, therefore, that this peace which they themselves so willingly sought might, without any cause of the breach thereof on our part given, be continued, and that wee might with more safety and expedition end our businesses in quiet, our Generall, with all his company, used all meanes possible gently to intreate them, bestowing upon each of them liberally good and necessary things to cover their nakednesse; withall signifying unto them we were no Gods, but men, and had neede of such things to cover our owne shame; teaching them to use them to the same ends, for which cause also wee did eate and drinke in their presence, giving them to understand that without that wee could not live, and therefore were but men as well as they.

Notwithstanding nothing could perswade them, nor remove that opinion which they had conceived of us, that wee should be Gods.

In recompence of those things which they had received of us, as shirts, linnen cloth, etc., they bestowed upon our Generall, and diverse of our company, diverse things, as feathers, cawles of networke, the quivers of their arrowes, made of fawne skins, and the very skins of beasts that their women wore upon their bodies. Having thus had their fill of this times visiting and beholding of us, they departed with joy to their houses, which houses are digged round within the earth, and have from the uppermost brimmes of the circle clefts of wood set up, and joined close together at the top, like our spires on the steeple

Source: Henry S. Burrage, ed., *Early English and French Voyages: Chiefly from Hakluyt, 1534–1608* (New York: Charles Scribner's Sons, 1930), pp. 159–61, 170–73.

of a Church; which being covered with earth, suffer no water to enter, and are very warme; the doore in the most part of them performes the office also of a chimney to let out the smoake: its made in bignesse and fashion like to an ordinary scuttle in a ship, and standing slopewise: their beds are the hard ground, onely with rushes strewed upon it, and lying round about the house, have their fire in the middest, which by reason that the house is but low vaulted, round, and close, giveth a marvelous reflexion to their bodies to heate the same. . . .

They are a people of a tractable, free, and loving nature, without guile or treachery; their bowes and arrowes (their only weapons, and almost all their wealth) they use very skillfully, but yet not to do any great harme with them, being by reason of their weaknesse more fit for children then for men, sending the arrowes neither farre off nor with any great force: and yet are the men commonly so strong of body, that that which 2 or 3 of our men could hardly beare, one of them would take upon his backe, and without grudging carrie it easily away, up hill and downe hill an English mile together: they are also exceeding swift in running, and of long continuance, the use whereof is so familiar with them, that they seldome goe, but for the most part runne. One thing we observed in them with admiration, that if at any time they chanced to see a fish so neere the shoare that they might reach the place without swimming, they would never, or very seldome, misse to take it.

After that our necessary businesses were well dispatched, our Generall, with his gentlemen and many of his company, made a journy up into the land, to see the manner of their dwelling, and to be the better acquainted with the nature and commodities of the country. There houses were all such as we have formerly described, and being many of them in one place, made severall villages here and there. The inland we found to be farre different from the shoare, a goodly country, and fruitfull soyle, stored with many blessings fit for the use of man: infinite was the company of very large and fat Deere which there we sawe by thousands, as we supposed, in a heard; besides a multitude of a strange kinde of Conies, by farre exceeding them in number: their heads and bodies, in which they resemble other Conies, are but small; his tayle, like the tayle of a Rat, exceeding long; and his feet like the pawes of a Want or moale; under his chinne, on either side, he hath a bagge, into which he gathereth his meate, when he hath filled his belly abroade, that he may with it, either feed his young, or feed himselfe when he lists not to travaile from his burrough; the people eate their bodies, and make great account of their skinnes, for their kings holidaies coate was made of them.

This country our Generall named *Albion*, and that for two causes; the one in respect of the white bancks and cliffes, which lie toward the sea; the other, that it might have some affinity, even in name also, with our own country, which was sometimes so called.

Before we went from thence, our Generall caused to be set up a monument of our being there, as also of her majesties and successors right and title to that kingdome; namely, a plate of brasse, fast nailed to a great and firme poste; whereon is engraven her graces name, and the day and yeare of our arrivall there, and of the free giving up of the province and kingdome, both by the king and people, into her majesties hands: together with her highnesse picture and armes, in a piece of six-pence currant English monie, shewing itselfe by a hole made of purpose through the plate; underneath was likewise engraven the name of our Generall, etc.

The Spaniards never had any dealing, or so much as set a foote in this country, the utmost of their discoveries reaching onely to many degrees Southward of this place.

And now, as the time of our departure was perceived by them to draw nigh, so did the sorrowes and miseries of this people seeme to themselves to increase upon them, and the more certaine they were of our going away, the more doubtful they shewed themselves what they might doe; so that we might easily judge that that joy (being exceeding great) wherewith they received us at our first arrivall, was cleane drowned in their excessive sorrow for our departing. For they did not onely loose on a sudden all mirth, joy, glad countenance, pleasant speeches, agility of body, familiar rejoycing one with another, and all pleasure what ever flesh and blood might bee delighted in, but with sighes and sorrowings, with heavy hearts and grieved minds, they powred out wofull complaints and moanes, with bitter teares and wringing of their hands, tormenting themselves. And as men refusing all comfort, they onely accounted themselves as cast-awayes, and those whom the gods were about to forsake: so that nothing we could say or do, was able to ease them of their so heavy a burthen, or to deliver them from so desperate a straite, as our leaving of them did seeme to them that it would cast them into.

Howbeit, seeing they could not still enjoy our presence, they (supposing us to be gods indeed) thought it their duties to intreate us that, being absent, we would yet be mindfull of them, and making signes of their desires that in time to come wee would see them againe, they stole upon us a sacrifice, and set it on fire erre we were aware, burning therein a chaine and a bunch of feathers. We laboured by all meanes possible to withhold or withdraw them, but could not prevaile, till at last we fell to prayers and singing of Psalmes, whereby they were allured immediatly to forget their folly, and leave their sacrifice unconsumed, suffering the fire to go out; and imitating us in all our actions, they fell a lifting of their eyes and hands to heaven, as they saw us do.

The 23 of July they took a sorrowfull farewell of us, but being loath to leave us, they presently ranne to the top of the hils to keepe us in their sight as long as they could, making fires before and behind, and on each side of them, burning therein (as is to be supposed) sacrifices at our departure.

DOCUMENT 1.6

Spanish Adventurers

Spanish Emigrants to the Indies, 1595–98

	Males	Females	Couples	"Don"	"Criados"	Work	Education	Wives Joining Husbands	Widows	Children
				69	718			30	48	522
Craftsmen						43				
Merchants						27				
Royal officials						8				
Notaries [*escribanos*]						4				
Pharmacists [*boticarios*]						2				
Physician						1				
Book seller						1				
Bachilleres							8			
Licenciados							10			
Doctores							2			
Going to:										
Peru	541	274								
Mexico	404	188								
Cartagena & Panama	158	120								
Cuba	138	19								
Total	1241	601	238							

Source: From Michael J. B. Allen and Robert L. Benson, eds., *First Images of America: The Impact of the New World on the Old,* vol. 2, (Berkeley: University of California Press, 1976), pp. 723–735.

2

Plantation Colonies

The vast wealth that Spain quickly realized from her American adventures helped to popularize and inspire a series of similar colonial enterprises. As the latecomers discovered, though, gold nuggets were not just lying about waiting to be harvested; nor were there hundreds of Native American societies with vast silver resources patiently awaiting the Europeans' arrival to be conquered and exploited. Indeed, what there was to be exploited was ordinary, yet nonetheless potentially valuable: fertile land and forests abounding with wildlife, timber products, and other natural resources. And as with the initial Spanish enterprises, little more than negotiated contracts designed to alleviate any responsibility of the Spanish crown for the financial burden of colonial enterprise, monarchs and societies from other countries had to find ways to send out forays on limited budgets. In so doing, the English seized upon the concept of the plantation, which had been used to organize the English conquest of Ireland. Private individuals received the right or privilege to develop and exploit resources. Thus was the case with Virginia, the first permanent English colony in North America.

Eventually the British realized that the real potential of the Americas lay in establishing agricultural settlements with English subjects permanently residing on and working vast tracts of land. With the success and profitability of the model in the sugar islands of the Caribbean, the plantation took on the characteristics of agrarian factories specializing in producing cash crops for a widening world market. Likewise, Virginia discovered tobacco as an avenue to wealth and profits. With the seemingly inexhaustible land resources available in some colonies, the issue for the British quickly became the need for enough workers to turn land into profits. One solution was, of course, African slavery. In the second section of this chapter the capture of Olaudah Equiano reveals the harsh realities of being stolen from one's home—never to return.

The English were not the only ones interested in the potential benefits to be gained from North America. The Dutch sought to develop a space for themselves and their agricultural and commercial activity in North America. As illustrated in the next document, the servants in Maryland, not far distant from New Amsterdam, seem to have made a decent life for themselves through their American adventure.

Along with the hands and the hearts of servants, slaves, and masters came their minds and cultures. There were those who saw in the Americas an opportunity to experiment with the organization of human society to achieve a better, more humane, and more effective form of government. This is evident in the **Fundamental Constitutions of Carolina,** *part of which were drafted by the English political philosopher John Locke. Seeds of democracy were sown in British North America, some of which would later grow and blossom in ways unanticipated by the original gardeners.*

Finally, George Washington's letter about his affairs illustrates that, after 150 years or so of British colonial activity in Virginia, a healthy society had evolved. He shared the ongoing business concerns of many plantation owners and was not adverse to soliciting from the motherland publications that might help him with the tasks of husbandry.

DOCUMENT 2.1

The Second Charter of Virginia, May 23, 1609

AND forasmuch as the good and prosperous Success of the said Plantation, cannot but chiefly depend next under the Blessing of God, and the Support of our Royal Authority, upon the provident and good Direction of the whole Enterprise, by a careful and understanding Council, and that it is not convenient, that all the Adventurers shall be so often drawn to meet and assemble, as shall foe requisite for them to have Meetings and Conference about the Affairs thereof; Therefore we Do ORDAIN, establish and confirm, that there shall be perpetually one COUNCIL here resident, according to the Tenour of our former Letters-Patents; Which Council shall have a Seal for the better Government and Administration of the said Plantation, besides the legal Seal of the Company or Corporation, as in our former Letters-Patents is also expressed. . . .

AND further, of our special Grace, certain Knowledge, and mere Motion, for Us, our Heirs and Successors, we do, by these Presents, GIVE and GRANT full Power and Authority to our said Council here resident, as well at this present time, as hereafter from time to time, to nominate, make, constitute, ordain and confirm, by such Name or Names, Stile or Stiles, as to them shall seem good, And likewise to revoke, discharge, change, and alter, as well all and singular Governors, Officers, and Ministers, which already have been made, as

Source: The Federal and State Constitutions Colonial Charters, and Other Organic Laws of the States, Territories, and Colonies Now or Heretofore Forming the United States of America, Compiled and Edited Under the Act of Congress of June 30, 1906 by Francis Newton Thorpe (Washington, DC: Government Printing Office, 1909). Available at http://www.yale.edu/lawweb/avalon/states/va02.htm.

also which hereafter shall be by them thought fit and needful to be made or used for the Government of the said Colony and Plantation:

AND also to make, ordain, and establish all Manner of Orders, Laws, Directions, Instructions, Forms and Ceremonies of Government and Magistracy, fit and necessary for and concerning the Government of the said Colony and Plantation; And the same, at all Times hereafter, to abrogate, revoke, or change, not only within the Precincts of the said Colony, but also upon the Seas, in going and coming to and from the said Colony, as they in their good Discretion, shall think to be fittest for the Good of the Adventurers and inhabitants there. . . .

Also we do for Us, our Heirs and Successors, DECLARE by these Presents, that all and every the Persons being our Subjects, which shall go and inhabit within the said Colony and Plantation, and every their Children and Posterity, which shall happen to be born within any of the Limits thereof, shall HAVE and ENJOY all Liberties, Franchizes, and Immunities of Free Denizens and natural Subjects within any of our other Dominions to all Intents and Purposes, as if they had been abiding and born within this our Realm of England, or in any other of our Dominions. . . .

AND forasmuch as it shall be necessary for all such our loving Subject as shall inhabit within the said Precincts of Virginia aforesaid, to determine to live together in the Fear and true Worship of Almighty God, Christian Peace and Civil Quietness each with other, whereby every one may with more Safety, Pleasure and Profit enjoy that whereunto they shall attain with great Pain and Peril; WE for Us, our Heirs, and Successors are likewise pleased and contented, and by these Presents do GIVE and GRANT unto the said Treasurer and Company, and their Successors, and to such Governors, Officers, and Ministers, as shall be by our said Council constituted and appointed according to the Natures and Limits of their Offices and Places respectively, that they shall and may from Time to Time, for ever hereafter, within the said Precincts of Virginia, or in the way by Seas thither and from thence, have full and absolute Power and Authority to correct, punish, pardon, govern, and rule all such the Subjects of Us, our Heires, and Successors as shall from Time to Time adventure themselves in any Voyage thither, or that shall at any Time hereafter, inhabit in the Precincts and Territories of the said Colony as aforesaid, according to such Orders, Ordinances, Constitutions, Directions, and Instructions, as by our said Council as aforesaid, shall be established; And in Defect thereof in case of Necessity, according to the good Discretions of the said Governor and Officers respectively, as well in Cases capital and criminal, as civil, both Marine and other; So always as the said Statutes, Ordinances and Proceedings as near as conveniently may be, be agreeable to the Laws, Statutes, Government, and Policy of this our Realm of England.

AND we do further of our special Grace, certain Knowledge, and mere Motion, GRANT, DECLARE, and ORDAIN, that such principal Governor, as from Time to Time shall duly and lawfully be authorized and appointed in Manner and Form in these Presents heretofore expressed, shall have full Power and Authority, to use and exercise Martial Law in Cases of Rebellion or Mutiny, in as large and ample Manner as our Lieutenants in our Counties within this our

Realm of England have or ought to have, by Force of their Commissions of Lieutenancy.

AND furthermore, if any Person or Persons, Adventurers or Planters of the said Colony, or any other at any Time or Times hereafter, shall transport any Monies, Goods, or Merchandises, out of any of our Kingdoms with a Pretence or Purpose to land, sell, or otherwise dispose of the same within the Limits or Bounds of the Said Colony, and yet nevertheless being at Sea, or after he hath landed: within any part of the said Colony, shall carry the same into any other foreign Country with a Purpose there to sell and dispose thereof; That then all the Goods and Chattels of the said Person or Persons so offending, and transported, together with the Ship or Vessel wherein such Transportation was made, shall be forfeited to Us, our Heirs, and Successors.

DOCUMENT 2.2

Capture of Olaudah Equiano

One day, when all our people were gone out to their works as usual, and only I and my dear sister were left to mind the house, two men and a woman got over our walls, and in a moment seized us both, and, without giving us time to cry out, or make resistance, they stopped our mouths, and ran off with us into the nearest wood. Here they tied our hands, and continued to carry us as far as they could, till night came on, when we reached a small house, where the robbers halted for refreshment, and spent the night. We were then unbound, but were unable to take any food; and, being quite overpowered by fatigue and grief, our only relief was some sleep, which allayed our misfortune for a short time. The next morning we left the house, and continued travelling all the day. For a long time we had kept the woods, but at last we came into a road which I believed I knew. I had now some hopes of being delivered; for we had advanced but a little way before I discovered some people at a distance, on which I began to cry out for their assistance; but my cries had no other effect than to make them tie me faster and stop my mouth, and then they put me into a large sack. They also stopped my sister's mouth, and tied her hands; and in this manner we proceeded till we were out of sight of these people. When we went to rest the following night, they offered us some victuals, but we refused it; and the only comfort we had was in being in one another's arms all that night, and bathing each other with our tears. But alas! we were soon deprived of even the small comfort of weeping together.

The next day proved a day of greater sorrow than I had yet experienced; for my sister and I were then separated, while we lay clasped in each other's arms. It was in vain that we besought them not to part us; she was torn from me, and immediately carried away, while I was left in a state of distraction not to be described. I cried and grieved continually; and for several days did not eat

Source: From Olaudah Equiano, *The Interesting Narrative of the Life of Olaudah Equiano: Written by Himself*, ed. Robert J. Allison (Boston: Bedford Books, 1995), pp. 47–55.

anything but what they forced into my mouth. At length, after many days' travelling, during which I had often changed masters, I got into the hands of a chieftain, in a very pleasant country. This man had two wives and some children, and they all used me extremely well, and did all they could do to comfort me; particularly the first wife, who was something like my mother. Although I was a great many days' journey from my father's house, yet these people spoke exactly the same language with us. This first master of mine, as I may call him, was a smith, and my principal employment was working his bellows, which were the same kind as I had seen in my vicinity. . . .

All the nations and people I had hitherto passed through resembled our own in their manners, customs, and language; but I came at length to a country, the inhabitants of which differed from us in all those particulars. I was very much struck with this difference, especially when I came among a people who did not circumcise, and ate without washing their hands. They cooked also in iron pots, and had European cutlasses and cross bows, which were unknown to us, and fought with their fists among themselves. Their women were not so modest as ours, for they ate, and drank, and slept with their men. But above all, I was amazed to see no sacrifices or offerings among them. In some of those places the people ornamented themselves with scars, and likewise filed their teeth very sharp. They wanted sometimes to ornament me in the same manner, but I would not suffer them; hoping that I might some time be among a people who did not thus disfigure themselves, as I thought they did. At last I came to the banks of a large river which was covered with canoes, in which the people appeared to live with their household utensils, and provisions of all kinds. I was beyond measure astonished at this, as I had never before seen any water larger than a pond or a rivulet; and my surprise was mingled with no small fear when I was put into one of these canoes, and we began to paddle and move along the river. We continued going on thus till night, and when we came to land, and made fires on the banks, each family by themselves; some dragged their canoes on shore, others stayed and cooked in theirs, and laid in them all night. Those on the land had mats, of which they made tents, some in the shape of little houses; in these we slept; and after the morning meal, we embarked again and proceeded as before. I was often very much astonished to see some of the women, as well as the men, jump into the water, dive to the bottom, come up again, and swim about.

Thus I continued to travel, sometimes by land, sometimes by water, through different countries and various nations, till, at the end of six or seven months after I had been kidnapped, I arrived at the sea coast. It would be tedious and uninteresting to relate all the incidents which befell me during this journey, and which I have not yet forgotten; of the various hands I passed through, and the manners and customs of all the different people among whom I lived—I shall therefore only observe, that in all the places where I was, the soil was exceedingly rich; the pumpkins, eadas, plantains, yams, &c. &c., were in great abundance, and of incredible size. There were also vast quantities of different gums, though not used for any purpose, and everywhere a great deal of tobacco. The cotton even grew quite wild, and there was plenty of red-wood. I saw no mechanics whatever in all the way, except such as I have mentioned. The chief employment in all these countries was agriculture, and both the males and females, as with us, were brought up to it, and trained in the arts of war.

The first object which saluted my eyes when I arrived on the coast, was the sea, and a slave ship, which was then riding at anchor, and waiting for its cargo. These filled me with astonishment, which was soon converted into terror, when I was carried on board. I was immediately handled, and tossed up to see if I were sound, by some of the crew; and I was now persuaded that I had gotten into a world of bad spirits, and that they were going to kill me. Their complexions, too, differing so much from ours, their long hair, and the language they spoke (which was very different from any I had ever heard), united to confirm me in this belief. Indeed, such were the horrors of my views and fears at the moment, that, if ten thousand worlds had been my own, I would have freely parted with them all to have exchanged my condition with that of the meanest slave in my own country. When I looked round the ship too, and saw a large furnance [sic] of copper boiling, and a multitude of black people of every description chained together, every one of their countenances expressing dejection and sorrow, I no longer doubted of my fate; and, quite overpowered with horror and anguish, I fell motionless on the deck and fainted. When I recovered a little, I found some black people about me, who I believed were some of those who had brought me on board, and had been receiving their pay; they talked to me in order to cheer me, but all in vain. I asked them if we were not to be eaten by those white men with horrible looks, red faces, and long hair. They told me I was not, and one of the crew brought me a small portion of spirituous liquor in a wine glass; but being afraid of him, I would not take it out of his hand. One of the blacks therefore took it from him and gave it to me, and I took a little down my palate, which, instead of reviving me, as they thought it would, threw me into the greatest consternation at the strange feeling it produced, having never tasted any such liquor before. Soon after this, the blacks who brought me on board went off, and left me abandoned to despair.

DOCUMENT 2.3

Information Relative to Taking up Land in New Netherland

In the Form of Colonies or Private Boweries (1650)
Cornelius Van Tienhoven, Secretary of the Province

If any man be disposed to begin, either by himself or others, colonies, boweries, or plantations in New Netherland, lying in the latitude of one and forty degrees and a half, he shall first have to inform himself fully of the situation of the lands lying on rivers, havens, and bays, in order thus to select the most suitable and particularly the most convenient grounds. It is therefore to be borne in mind that the lands in New Netherland are not all level and flat and adapted to raising of

Source: Available at www.whc.neu.edu/prototype/texts/cose1_1t.html.

grain, inasmuch as they are, with the exception of some few flats, generally covered with timber [and] in diverse places also with large and small stones.

In order, then, first to describe those lands which are actually the most convenient and best adapted for early occupancy—where and how [they are] located—I shall enumerate the following places, and commend the remainder to the consideration of proprietors of this country.

I begin, then, at the most easterly corner of Long Island, being a point situated on the main ocean [and] enclosing within, [to the] westward, a large inland sea adorned with diverse fair havens and bays fit for all sorts of craft. This point is entirely covered with trees, without any flats, and is somewhat hilly and stony; [it is] very convenient for cod fishing, which is most successfully followed by the natives during the season. This point is also well adapted to secure the trade of the Indians in wampum (the mine of New Netherland), since in and about the abovementioned sea and the islands therein situated lie the cockles whereof wampum is made—from which great profit could be realized by those who would plant a colony or hamlet on the aforesaid hook for the cultivation of the land, for raising all sorts of cattle, for fishing, and the wampum trade. It would be necessary, in such [a] case, to settle on the aforesaid land some persons thoroughly conversant with agriculture and others with the fishery.

Oyster Bay [is] so called from the great abundance of fine and delicate oysters which are found there. This bay is about a short mile across (or in width, at the mouth), deep and navigable, without either rocks or sands. [It] runs westward in proportion and divides itself into two rivers, which are broad and clear; on which said rivers lie fine maize lands, formerly cultivated by the Indians, some of which they still work. (They could be had for a trifle.) This land is situated on such a beautiful bay and rivers that it could at little cost be converted into good farms fit for the plow; there are here, also, some fine hay valleys.

DOCUMENT 2.4

"They Live Well in the Time of their Service"

George Alsop Writes of Servants in Maryland, 1663
George Alsop

Now those Servants which come over into this Province, being Artificers [craftsmen], they never (during their Servitude) work in the Fields, or do any other imployment save that which their Handicraft and Mechanick endeavours are capable of putting them upon, and are esteem'd as well by their Masters, as those that imploy them, above measure. He that's a Tradesman here in *Mary-Land* (though a Servant), lives as well as most common Handicrafts do in *London*, though they may want something of that Liberty which Freemen have, to go and come at their pleasure. . . . He that lives in the nature of a Servant in this

Source: From George Alsop, *A Character of the Province of Maryland* (1666), ed. Newton D. Mereness (Cleveland: Burrows Brothers Co., 1902), 52–61. Posted at historymatters.gmu.edu/d/5815/.

Province, must serve but four years by the Custom of the Country; and when the expiration of his time speaks him a Freeman, there's a law in the Province, that enjoyns his Master whom he hath served to give him Fifty Acres of Land, Corn to serve him a whole year, three Sutes of Apparel, with things necessary to them, and Tools to work withall; so that they are no sooner free, but they are ready to set up for themselves, and when once entred, they live passingly well.

The Women that go over into this Province as Servants, have the best luck here as in any place of the world besides; for they are no sooner on shoar, but they are courted into a Copulative Matrimony, which some of them (for aught I know) had they not come to such a Market with their Virginity, might have kept it by them untill it had been mouldy, unless they had to let it out by a yearly rent to some of the Inhabitants of *Lewknors-lane* [a disreputable neighborhood in London]. . . . Men have not altogether so good luck as Women in this kind, or natural preferment, without they be good Rhetoricians, and well vers'd in the Art of perswasion then (probably) they may ryvet themselves in the time of their Servitude into the private and reserved favour of their Mistress, if Age speak their Master deficient.

In short, touching the Servants of this Province, they live well in the time of their Service, and by their restrainment in that time, they are made capable of living much better when they come to be free; which in several other parts of the world I have observed, That after some servants have brought their indented and limited time to a just and legal period by Servitude, they have been much more incapable of supporting themselves from sinking into the Gulf of a slavish, poor, fettered, and intangled life, then all the fastness of their prefixed time did involve them in before.

DOCUMENT 2.5

The Fundamental Constitutions of Carolina, March 1, 1669

Our sovereign lord the King having, out of his royal grace and bounty, granted unto us the province of Carolina, with all the royalties, properties, jurisdictions, and privileges of a county palatine, as large and ample as the county palatine of Durham, with other great privileges; for the better settlement of the government of the said place, and establishing the interest of the lords proprietors with equality and without confusion; and that the government of this province may be made most agreeable to the monarchy under which we live and of which this province is a part; and that we may avoid erecting a numerous democracy, we, the lords and proprietors of the province aforesaid, have agreed to this following form of government, to be perpetually established amongst us, unto which we do oblige ourselves, our heirs and successors, in the most binding ways that can be devised.

Source: From Francis Newton Thorpe, ed., *The Federal and State Constitutions, Colonial Charters, and Other Organic Laws of the States, Territories, and Colonies Now or Heretofore Forming the United States of America* (Washington, DC: GPO, 1909). Available at www.yale.edu/lawweb/avalon/states/nc05.htm/.

* * *

Seventy-one. There shall be a parliament, consisting of the proprietors or their deputies, the landgraves, and caziques, and one freeholder out of every precinct, to be chosen by the freeholders of the said precinct, respectively. They shall sit all together in one room, and have every member one vote.

Seventy-two. No man shall be chosen a member of parliament who has less than five hundred acres of freehold within the precinct for which he is chosen; nor shall any have a vote in choosing the said member that hath less than fifty acres of freehold within the said precinct.

* * *

Seventy-six. No act or order of parliament shall be of any force, unless it be ratified in open parliament, during the same session, by the palatine or his deputy, and three more of the lords proprietors or their deputies; and then not to continue longer in force but until the next biennial parliament, unless in the mean time it be ratified under the hands and seals of the palatine himself, and three more of the lords proprietors themselves, and by their order published at the next biennial parliament.

Seventy-seven. Any proprietor or his deputy may enter his protestation against any act of the parliament, before the palatine or his deputy's consent be given as aforesaid, if he shall conceive the said act to be contrary to this establishment, or any of these fundamental constitutions of the Government. And in such case, after full and free debate, the several estates shall retire into four several chambers; the palatine and proprietors into one; the landgraves into another; the caziques into another; and those chosen by the precincts into a fourth; and if the major part of any of the four estates shall vote that the law is not agreeable to this establishment, and these fundamental constitutions of the government, then it shall pass no further, but be as if it had never been proposed.

* * *

Ninety-three. It being of great consequence to the plantation that port-towns should be built and preserved; therefore, whosoever shall lade or unlace any commodity at any other place than a port-town, shall forfeit to the lords proprietors, for each ton so laden or unladen, the sum of ten pounds sterling; except only such goods as the palatine's court shall license to be laden or unladen elsewhere.

Ninety-four. The first port-town upon every river shall be in a colony, and be a port-town forever.

Ninety-five. No man shall be permitted to be a freeman of Carolina, or to have any estate or habitation within it, that doth not acknowledge a God, and that God is publicly and solemnly to be worshipped.

* * *

Ninety-seven. But since the natives of that place, who will be concerned in our plantation, are utterly strangers to Christianity, whose idolatry, ignorance, or mistake gives us no right to expel or use them ill; and those who remove from other parts to plant there will unavoidably be of different opinions concerning matters of religion, the liberty whereof they will expect to have allowed them, and it will not be reasonable for us, on this account, to keep them out, that civil peace may be maintained amidst diversity of opinions, and our agreement and compact with all men may be duly and faithfully observed; the violation whereof, upon what presence soever, cannot be without great offence to Almighty God, and great scandal to the true religion which we profess; and also that Jews, heathens, and other dissenters from the purity of Christian religion may not be scared and kept at a distance from it, but, by having an opportunity of acquainting themselves with the truth and reasonableness of its doctrines, and the peaceableness and inoffensiveness of its professors, may, by good usage and persuasion, and all those convincing methods of gentleness and meekness, suitable to the rules and design of the gospel, be won ever to embrace and un-feignedly receive the truth; therefore, any seven or more persons agreeing in any religion, shall constitute a church or profession, to which they shall give some name, to distinguish it from others.

* * *

One hundred and ten. Every freeman of Carolina shall have absolute power and authority over his negro slaves, of what opinion or religion soever.

One hundred and eleven. No cause, whether civil or criminal, of any freeman, shall be tried in any court of judicature, without a jury of his peers.

DOCUMENT 2.6

George Washington and Tobacco

George Washington to Robert Cary & Company, October 24, 1760, Account Book 1

George Washington

York River, October 24, 1760.

Gentn: I forebore in my Letter of the 28th. Ulto. to mention what quantity of To-bacco you might probably receive from myself and Ward from our Plantation on York River till I came down here, and now I am almost as much at a loss, as I was then, to guess; so bad is the Tobacco, and so short are the Crops (where proper care is taken to cull it, and that I have strictly chargd all my Overseers to do, being determind never to Ship any but the very best sorts). However, this

Source: George Washington, "George Washington to Robert Cary & Company, October 24, 1760, Account Book 1," *The Writings of George Washington from the Original Manuscript Sources*, ed. John C. Fitzpatrick. Available at memory.loc.gov/cgi-bin/query/r?ammem/mgw:@field(DOCID+@lit(gw020241)).

you may be assurd of, that the greatest share of what is made shall go consignd to you and I am not without hopes that I shall be able to Ship you about 30 Hhds. on my own Acct. and perhaps 40 or more on my Wards.

On the other side you will receive Invoices of such Goods as will be wanting for my own and Mr. Jno. Parke Custis's Plantations on this River which please to send as there directed, under distinct Marks, and chargd to our respective Accounts but both consigned to our Common Steward, Mr. Joseph Valentine with Copies of the Invoices (Originals to me) that he may commit no errors in appropriating the several Articles to our respective uses.

Your Letter of the 27th. of June Inclosing the Charge of Insurance of 15 Hhds. Tobacco pr. the Russian Merchant is come to hand, and my Letter of the 10th. of August last will direct how the proceeds of that, and all former Tobacco's should be applied. I hope the quantity of Tobo. mentiond by you, to be on hand, has not affected the Sales of the 15 Hhds. and I think I can venture to pronounce, your market will not be glutted with the present Crop. You have doubtless been fully informd by many of your Friends of the misfortune attending your Charterd Ship, it will be needless therefore for me to touch upon the Subject.

I have at different times sent for Hale's Husbandry but never yet got it, which I begin to attribute to a wrong description of the Title, having never till lately seen the Book; you will know it now by "A Compleat Body of Husbandry compiled from the Original Papers of the late Thomas Hale Esqr., enlargd from the Collection of others, &ca.". If any oppertunty shoud offer into Potomack before Johnston may Sail in the Spring or, if any Ship shoud be bound for Rappanhannock River, please to send it to me; together with Hartlibs Legacy of Husbandry and if it shoud so happen, that the first oppertunity presents itself for the latter River, be pleasd then to address the Books, and following things to the care of Fielding Lewis Esqr. at Fredericksburg. viz. Circumferentor; Pocket Book; Garden Seeds, Accordg. to mine of the 28th. Ulto. and Hop Clover: let be 4 Bushels. and to them pray add abt. 20 Bushels of the best, and true Ray Grass Seed for all of them are Articles I woud gladly get to hand as soon as possible. I mentioned in a former Letter, and perhaps it may not be amiss to remind you here, of the necessity of putting all these Seeds in the Cabbin, or some place where the closeness, and heat of the Ship may not destroy the Vegetative virtue of them, which scarce ever fails to happen in a contrary Case. I am Gentn. etc.

3

Religious Worlds and Encounters

While gold and glory motivated many to launch colonial enterprises or establish plantations, others saw in the seemingly vacant and inviting land a stage for establishing perfect religious communities dedicated to the ever evolving understanding of God. Such was the case with the establishment of Plymouth Plantation. Yet the land was not vacant and, just as with others who had started with that assumption, the various servants of God had to confront peoples already present and sort out their relationship with them, physically and spiritually.

The great hope that the New World would offer opportunities to establish communities so aligned with faith that they stood as perfect models of human relationships with the divine is expressed in John Winthrop's career and thoughts. To establish a "city upon a hill," as he envisioned, was indeed a powerful and persistent ingredient in what many consider today to be a principal element in American national character. Yet all was not perfect within the city of God. The issue of buying and selling fellow human beings presented some dilemmas, if only in hindsight. While the British struggled to define relationships with native inhabitants, the French and Spanish were also seeking to blend their religions and culture with native American societies in the north and far distant west to forge their own definition of national character.

DOCUMENT 3.1

Natives of New England

Rev. Francis Higginson, 1629

Now thus you know what New-England is, as also with the commodities and discommodities thereof. Now I will show you a little of the inhabitants thereof, and their government.

For their governors they have kings, which they call saggamores, some greater and some lesser, according to the number of their subjects. The greater saggamores about us cannot make above three hundred men, and other less saggamores have not above fifteen subjects, and others near about us but two.

Their subjects, about twelve years since, were swept away by a great and grievous plague that was amongst them, so that there are very few left to inhabit the country.

The Indians are not able to make use of the one fourth part of the land; neither have they any settled places, as towns, to dwell in; nor any ground as they challenge for their own possession, but change their habitation from place to place.

For their statures, they are a tall and strong-limbed people. Their colors are tawny. They go naked, save only they are in part covered with beasts' skins on one of their shoulders, and wear something before their privities. Their hair is generally black, and cut before, like our gentlewomen, and one lock longer than the rest, much like to our gentlemen, which fashion I think came from hence into England.

For their weapons, they have bows and arrows, some of them headed with bone, and some with brass. I have sent you some of them for an example.

The men, for the most part, live idly; they do nothing but hunt and fish. Their wives set their corn, and do all their other work. They have little household stuff, as a kettle, and some other vessels like trays, spoons, dishes and baskets.

Their houses are very little and homely, being made with small poles pricked into the ground, and so bended and fastened at the tops, and on the sides they are matted with boughs and covered on the roof with sedge and old mats; and for their beds that they take their rest on, they have a mat.

They do generally profess to like well of our coming and planting here; partly because there is abundance of ground that they cannot possess nor make use of, and partly because our being here will be a means both of relief to them when they want, and also a defence from their enemies, wherewith (I say) before this Plantation began, they were often endangered.

For their religion, they do worship two Gods, a good God and an evil God. The good God they call Tantum, and their evil God, whom they fear will do them hurt, they call Squantum.

For their dealing with us, we neither fear them nor trust them; for forty of our musketeers will drive five hundred of them out of the field. We use them kindly. They will come into our houses sometimes by half a dozen or half a score at a time when we are at victuals, but will ask or take nothing but what we give them.

We purpose to learn their language as soon as we can, which will be a means to do them good.

Source: From Alexander Young, ed., *Chronicles of the First Planters of the Colony of Massachusetts Bay, from 1623 to 1636* (Boston: Charles C. Little and James Brown, 1846?), pp. 256–58.

DOCUMENT 3.2

A Model of Christian Charity, 1630

Governor John Winthrop

It rests now to make some application of this discourse, by the present design, which gave the occasion of writing of it. Herein are four things to be propounded; first the persons, secondly, the work, thirdly the end, fourthly the means.

First, for the persons. We are a company professing ourselves fellow members of Christ, in which respect only, though we were absent from each other many miles, and had our employments as far distant, yet we ought to account ourselves knit together by this bond of love and live in the exercise of it, if we would have comfort of our being in Christ. This was notorious in the practice of the Christians in former times; as is testified of the Waldenses, from the mouth of one of the adversaries Aeneas Sylvius "mutuo ament pene antequam norunt"—they use to love any of their own religion even before they were acquainted with them.

Secondly for the work we have in hand. It is by a mutual consent, through a special overvaluing providence and a more than an ordinary approbation of the churches of Christ, to seek out a place of cohabitation and consortship under a due form of government both civil and ecclesiastical. In such cases as this, the care of the public must oversway all private respects, by which, not only conscience, but mere civil policy, doth bind us. For it is a true rule that particular estates cannot subsist in the ruin of the public.

Thirdly, the end is to improve our lives to do more service to the Lord; the comfort and increase of the body of Christ, whereof we are members, that ourselves and posterity may be the better preserved from the common corruptions of this evil world, to serve the Lord and work out our salvation under the power and purity of his holy ordinances.

Fourthly, for the means whereby this must be effected. They are twofold, a conformity with the work and end we aim at. These we see are extraordinary, therefore we must not content ourselves with usual ordinary means. Whatsoever we did, or ought to have done, when we lived in England, the same must we do, and more also, where we go. That which the most in their churches maintain as truth in profession only, we must bring into familiar and constant practice; as in this duty of love, we must love brotherly without dissimulation, we must love one another with a pure heart fervently. We must bear one another's burdens. We must not look only on our own things, but also on the things of our brethren.

Neither must we think that the Lord will bear with such failings at our hands as he doth from those among whom we have lived; and that for these three reasons:

Source: "A Model of Christian Charity–by Gov. John Winthrop, 1630," www.winthropsociety.org/charity.htm.

First, in regard of the more near bond of marriage between Him and us, wherein He hath taken us to be His, after a most strict and peculiar manner, which will make Him the more jealous of our love and obedience. So He tells the people of Israel, you only have I known of all the families of the earth, therefore will I punish you for your transgressions.

Secondly, because the Lord will be sanctified in them that come near Him. We know that there were many that corrupted the service of the Lord; some setting up altars before his own; others offering both strange fire and strange sacrifices also; yet there came no fire from heaven, or other sudden judgment upon them, as did upon Nadab and Abihu, whom yet we may think did not sin presumptuously.

Thirdly, when God gives a special commission He looks to have it strictly observed in every article; When He gave Saul a commission to destroy Amaleck, He indented with him upon certain articles, and because he failed in one of the least, and that upon a fair pretense, it lost him the kingdom, which should have been his reward, if he had observed his commission.

Thus stands the cause between God and us. We are entered into covenant with Him for this work. We have taken out a commission. The Lord hath given us leave to draw our own articles. We have professed to enterprise these and those accounts, upon these and those ends. We have hereupon besought Him of favor and blessing. Now if the Lord shall please to hear us, and bring us in peace to the place we desire, then hath He ratified this covenant and sealed our commission, and will expect a strict performance of the articles contained in it; but if we shall neglect the observation of these articles which are the ends we have propounded, and, dissembling with our God, shall fall to embrace this present world and prosecute our carnal intentions, seeking great things for ourselves and our posterity, the Lord will surely break out in wrath against us, and be revenged of such a people, and make us know the price of the breach of such a covenant.

Now the only way to avoid this shipwreck, and to provide for our posterity, is to follow the counsel of Micah, to do justly, to love mercy, to walk humbly with our God. For this end, we must be knit together, in this work, as one man. We must entertain each other in brotherly affection. We must be willing to abridge ourselves of our superfluities, for the supply of others' necessities. We must uphold a familiar commerce together in all meekness, gentleness, patience and liberality. We must delight in each other; make others' conditions our own; rejoice together, mourn together, labor and suffer together, always having before our eyes our commission and community in the work, as members of the same body. So shall we keep the unity of the spirit in the bond of peace. The Lord will be our God, and delight to dwell among us, as His own people, and will command a blessing upon us in all our ways, so that we shall see much more of His wisdom, power, goodness and truth, than formerly we have been acquainted with. We shall find that the God of Israel is among us, when ten of us shall be able to resist a thousand of our enemies; when He shall make us a praise and glory that men shall say of succeeding plantations, "may the Lord make it like that of New England." For we must consider that we shall be as a city upon a hill. The eyes of all people are upon us. So that if we shall deal falsely with our God in this work we have undertaken, and so cause Him to withdraw His present help from us, we shall be made a story and a by-word through the world. We shall open the mouths of enemies to speak evil of the ways of God, and all professors for God's sake. We shall shame the faces of many of God's worthy servants, and cause their prayers to be turned into curses upon us till we be consumed out of the good land whither we are going.

And to shut this discourse with that exhortation of Moses, that faithful servant of the Lord, in his last farewell to Israel, Deut. 30. "Beloved, there is now set before us life and death, good and evil," in that we are commanded this day to love the Lord our God, and to love one another, to walk in his ways and to keep his Commandments and his ordinance and his laws, and the articles of our Covenant with Him, that we may live and be multiplied, and that the Lord our God may bless us in the land whither we go to possess it. But if our hearts shall turn away, so that we will not obey, but shall be seduced, and worship other Gods, our pleasure and profits, and serve them; it is propounded unto us this day, we shall surely perish out of the good land whither we pass over this vast sea to possess it.

> Therefore let us choose life,
> that we and our seed may live,
> by obeying His voice and cleaving to Him,
> for He is our life and our prosperity.

DOCUMENT 3.3

The First Thanksgiving Proclamation, June 20, 1676

The Holy God having by a long and Continual Series of his Afflictive dispensations in and by the present Warr with the Heathen Natives of this land, written and brought to pass bitter things against his own Covenant people in this wilderness, yet so that we evidently discern that in the midst of his judgements he hath remembered mercy, having remembered his Footstool in the day of his sore displeasure against us for our sins, with many singular Intimations of his Fatherly Compassion, and regard; reserving many of our Towns from Desolation Threatened, and attempted by the Enemy, and giving us especially of late with many of our Confederates many signal Advantages against them, without such Disadvantage to ourselves as formerly we have been sensible of, if it be the Lord's mercy that we are not consumed, It certainly bespeaks our positive Thankfulness, when our Enemies are in any measure disappointed or destroyed; and fearing the Lord should take notice under so many Intimations of his returning mercy, we should be found an Insensible people, as not standing before Him with Thanksgiving, as well as lading him with our Complaints in the time of pressing Afflictions:

Source: University of Oklahoma Law Center, University of Oklahoma, College of Law, *A Chronology of U.S. Historical Documents*, www.law.ou.edu/hist/thanksgiv.html.

The Council has thought meet to appoint and set apart the 29th day of this instant June, as a day of Solemn Thanksgiving and praise to God for such his Goodness and Favour, many Particulars of which mercy might be Instanced, but we doubt not those who are sensible of God's Afflictions, have been as diligent to espy him returning to us; and that the Lord may behold us as a People offering Praise and thereby glorifying Him; the Council doth commend it to the Respective Ministers, Elders and people of this Jurisdiction; Solemnly and seriously to keep the same Beseeching that being perswaded by the mercies of God we may all, even this whole people offer up our bodies and soulds [sic] as a living and acceptable Service unto God by Jesus Christ.

DOCUMENT 3.4

The Dangers Threatening Canada

Memoir for the Marquis de Seignelay Regarding the Dangers That Threaten Canada and the Means to Remedy Them, Januari 1687

Canada is encompassed by many powerful Colonies of English who labor incessantly to ruin it by exciting all our Indians, and drawing them away with their peltries for which said English give them a great deal more merchandise than the French, because the former pay no duty to the King of England. That profit attracts towards them, also, all our Coureurs de bois and French libertines who carry their peltries to them, deserting our Colony and establishing themselves among the English who take great pains to encourage them.

They employ these French deserters to advantage in bringing the Far Indians to them who formerly brought their peltries into our Colony, whereby our trade is wholly destroyed.

The English have begun by the most powerful and best disciplined Indians of all America, whom they have excited entirely against us by their avowed protection and manifest usurpation of the sovereignty they claim over the country of those Indians which appertains beyond contradiction to the King for nearly a century without the English having, up to this present time, had any pretence thereto.

They also employ the Iroquois to excite all our other Indians against us. They sent those last year to attack the Hurons and the Outawas, our most ancient subjects; from whom they swept by surprise more than 75 prisoners, including some of their principal Chiefs; killed several others, and finally offered peace and the restitution of their prisoners, if they would quit the French and acknowledge the English.

They sent those Iroquois to attack the Illinois and the Miamis, our allies, who are in the neighborhood of Fort Saint Louis, built by M. de La Salle on the Illinois River which empties into the River Colbert or Mississipi; those Iroquois massacred and burnt a great number of them, and carried off many prisoners

Source: "Memoir for the Marquis de Seignelay Regarding the Dangers That Threaten Canada and the Means to Remedy Them, Januari 1687," www.let.rug.nl/~usa/D/1651-1700/france/seign.htm.

with threats of entire extermination if they would not unite with them against the French. . . .

War is likewise necessary for the establishment of the Religion, which will never spread itself there except by the destruction of the Iroquois: so that on the success of hostilities, which the Governor-General of Canada proposes to commence against the Iroquois on the 15th of May next, depends either the ruin of the Country and of the Religion if he be not assisted, or the Establishment of the Religion, of Commerce and the King's Power over all North America, if granted the required aid.

If men consider the Merit in the eyes of God, and the Glory and utility which the King will derive from that succor, it is easy to conclude that expense was never better employed since, independent of the salvation of the quantity of souls in that vast County to which His Majesty will contribute by establishing the faith there, he will secure to himself an Empire of more than a thousand leagues in extent, from the Mouth of the River Saint Lawrence to that of the river Mississippi in the Gulf of Mexico; a country discovered by the French alone, to which other Nations have no right, and from which great Commercial advantages, and a considerable augmentation of His Majesty's Revenues will eventually be derived.

DOCUMENT 3.5

The Selling of Joseph

Samuel Sewall

The Numerousness of Slaves at this day in the Province, and the Uneasiness of them under their Slavery, hath put many upon thinking whether the Foundation of it be firmly and well laid; so as to sustain the Vast Weight that is built upon it. It is most certain that all Men, as they are the Sons of *Adam*, are Coheirs; and have equal Right unto Liberty, and all other outward Comforts of Life. *GOD hath given the Earth* [with all its Commodities] *unto the Sons of* Adam, *Psal* 115. 16. *And hath made of One Blood, all Nations of Men, for to dwell on all the face of the Earth, and hath determined the Times before appointed, and the bounds of their habitation: That they should seek the Lord. Forasmuch then as we are the Offspring of GOD* &c. *Act* 17. 26, 27, 29. Now although the Title given by the last ADAM, doth infinitely better Mens Estates, respecting GOD and themselves; and grants them a most beneficial and inviolable Lease under the Broad Seal of Heaven, who were before only Tenants at Will: Yet through the Indulgence of GOD to our First Parents after the Fall, the outward Estate of all and every of their Children, remains the same, as to one another. So that Originally, and Naturally, there is no such thing as Slavery. *Joseph* was rightfully no more a Slave to his Brethren, than they were to him: and they had no more Authority to *Sell* him, than they had to *Slay* him. And if *they* had nothing to do to Sell him; the *Ishmaelites*

Source: From Samuel Sewall, *The Selling of Joseph: A Memorial*, ed. Sidney Kaplan (Amherst: University of Massachusetts Press, 1969), pp. 7–12.

bargaining with them, and paying down Twenty pieces of Silver, could not make a Title. Neither could *Potiphar* have any better Interest in him than the *Ishmaelites* had. *Gen. 37. 20, 27, 28.* For he that shall in this case plead *Alteration of Property*, seems to have forfeited a great part of his own claim to Humanity. There is no proportion between Twenty Pieces of Silver, and LIBERTY. The Commodity it self is the Claimer. If *Arabian* Gold be imported in any quantities, most are afraid to meddle with it, though they might have it at easy rates; lest if it should have been wrongfully taken from the Owners, it should kindle a fire to the Consumption of their whole Estate. 'Tis pity there should be more Caution used in buying a Horse, or a little lifeless dust; than there is in purchasing Men and Women: Whenas they are the Offspring of GOD, and their Liberty is, . . . *Auro pretiosior Omni.*

And seeing GOD hath said, *He that Stealeth a Man and Selleth him, or if he be found in his hand, he shall surely be put to Death.* Exod. 21. 16. This Law being of Everlasting Equity, wherein Man Stealing is ranked amongst the most atrocious of Capital Crimes: What louder Cry can there be made of that Celebrated Warning, **Caveat Emptor!**

And all things considered, it would conduce more to the Welfare of the Province, to have White Servants for a Term of Years, than to have Slaves for Life. Few can endure to hear of a Negro's being made free; and indeed they can seldom use their freedom well; yet their continual aspiring after their forbidden Liberty, renders them Unwilling Servants. And there is such a disparity in their Conditions, Colour & Hair, that they can never embody with us, and grow up into orderly Families, to the Peopling of the Land: but still remain in our Body Politick as a kind of extravasat Blood. As many Negro men as there are among us, so many empty places there are in our Train Bands, and the places taken up of Men that might make Husbands for our Daughters. And the Sons and Daughters of *New England* would become more like *Jacob,* and *Rachel,* if this Slavery were thrust quite out of doors. Moreover it is too well known what Temptations Masters are under, to connive at the Fornication of their Slaves; lest they should be obliged to find them Wives, or pay their Fines. It seems to be practically pleaded that they might be Lawless; 'tis thought much of, that the Law should have Satisfaction for their Thefts, and other Immoralities; by which means, *Holiness to the Lord,* is more rarely engraven upon this sort of Servitude. It is likewise most lamentable to think, how in taking Negros out of *Africa,* and Selling of them here, That which GOD has joyned together men do boldly rend asunder; Men from their Country, Husbands from their Wives, Parents from their Children. How horrible is the Uncleanness, Mortality, if not Murder, that the Ships are guilty of that bring great Crouds of these miserable Men, and Women. Methinks, when we are bemoaning the barbarous Usage of our Friends and Kinsfolk in *Africa:* it might not be unseasonable to enquire whether we are not culpable in forcing the *Africans* to become Slaves amongst our selves. And it may be a question whether all the Benefit received by *Negro* Slaves, will balance the Accompt of Cash laid out upon them; and for the Redemption of our own enslaved Friends out of *Africa.* Besides all the Persons and Estates that have perished there.

DOCUMENT 3.6

De Anza into California

May 2, 1772

The fervent desire which at all times moves me to serve his Majesty and advance his conquests, impels me to beg of your Excellency, in case you learn that it is to be granted to anyone, permission to make the necessary efforts to see if we can open communication between the port of Monterey and the province of Sonora. This has always been considered as impossible or very difficult, but without the best foundation, for in this region no examination has ever been made sufficiently exact to justify such an opinion. Indeed, there are today plenty of indications that it might be effected at slight cost, although with some effort on our part. . . .

In 1769, the same year in which the expedition was made to find the Monte Rey mentioned, I learned through the heathen Pima tribe, which maintains communication with us and lives fifty leagues from this presidio, and the same distance or a little more from the junction of this river with the Colorado, that the vast tribes which live there had told them that on the other side of the Colorado, at some distance, white men were passing, a thing which they had never seen before. Having been assigned to the expedition which was then being made against the Pimas and the Seris, I reported this news to the governor of the provinces, to my Colonel, Don Domingo Elizondo, commander of the expedition, and to officials who reside in that capital, and, finally, to the Señor Visitor-general, Don Joseph de Gálvez, at the time of his coming to this province that year. In the same year this tribe repeated the story to the very reverend father Fray Francisco Garcés, missionary de propaganda fide, who went to visit it, and who now is engaged in his ministry in the pueblo of San Xavier del Bac, distant from here fifteen leagues. And on another occasion the same tribe has recently repeated the same thing to me, which it never had done before

To all this it is to be added that this zealous missionary, with the aim of preparing the heathen situated in the northwest and west to receive the Holy Evangel, went in to them alone and with inexpressible hardships in the month of August of last year. Having been at the junction of the Colorado and Gila rivers, he remained on these streams many days, conversing with the tribes who live there, by whom he was well received because of their natural docility. And through the Yuma tribe, which embraces a large part of the Colorado, he learned, without asking, that at no great distance from them there were white people. Those who had chanced to see them begged him by signs, which was the common language, that he should show them the compass, the glass for making fire, and other instruments which we use but which the father did not have, and which, if they had not seen them in that country, they could not have

Source: Herbert Eugene Bolton, *Anza's California Expeditions*, vol. 5: *Correspondence* (New York: Russell & Russell, 1966), pp. 3–7.

known about, for from this region no one has gone into their land, nor do they come out to ours, on account of the many enemies who keep the way closed to them

Likewise, they gave this father to understand that to the north and east of them there were also people of our kind, distinct from those whom they indicated to the west, and that some of their relatives maintained communication with the Indians who lived in the pueblos near to those of the Spaniards. These we judge must be those who live in New Mexico, for otherwise, it would seem, they must be strangers.

From the same Colorado River this father discovered a great mountain chain of blue color, and although he did not cross it he thinks that it may be the one which our troops skirted when they went to Monte Rey. And if it is on the other side of the river, as is believed, the lack of water on the way will presumably be much less than has been stated hitherto, because everybody has thought it to be through level country. Indeed, up to now, at least in these parts, we have had no notice of this sierra, and I believe that this is because those who have gone to the Colorado have always inclined toward the coast, and since they did not go up to the north they could not see it.

In view of all these considerations, this reverend father and I are convinced that the distance from here to Monte Rey can not be so great as formerly has been estimated, and that it will not be impossible to overcome any obstacles encountered on the way. Therefore, if all this should merit the approval of your Excellency, I hope that you will charge the president of these missions to grant the father mentioned permission to accompany me, for I am in accord with him to sacrifice myself to this purpose and to whatever may redound to the service of his Majesty and the glory of your Excellency.

4

British North Americans

As British North America evolved, some elements of British culture were transferred to the colonies, but some were not; and even those British ideas, concepts, and values that were successfully transplanted took on new meanings and different shapes in the new world. The fact that ambitious and hardworking individuals could own land and ply their trade in a market that needed their services created many economic opportunities in the Americas that were not so available in Europe. Having a home usually meant having a family, and that meant that new and old attitudes about family roles were going to be sorted out in the colonies.

The mutual responsibilities in families were played out in the evolution of the concept of mutual responsibilities in colonies. The strong desire for and the continual experimentation with self-government shines through in the North Carolina Biennal Act of 1715.

As the world shrank through progressive developments in transportation and communications, the prospect of world wars for empire arose. Great Britain went through a series of wars against France and Spain for dominance in Africa, Asia, and the Americas. Though British North Americans might consider themselves loyal subjects of the Crown, the practical realities of being on the frontier become evident in James Oglethorpe's account of the Spanish invasion of Georgia.

Being within earshot of gunfire was one part of the struggle to sustain colonial activities. The British also felt it essential to devise systems to educate successive generations as British subjects and, thus, established a number of colleges in the colonies. Of course, the curriculum at those colleges would to some degree attempt to reinforce existing old world academic and intellectual concepts in the minds of new world students.

Not everyone had an opportunity to attend college. As the indentured servant system grew and evolved, it became a mixed blessing for those who chose that path to the Americas. Some servants were virtually bought and sold *like slaves, while others were able to free themselves from their debt by pro-viding the amount of labor for which they had bargained. Thus, the system was wrought with both risks of hardships and rewards.*

To secure the basic infrastructure that was necessary to stimulate and sustain economic activity in the colonies was a constant challenge. Throughout the early colonial period, a variety of methods were used to raise money nec-essary to build roads and bridges. One such method, established rather early in the nation's history, was the lottery, which is utilized by many states and or-ganizations for similar purposes today.

DOCUMENT 4.1

An Account of West Jersey and Pennsylvania, 1698

Gabriel Thomas

Of Lawyers and Physicians I shall say nothing, because this Countrey is very Peaceable and Healthy; long may it so continue and never have occasion for the Tongue of the one, nor the Pen of the other, both equally destructive to Mens Es-tates and Lives; besides forsooth, they, Hang-Man like, have a License to Mur-der and make Mischief. Labouring-Men have commonly here, between 14 and 15 Pounds a Year, and their Meat, Drink, Washing and Lodging; and by the Day their Wages is generally between Eighteen Pence and a Half a Crown, and Diet also; But in Harvest they have usually between Three and Four Shillings each Day, and Diet. The Maid Servants Wages is commonly betwixt Six and Ten Pounds per Annum, with very good Accommodation. And for the Women who get their Livelihood by their own Industry, their Labour is very dear, . . .

Corn and Flesh, and what else serves Man for Drink, Food and Rayment, is much cheaper here than in England, or elsewhere; but the chief reason why Wages of Servants of all sorts is much higher here than there, arises from the great Fertility and Produce of the Place; besides, if these large Stipends were re-fused them, they would quickly set up for themselves, for they can have Provi-sion very cheap, and Land for a very small matter, or next to nothing in comparison of the Purchase of Lands in England; and the Farmers there, can better afford to give that great Wages than the Farmers in England can, for sev-eral Reasons very obvious.

As First, their Land costs them (as I said but just now) little or nothing in comparison, of which the Farmers commonly will get twice the encrease of Corn for every Bushel they sow, that the Farmers in England can from the rich-est Land they have.

In the Second place, they have constantly good price for their Corn, by rea-son of the great and quick vent [trade] into Barbadoes and other Islands;

Source: Gabriel Thomas, *An Historical Description of the Province and Country of West-New-Jersey in America* (London, 1698); reprinted in part in Albert Bushnell Hart, ed., *American History Told by Con-temporaries* (New York, 1898), vol. 1, 573–75. Available at franklaughter.tripod.com/cgi-bin/histprof/misc/1698thomas.html.

through which means Silver is become more plentiful than here in England, considering the Number of People, and that causes a quick Trade for both Corn and Cattle; and that is the reason that Corn differs now from the Price formerly, else it would be at half the Price it was at then; for a Brother of mine (to my own particular knowledge) sold within the compass of one Week, about One Hundred and Twenty fat Beasts, most of them good handsom large Oxen.

Thirdly, They pay no Tithes, and their Taxes are inconsiderable; the Place is free for all Persuasions, in a Sober and Civil way; for the Church of England and the Quakers bear equal Share in the Government. They live Friendly and Well together; there is no Persecution for Religion, nor ever like to be; 'tis this that knocks all Commerce on the Head, together with high Imposts, strict Laws, and cramping Orders. Before I end this Paragraph, I shall add another Reason why Womens Wages are so exorbitant; they are not yet very numerous, which makes them stand upon high Terms for their several Services, . . .

DOCUMENT 4.2

The Duties of Husbands and Wives

Benjamin Wadsworth

Concerning the duties of this relation we may assert a few things. It is their duty to dwell together with one another. Surely they should dwell together; if one house cannot hold them, surely they are not affected to each other as they should be. They should have a very great and tender love and affection to one another. This is plainly commanded by God. This duty of love is mutual; it should be performed by each, to each of them. When, therefore, they quarrel or disagree, then they do the Devil's work; he is pleased at it, glad of it. But such contention provokes God; it dishonors Him; it is a vile example before inferiors in the family; it tends to prevent family prayer.

As to outward things. If the one is sick, troubled, or distressed, the other should manifest care, tenderness, pity, and compassion, and afford all possible relief and succor. They should likewise unite their prudent counsels and endeavors, comfortably to maintain themselves and the family under their joint care.

Husband and wife should be patient one toward another. If both are truly pious, yet neither of them is perfectly holy, in such cases a patient, forgiving, forbearing spirit is very needful. . . .

The husband's government ought to be gentle and easy, and the wife's obedience ready and cheerful. The husband is called the head of the woman. It belongs to the head to rule and govern. Wives are part of the house and family, and ought to be under the husband's government. Yet his government should not be with rigor, haughtiness, harshness, severity, but with the greatest love,

Source: Benjamin Wadsworth, *A Well-Ordered Family* (Boston, 1712). Available at "About the Duties of Husbands and Wives," personal.pitnet.net/primarysources/marriage.html.

gentleness, kindness, tenderness that may be. Though he governs her, he must not treat her as a servant, but as his own flesh; he must love her as himself.

Those husbands are much to blame who do not carry it lovingly and kindly to their wives. O man, if your wife is not so young, beautiful, healthy, well-tempered, and qualified as you would wish; if she did not bring a large estate to you, or cannot do so much for you, as some other women have done for their husbands; yet she is your wife, and the great God commands you to love her, not be bitter, but kind to her. What can be more plain and expressive than that?

Those wives are much to blame who do not carry it lovingly and obediently to their own husbands. O woman, if your husband is not as young, beautiful, healthy, so well-tempered, and qualified as you could wish; if he has not such abilities, riches, honors, as some others have; yet he is your husband, and the great God commands you to love, honor, and obey him. Yea, though possibly you have greater abilities of mind than he has, was of some high birth, and he of a more common birth, or did bring more estate, yet since he is your husband, God has made him your head, and set him above you, and made it your duty to love and revere him.

Parents should act wisely and prudently in the matching of their children. They should endeavor that they may marry someone who is most proper for them, most likely to bring blessings to them.

DOCUMENT 4.3

The North Carolina Biennal Act, 1715

1. Whereas His Excellency the Palatine and the rest of the true and Absolute Lord's Proprietors of Carolina, having duely considered the priviledges and immunities wherewith the Kingdom of Great Brittain is endued and being desirous that this their province may have such as may thereby enlarge the Settlement and that the frequent sitting of Assembly is a principal, safeguard of their People's priviledges, have thought fit to enact. And Be It Therefore Enacted by the said Pallatine and Lords Proprietors by and with the advice and consent of this present Grand Assembly now met at Little River for the North East part of the said province:

* * *

3. And Be It Further Enacted that it is and may be lawfull for the inhabitants and freemen in each Precinct in every other County or Counties that now is or shall be hereafter erected in this Government aforesaid to meet as aforesaid at such place as shall be judged most convenient by the Marshall of such county, unless he be otherwise ordered by the special commands of the Governor or Commander in Chief to choose two freeholders out of every precinct in the county aforesaid to sit and vote in the said Assembly.

Source: "The North Carolina Biennal Act (1715)," odur.let.rug.nl/~usa/D/1701-1725/northcarolina/ba.htm.

4. And Be It Further Enacted that the Burgesses so chosen in each precinct for the Biennial Assembly shall meet and sitt the first Monday in November then next following, every two years, at the same place the Assembly last satt except the Pallatines Court shall by their proclamation published Twenty days before the said meeting appoint some other place and there with the consent and concurrence of the Pallatine Court shall make and ordain such Laws as shall be thought most necessary for the Good of this Government. Provided allways and nevertheless that the Powers granted to the Lord's Proprietors from the Crown of Calling, proroguing and dissolving Assemblys are not hereby meant or intended to be invaded, limited or restrained.

5. And It Is Hereby Further Enacted by the Authority aforesaid that no person whatsoever Inhabitant of this Government born out of the allegiance of His Majesty and not made free; no Negroes, Mulattoes, Mustees or Indians shall be capable of voting for Members of Assembly; and that no other person shall be allowed or admitted to vote for Members of Assembly in this Government unless he be of the Age of one and twenty years and has been one full year in the Government and has paid one year's levy preceding the Election.

DOCUMENT 4.4

Surviving a Spanish Invasion

Order for Thanksgiving to Almighty God, for having put an End to the *Spanish Invasion*,

A PROCLAMATION.

ALMIGHTY GOD hath in all Ages shown His Power and Mercy in the Miraculous and Gracious Deliverance of His Church, and in the Protection of Righteous and Religious Kings, and States professing His holy and eternal Truth, from the open Invasions, wicked Conspiracies and malicious Practices, of all the Enemies thereof. He hath by the Manifestation of [*Omitted text*] Providence delivered us from the hands of the *Spaniards*, they with fourteen Sail of small Gallies and other Craft came into *Cumberland Sound;* but Fear and Terror from the Lord, came upon them and they fleed. The *Spaniards* also, with another mighty Fleet of 36 Ships and Vessels came into *Jekyll Sound,* and after a sharp Fight became Masters thereof; we having only four Vessels to oppose their whole Force, and God was the Shield of our People. Since in so unequal a Fight, which was stoutly maintained for the space of four Hours, not one of ours was killed, though many of

Source: Governor James Oglethorpe. Thankgiving proclamation, New York Gazette, 1742. Library of Congress, American Memory, Printed Ephemera Collection; Portfolio 102, Folder 37. Digital ID: rbpe 10203700 http://hdl.loc.gov/loc.rbc/rbpe.10203700, found at: http://memory.loc.gov/cgibin/query/ r?ammem/rbpebib:@OR(@field(AUTHOR+@3(New+York+Gazette++))+@field(OTHER+@3(New+ York+Gazette++)))

theirs Perished, and five were killed by one Shot only. They Landed 4500 Men upon this *Island*, according to the Accounts of the Prisoners, and even of *Englishmen* who escaped from them. The first Party Marched up thro' the Woods to this Town, and was within sight thereof, when God delivered them into the Hands of a few of ours. They Fought and were dispersed and fleed. Another Party which supported them also Fought, but were soon dispersed. We may with Truth say, that the Hand of the Lord Fought for us; for in the two Fights more than 500 fleed before 50, and yet they for a time Fought with Courage, and the Granadiers particularly, charged with great Resolution, but their Shot did not take Place, in so much that none of ours were killed; but they were broken and pursued with great Slaughter, so that by the Reports of the Prisoners, since taken, upwards of 200 Men never returned to their Camp. They also came up with their half Gallies toward this Town, and retired without so much as Firing one Shot, and then Fear came upon them and they fleed, leaving behind them some Cannon, and many Things they had taken. Twenty Eight Sail attacked *Fort William*, in which was only 50 Men, and after three Hours Fight, went away, and left the Province: They having been pursued as far as St. *John's* so that by this whole Expedition and great Armaments, no more than two of ours were taken and 2 killed. Therefore with Truth we may say, that the Lord hath done great Things for us, who hath delivered us out of the Hands of a Numerous Enemy; who had already Swallowed us up in their Thoughts and boasted that they would Torture and Burn us. But the Lord was our Shield, and we of a Truth may say, that it was not our Strength nor Might that delivered us, but that it was the Lord; Therefore it is Meat and Fitting, that we should return Thanks unto God our Deliverer.

HAVING taken the Premises into Consideration, I do hereby Order that Sunday the 25th. Instant be observed as a Day of publick Thanksgiving to Almighty God for his great deliverance in having put an End to the *Spanish Invasion,* and that all Persons do Solemnize the same in a *Christian* and *Religious* Manner, and abstain from Drunkenness and any other wicked or dissolate Testimonies of Joy.

GIVEN under my Hand and Seal, this 24th Day of July, *at* Frederica *in* Georgia, Anno Domini 1742.

[Signed by *James Oglethorp?*]

DOCUMENT 4.5

Regulations at Yale College, 1745

That none may Expect to be admitted into this College unless upon Examination of the Praesident and Tutors, They shall be found able Extempore to Read, Construe and Parce Tully, Virgil and the Greek Testament: and to write True Latin Prose and to understand the Rules of Prosodia, and Common Arithmetic, and shall bring Sufficient Testamony of his Blameless and inoffensive Life.

Source: Excerpted from Franklin B. Dexter, *Biographical Sketches of the Graduates of Yale College* (1896), 2:2–18. Available at personal.pitnet.net/primarysources/yale.html.

That no Person shall be admitted a Freshman into this College who is more than Twenty one Years old, unless by the special allowance of ye President and Fellows or their Committee.

That no Person shall be admitted Undergraduate in this College until his Father, Guardian or some proper Person hath given a Sufficient Bond to the Steward of the College, to pay the Quarter Bills of the s^d Scholar allowed by the authority of College from Time to Time as long as He shall continue a Member of s^d College. . . .

All Scholars Shall Live Religious, Godly and Blameless Lives according to the Rules of God[']s Word, diligently Reading the holy Scriptures the Fountain of Light and Truth; and constan[t]lly attend upon all the Duties of Religion both in Publick and Secret. . . .

Every Student Shall diligently apply himself to his Studies in his Chamber as well as attend upon all Public Exercises appointed by the President or Tutors, and no Student Shall walk abroad, or be absent from his Chamber, Except Half an hour after Breakfast, and an hour and an half after Dinner, and from prayers at Night to Nine o' the Clock, without Leave, upon Penalty of Two Pence or more to Six pence, at the Discretion of ye President and Tutors. . . .

If any Scholar Shall be Guilty of Blasphemy, Fornication, Robbery, Forgery, or any other such Great and Atrocious Crime he Shall be Expelled forthwith.

If any Scholar Shall deny the Holy Scriptures or any part of Them to be the Word of God: or be guilty of Heresy or any Error directly Tending to Subvert the Fundamentals of Christianity, and continuing Obstinate Therein after the first and Second Admonition, He shall be Expelled.

If any Scholar shall be Guilty of Profane Swearing, Cursing, Vowing, any Petty or Implicit Oath, Profane or Irreverent Use of the Names, Attributes, Ordinances or Word of God; Disobedient or Contumacious or Refractory Carriage toward his Superiours, Fighting, Striking, Quarrelling, Challenging, Turbulent Words or Behaviour, Drunkenness, Uncleaness, lacivious Words or Actions, wearing woman's Apparel, Defrauding, Injustice, Idleness, Lying, Defamation, Tale bareing or any other Such like immoralities, He Shall be Punished by Fine, Confession, Admonition or Expulsion, as the nature and Circumstances of the case may Require.

DOCUMENT 4.6

Indentured Servants

Gottlieb Mittelberger

Both in Rotterdam and in Amsterdam the people are packed densely, like herrings so to say, in the large sea-vessels. One person receives a place of scarcely 2 feet width and 6 feet length in the bedstead, while many a ship carries four to

Source: From "Gottlieb Mittelberger on the Misfortune of Indentured Servants (1754)," from Gottlieb Mittelberger's Journey to Pennsylvania in the Year 1750 and Return to Germany in the Year 1754, trans. Carl Theo. Eben (Philadelphia: John Jos. McVey, 1898), pp. 19–29; www.let.rug.nl/~usa/D/1601-1650/mittelberger/servan.htm.

six hundred souls; not to mention the innumerable implements, tools, provisions, water-barrels and other things which likewise occupy much space. . . .

But during the voyage there is on board these ships terrible misery, stench, fumes, horror, vomiting, many kinds of sea-sickness, fever, dysentery, headache, heat, constipation, boils, scurvy, cancer, mouth-rot, and the like, all of which come from old and sharply salted food and meat, also from very bad and foul water, so that many die miserably. . . .

I myself had to pass through a severe illness at sea, and I best know how I felt at the time. These poor people often long for consolation, and I often entertained and comforted them with singing, praying and exhorting; and whenever it was possible and the winds and waves permitted it, I kept daily prayer-meetings with them on deck. Besides, I baptized five children in distress, because we had no ordained minister on board. I also held divine service every Sunday by reading sermons to the people; and when the dead were sunk in the water, I commended them and our souls to the mercy of God. . . .

No one can have an idea of the sufferings which women in confinement have to bear with their innocent children on board these ships. Few of this class escape with their lives; many a mother is cast into the water with her child as soon as she is dead. One day, just as we had a heavy gale, a woman in our ship, who was to give birth and could not give birth under the circumstances, was pushed through a loop-hole [port-hole] in the ship and dropped into the sea, because she was far in the rear of the ship and could not be brought forward.

Children from 1 to 7 years rarely survive the voyage. I witnessed misery in no less than 32 children in our ship, all of whom were thrown into the sea. The parents grieve all the more since their children find no resting-place in the earth, but are devoured by the monsters of the sea.

That most of the people get sick is not surprising, because, in addition to all other trials and hardships, warm food is served only three times a week, the rations being very poor and very little. Such meals can hardly be eaten, on account of being so unclean. The water which is served out on the ships is often very black, thick and full of worms, so that one cannot drink it without loathing, even with the greatest thirst. Toward the end we were compelled to eat the ship's biscuit which had been spoiled long ago; though in a whole biscuit there was scarcely a piece the size of a dollar that had not been full of red worms and spiders nests. . . .

When the ships have landed at Philadelphia after their long voyage, no one is permitted to leave them except those who pay for their passage or can give good security; the others, who cannot pay, must remain on board the ships till they are purchased, and are released from the ships by their purchasers. The sick always fare the worst, for the healthy are naturally preferred and purchased first; and so the sick and wretched must often remain on board in front of the city for 2 or 3 weeks, and frequently die, whereas many a one, if he could pay his debt and were permitted to leave the ship immediately, might recover and remain alive.

The sale of human beings in the market on board the ship is carried on thus: Every day Englishmen, Dutchmen and High-German people come from the city of Philadelphia and other places, in part from a great distance, say 20, 30, or 40 hours away, and go on board the newly arrived ship that has brought and offers for sale passengers from Europe, and select among the healthy persons such as they deem suitable for their business, and bargain with them how long they will serve for their passage money, which most of them are still in debt for. When they have come to an agreement, it happens that adult persons bind themselves in writing to serve 3, 4, 5 or 6 years for the amount due by them, according to their age and strength. But very young people, from 10 to 15 years, must serve till they are 21 years old.

Many parents must sell and trade away their children like so many head of cattle; for if their children take the debt upon themselves, the parents can leave the ship free and unrestrained; but as the parents often do not know where and to what people their children are going, it often happens that such parents and children, after leaving the ship, do not see each other again for many years, perhaps no more in all their lives.

It often happens that whole families, husband, wife, and children, are separated by being sold to different purchasers, especially when they have not paid any part of their passage money.

DOCUMENT 4.7

A Lottery Scheme

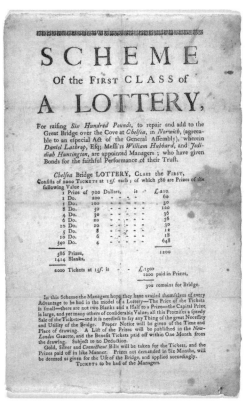

5

Storm Clouds

As the motherland, Great Britain had collective and institutional goals for the development of the British North American colonies. The possession of colonies fit into the existing economic theories of mercantilism and beliefs about national power and wealth. Moreover, whether the colonists accepted it in part, or not at all, policy makers in Great Britain were aware of the forces that threatened England's economic and physical existence and saw in the colonies a role for enhancing England's national security.

Not everyone in the colonies shared the same vision or understanding of the colonial role within the empire. People who had ventured to North America in hopes of achieving goals unobtainable in England were sometimes surprised and frustrated to learn that the same power elites who manipulated power and wealth to exclude competition in England also stacked the deck against upstarts and challengers in the colonies. But the colonies were not England. Little removed from the frontier environment and physically distant from England, a degree of freedom and independent thinking was inevitable, as evidenced by violent outbursts from disappointed classes and disgruntled would-be leaders like Nathaniel Bacon.

For the British, disturbances in the colonies raised questions of security and control, issues complicated by the fact that colonial authority was vested simultaneously in Parliament and the British throne. One of the ways to control the colonies, of course, would be to affix firmly on the colonies privileges of power and definitions of justice that sustained Parliamentary and Royal authority in Great Britain. However, as in the case of John Peter Zenger, juries in British North America could sometimes be persuaded otherwise, thus contributing to the increase of independent action and resistance to arbitrary authority.

Beginning in the 1750s the aspirations of British North Americans to achieve an enhanced version of the rights of English subjects or to expand on the concept of English democracy set the colonies on a collision course with the British government, faced as it was with the practical necessity of securing *the colonies in an increasingly hostile world and of finding ways to defray the costs of colonial government. Controlling the trade and economy of the colonies seemed a reasonable step to policy makers in Britain. Such steps, however, seemed a worst-case scenario to and for a people who had left Europe to secure greater economic opportunities. Hence, George Mason questions the propriety of British economic and fiscal policies while maintaining the dependence of America on Britain and the breadth of the ties that bind the two societies together. Moreover, William Pitt notes in his speech that, given the abuse of the Stamp Act, it should not be surprising that good English subjects protested it and sought relief from the tax. Finally, John Adams's reflections on his defense of Captain Preston and the other British soldiers indicted for murder in the emotionally super-charged Boston Massacre case illustrates another element in the evolution of an American consciousness. In the face of such strong emotions, placing the concept of justice above all other considerations illustrated the maturity of the would-be American political leadership and contributed to the evolution of American values that would form the bedrock of a republican form of government.*

DOCUMENT 5.1

Treasure by Foreign Trade

Thomas Mun

THE MEANS TO ENRICH THIS KINGDOM, AND TO INCREASE OUR TREASURE

Although a Kingdom may be enriched by gifts received, or by purchase taken from some other Nations, yet these are things uncertain and of small consideration when they happen. The ordinary means therefore to increase our wealth and treasure is by Foreign Trade, wherein wee must ever observe this rule; to sell more to strangers yearly than wee consume of theirs in value. For suppose that when this Kingdom is plentifully served with the Cloth, Lead, Tin, Iron, Fish and other native commodities, we doe yearly export the overplus to foreign Countries to the value of twenty two hundred thousand pounds; by which means we are enabled beyond the Seas to buy and bring in foreign wares for our use and Consumptions, to the value of twenty hundred thousand pounds: By this order duly kept in our trading, we may rest assured that the kingdom shall be enriched yearly two hundred thousand pounds, which must be brought to us in so much Treasure; because that part of our stock which is not returned to us in wares must necessarily be brought home in treasure.

Source: From Thomas Mun, *England's Treasure by Foreign Trade* (1664; 1895); available at campus. northpark.edu/history/classes/Sources/Mun.html.

THE EXPORTATION OF OUR MONEYS IN TRADE OF MERCHANDIZE IS A MEANS TO INCREASE OUR TREASURE

This Position is so contrary to the common opinion, that it will require many and strong arguments to prove it before it can be accepted of the Multitude, who bitterly exclaim when they see any monies carried out of the Realm; affirming thereupon that wee have absolutely lost so much Treasure, and that this is an act directly against the long continued laws made and confirmed by the wisdom of this Kingdom in the High Court of Parliament, and that many places, nay Spain itself which is the Fountain of Money, forbids the exportation thereof, some cases only excepted.

First, I will take that for granted which no man of judgment will deny, that we have no other means to get Treasure but by foreign trade, for Mines we have none which do afford it, and how this money is gotten in the managing of our said Trade I have already showed, that it is done by making our commodities which are exported yearly to over balance in value the foreign wares which we consume; so that it resteth only to show how our moneys may be added to our commodities, and being jointly exported may so much the more increase our Treasure.

We have already supposed our yearly consumptions of foreign wares to be for the value of twenty hundred thousand pounds, and our exportations to exceed that two hundred thousand pounds, which sum wee have thereupon affirmed is brought to us in treasure to balance the account. But now if we add three hundred thousand pounds more in ready money unto our former exportations in wares, what profit can we have (will some men say) although by this means we should bring in so much ready money more than wee did before, seeing that wee have carried out the like value.

To this the answer is, that when we have prepared our exportations of wares, and sent out as much of everything as wee can spare or vent abroad; It is not therefore said that then we should add our money thereunto to fetch in the more money immediately, but rather first to enlarge our trade by enabling us to bring in more foreign wares, which being sent out again will in due time much increase our Treasure.

For although in this manner we do yearly multiply our importations to the maintenance of more Shipping and Mariners, improvement of His Majesties Customs and other benefits; yet our consumption of those foreign wares is no more than it was before; so that all the said increase of commodities brought by the means of our ready money sent out as is afore written, doth in the end become an exportation unto this of a far greater value than our said moneys were.

The answer is (keeping our first ground) that if our consumption of foreign wares be no more yearly than is already supposed, and that our exportations be so mightily increased by this manner of Trading with ready money, as is before declared: It is not then possible but that all the over balance or difference should return either in money or in such wares as we must export again, which, as is already plainly showed will be still a greater means to increase our Treasure.

For it is in the stock of the Kingdom as in the estates of private men, who having store of wares, do not therefore say that they will not venture out or trade with their money (for this were ridiculous) but do also turn that into wares, whereby they multiply their Money, and so by a continual and orderly change of one into the other grow rich, and when they please turn all their estates into Treasure; for they that have Wares cannot want money. Neither is it said that Money is the Life of Trade, as if it could not subsist without the same; for we know that there was great trading by way of commutation or barter when there was little money stirring in the world. The Italians and some other Nations have such remedies against this want, that it can neither decay nor hinder their trade, for they transfer bills of debt, and have Banks both publick and private, wherein they do assign their credits from one to another daily for very great sums with ease and satisfaction by writings only, whilst in the mean time the Mass of Treasure which gave foundation to these credits is employed in Foreign Trade as a Merchandize, and by the said means they have little other use of money in those countries more than for their ordinary expenses. It is not therefore the keeping of our money in the Kingdom, but the necessity and use of our wares in foreign Countries, and our want of their commodities that causeth the vent and consumption of all sides, which makes a quick and ample Trade. If we were once poor, and now having gained some store of money by trade with resolution to keep it still in the Realm, shall this cause other Nations to spend more of our commodities than formerly they have done, whereby we might say that our trade is Quickened and Enlarged? No verily, it will produce no such good effect, but rather, according to the alteration of times by their true causes, we may expect the contrary; for all men do consent that plenty of money in a Kingdom doth make the native commodities dearer, which as it is to the profit of some private men in their revenues, so is it directly against the benefit of the Public in the quantity of the trade; for as plenty of money makes wares dearer, so dear wares decline their use and consumption.

DOCUMENT 5.2

Bacon's Declaration in the Name of the People, 1676

Nathaniel Bacon

For having upon specious pretenses of Publick works raised unjust Taxes upon the Commonalty for the advancement of private Favourts and other sinnister ends but noe visible effects in any measure adequate.

Source: Nathaniel Bacon, "Declaration of the People" (1676), reprinted in *Virginia Magazine of History and Biography* 1.1 (1893): 59–61. Available at azimuth.harcourtcollege.com/history/ayers/chapter3/ 3.2.declaration.html. The *American Passages* textbook and website are published by Harcourt College Publishers, a Harcourt Higher Learning company. Copyright 1999. All rights reserved.

For not having dureing the long time of his Government in any measure advanced this hopeful Colony either by Fortification, Townes or Trade.

For having abused and rendered Contemptible the Majesty of Justice, of advancing to places of judicature scandalous and Ignorant favourits.

For having wronged his Maties Prerogative and Interest by assuming the monopoley of the Beaver Trade.

By having in that unjust gain Bartered and sould his Ma^ts Country and the lives of his Loyall Subjects to the Barbarous Heathen.

For having protected favoured and Imboldened the Indians against his Ma^ts most Loyall subjects never contriveing requireing or appointing any due or proper meanes of satisfaction for their many Invassions Murthers and Robberies Committed upon us.

For having when the Army of the English was Just upon the Track of the Indians, which now in all places Burne Spoyle and Murder, and when wee might with ease have destroyed them who then were in open Hostility for having expresly Countermanded and sent back our Army by passing his word for the peaceable demeanour of the said Indians, who immediately prosecuted their evill Intentiions Committing horrid Murders and Robberies in all places being protected by the said Engagement and word passâd of him the said Sâr William Berkley having ruined and made desolate a great part of his Ma^ts Country, have now drawne themselves into such obscure and remote places and are by their successes soe imboldened and confirmed and by their Confederacy soe strengthened that the cryes of Bloud are in all places and the Terrour and censternation of the People soe great, that they are now become not only a difficult, but a very formidable Enemy who might with Ease have been destroyed &c. When upon the Loud Outcries of Blood the Assembly had with all care raised and framed an army for the prevention of future Mischiefs and safeguard of his Ma^ts Colony.

For having with only the privacy of some few favourits without acquainting the People, only by the Alteration of a Figure forged a Commission by wee know not what hand, not only without but against the Consent of the People, for raising and effecting of Civill Wars and distractions, which being happily and w^thout Bloodshed prevented.

For having the second tyme attempted the dame thereby, calling downe our Forces from the defence of the Frontiers, and most weake Exposed Places, for the prevention of civill Mischief and Ruine amongst ourselves, whilst the barbarous Enemy in all places did Invade murder and spoyle us by his Ma^ts most faithfull subjects.

Of these aforesaid Articles wee accuse Sâr William Berkley, as guilty of each and every one of the same, and as one, who hath Traiterously attempted, violated and Injured his Maties Interst here, by the losse of a great Part of his Colony, and many of his Faithfull and Loyall subjects by him betrayed, and in a barbarous and shamefull manner exposed to the Incursions and murthers of the Heathen.

DOCUMENT 5.3

Freedom of the Press

Mr. Hamilton. If a libel is understood in the large and unlimited sense urged by Mr. Attorney, there is scarce a writing I know that may not be called a libel, or scarce a person safe from being called to an account as a libeler. For Moses, meek as he was, libeled Cain; and who is it that has not libeled the Devil?

For according to Mr. Attorney it is no justification to say that one has a bad name. Echard has libeled our good King William; Burnet has libeled, among others, King Charles and King James; and Rapin has libeled them all. How must a man speak or write; or what must he hear, read, or sing; or when must he laugh so as to be secure from being taken up as a libeler?

I sincerely believe that were some persons to go through the streets of New York nowadays and read a part of the Bible, if it was not known to be such, Mr. Attorney (with the help of his *innuendos*) would easily turn it into a libel. As for instance Isaiah 9:16: "The leaders of the people cause them to err; and they that are led by them are destroyed." Should Mr. Attorney go about to make this a libel, he would read it thus: The leaders of the people (*innuendo, the Governor and Council of New York*) cause them (*innuendo, the people of this Province*) to err, and they (*the people of this Province meaning*) that are led by them (*the Governor and Council meaning*) are destroyed (*innuendo, are deceived into the loss of their liberty*), which is the worst kind of destruction. . . .

Gentlemen: The danger is great in proportion to the mischief that may happen through our too great credulity. A proper confidence in a court is commendable, but as the verdict (whatever it is) will be yours, you ought to refer no part of your duty to the discretion of other persons. If you should be of the opinion that there is no falsehood in Mr. Zenger's papers, you will, nay (pardon me for the expression) you ought, to say so—because you do not know whether others (I mean the Court) may be of that opinion. It is your right to do so, and there is much depending upon your resolution as well as upon your integrity.

The loss of liberty, to a generous mind, is worse than death. And yet we know that there have been those in all ages who, for the sake of preferment, or some imaginary honor, have freely lent a helping hand to oppress, nay to destroy, their country.

This brings to my mind that saying of the immortal Brutus when he looked upon the creatures of Caesar, who were very great men but by no means good men. "You Romans," said Brutus, "if yet I may call you so, consider what you are doing. Remember that you are assisting Caesar to forge those very chains that one day he will make you yourselves wear." This is what every man (who values freedom) ought to consider. He should act by judgment and not by affection or self-interest; for where those prevail, no ties of either country or kindred are regarded; as upon the other hand, the man who loves his country

Source: Vincent Buranelli, ed., *The Trial of Peter Zenger* (New York: New York University Press, 1957), pp. 125–32.

prefers its liberty to all other considerations, well knowing that without liberty life is a misery. . . .

Power may justly be compared to a great river. While kept within its due bounds it is both beautiful and useful. But when it overflows its banks, it is then too impetuous to be stemmed; it bears down all before it, and brings destruction and desolation wherever it comes. If, then, this is the nature of power, let us at least do our duty, and like wise men (who value freedom) use our utmost care to support liberty, the only bulwark against lawless power, which in all ages has sacrificed to its wild lust and boundless ambition the blood of the best men that ever lived.

I hope to be pardoned, Sir, for my zeal upon this occasion. It is an old and wise caution that when our neighbor's house is on fire we ought to take care of our own. For though (blessed be God) I live in a government where liberty is well understood and freely enjoyed, yet experience has shown us all (I am sure it has to me) that a bad precedent in one government is soon set up for an authority in another. And therefore I cannot but think it my, and every honest man's, duty that (while we pay all due obedience to men in authority) we ought at the same time to be upon our guard against power wherever we apprehend that it may affect ourselves or our fellow subjects.

I am truly very unequal to such an undertaking on many accounts. You see that I labor under the weight of many years, and am bowed down with great infirmities of body. Yet, old and weak as I am, I should think it my duty, if required, to go to the utmost part of the land where my services could be of any use in assisting to quench the flame of prosecutions upon informations, set on foot by the government to deprive a people of the right of remonstrating (and complaining too) of the arbitrary attempts of men in power.

Men who injure and oppress the people under their administration provoke them to cry out and complain, and then make that very complaint the foundation for new oppressions and prosecutions. I wish I could say that there were no instances of this kind.

But to conclude. The question before the Court and you, Gentlemen of the Jury, is not of small or private concern. It is not the cause of one poor printer, nor of New York alone, which you are now trying. No! It may in its consequence affect every free man that lives under a British government on the main of America. It is the best cause. It is the cause of liberty. And I make no doubt but your upright conduct this day will not only entitle you to the love and esteem of your fellow citizens, but every man who prefers freedom to a life of slavery will bless and honor you as men who have baffled the attempt of tyranny, and by an impartial and uncorrupt verdict have laid a noble foundation for securing to ourselves, our posterity, and our neighbors, that to which nature and the laws of our country have given us a right—the liberty of both exposing and opposing arbitrary power (in these parts of the world at least) by speaking and writing truth.

Here Mr. Attorney observed that Mr. Hamilton had gone very much out of the way, and had made himself and the people very merry; but that he had been citing cases not at all to the purpose. All that the jury had to consider was Mr. Zenger's printing and publishing two scandalous libels that very highly reflected on His Excellency and the principal men concerned in the administration of this government—which is confessed. That is, the printing and publishing of the journals set forth in the information is confessed. He concluded that as Mr. Hamilton had confessed the printing, and there could be no doubt but they were scandalous papers highly reflecting upon His Excellency and on the principal magistrates in the Province—therefore he made no doubt but that the jury would find the defendant guilty, and would refer to the Court for their directions.

Mr. Chief Justice. Gentlemen of the Jury: The great pains Mr. Hamilton has taken to show how little regard juries are to pay to the opinion of judges, and his insisting so much upon the conduct of some judges in trials of this kind, is done no doubt with a design that you should take but very little notice of what I might say upon this occasion. I shall therefore only observe to you that as the facts or words in the information are confessed, the only thing that can come in question before you is whether the words as set forth in the information make a libel. And that is a matter of law, no doubt, and which you may leave to the Court.

Mr. Hamilton. I humbly beg Your Honor's pardon, I am very much misapprehended if you suppose that what I said was so designed.

Sir, you know I made an apology for the freedom that I found myself under a necessity of using upon this occasion. I said there was nothing personal designed. It arose from the nature of our defense.

The jury withdrew, and returned in a small time. Being asked by the clerk whether they were agreed on their verdict, and whether John Peter Zenger was guilty of printing and publishing the libels in the information mentioned, they answered by Thomas Hunt, their foreman, "Not guilty." Upon which there were three huzzas in the hall, which was crowded with people; and the next day I was discharged from my imprisonment.

DOCUMENT 5.4

Letter to London Merchants

George Mason

Virginia
Potomack
River June 6th 1766

To the Committee of Merchants in London

GENTLEMEN

There is a Letter of yours dated the 28th of Febry last, lately printed in the public Papers here; which tho' addressed to a particular Set of men, seems intended for the Colonys in general; and being upon a very interesting Subject, I shall,

Source: George Mason, "Mason's Letter to London Merchants," June 6, 1766, at Gunston Hall Plantation website, gunstonhall.org/documents/merchants.html.

without further Preface or Apology, exercise the Right of a Freeman, in making such Remarks upon it as I think proper.

The Epithets of Parent & Child have been so long applyed to Great Britain & her Colonys, that Individuals have adopted them, and we rarely see anything, from your Side of the Water, free from the authoritative Style of a Master to a School-Boy. "We have, with infinite Difficulty & Fatigue got you excused this one Time; pray be a good boy for the future; do what your Papa and Mamma bid you, & hasten to return them your most grateful Acknowledgements for condescending to let you keep what is your own; and then all your Acquaintance will love you, & praise you, & give you pretty things; and if you shou'd, at any Time hereafter, happen to transgress, your Friends will all beg for you, and be Security for your good Behaviour; but if you are a naughty Boy, & turn obstinate, & don't mind what your Papa & Mamma say to you, but presume to think their Commands (let them be what they will) unjust or unreasonable, or even seem to ascribe their present Indulgence to any other Motive than Excess of Moderation & Tenderness, and pretend to judge for yourselves, when you are not arrived at the Years of Discretion, or capable of distinguishing between Good & Evil; then every-body will hate you, & say you are a graceless & undutiful Child; your Parents & Masters will be obliged to whip you severely, & your Friends will be ashamed to say any thing in your Excuse: nay they will be blamed for your Faults. See your work—See what you have brought the Child to—If he had been well scourged at first for opposing our absolute Will & Pleasure, & daring to think he had any such thing as Property of his own, he wou'd not have had the Impudence to repeat the Crime."

"My dear Child, we have laid the Alternative fairly before you, you can't hesitate in the Choice, and we doubt not you will observe such a Conduct as your Friends recommend." Is not this a little ridiculous, when applyed to three Millions of as loyal & useful Subjects as any in the British dominions, who have been only contending for their Birth-right, and have now only gained, or rather kept, what cou'd not, with common Justice, or even Policy, be denied them? But setting aside the Manner, let me seriously consider the Substance & Subject of your Letter.

Can the Honour of Parliament be maintained by persisting in a Measure evidently wrong? Is it any Reflection upon the Honour of Parliament to shew itself wiser this Year than the last, to have profited by Experience, and to correct the Errors which Time & endubitable Evidence have pointed out? If the Declaratory Act, or Vote of Right, has asserted any unjust, oppressive, or unconstitutional Principles, to become "waste paper" wou'd be the most innocent use that cou'd be made of it: by the Copys we have seen here, the legislative authority of Great Britain is fully & positively asserted in all Cases whatsoever. But a just & necessary Distinction between Legislation & Taxation hath been made by the greatest & wisest Men in the Nation; so that if the Right to the latter had been disclaimed, it wou'd not have impeached or weakened the Vote of Right; on the contrary it wou'd have strengthened it; for Nothing (except hanging the Author of the Stamp Act) wou'd have contributed more to restore that Confidence which a weak or corrupt Ministry had so greatly impaired.

We do not deny the supreme Authority of Great Britain over her Colonys, but it is a Power which a wise Legislature will exercise with extreme Tenderness & Caution, and carefully avoid the least Imputation or Suspicion of Partiality. Wou'd to God that this Distinction between us & your fellow Subjects residing in Great Britain, by depriving us of the ancient Tryal, by a Jury of our Equals, and substituting in its' place an arbitrary Civil Law Court—to put it in the Power of every Sycophant & Informer ("the most mischievous, wicked abandoned & profligate Race" says an eminent writer upon British Politics, "that ever God permited to plague Mankind") to drag a Freeman a thousand Miles from his own Country (whereby he may be deprived of the Benefit of Evidence) to defend his property before a Judge, who, from the Nature of his office, is a Creature of the Ministry, liable to be displaced at their Pleasure, whose Interest it is to encourage Informers, as his Income may in a great Measure depend upon His Condemnations, and to give such a Judge a Power of excluding the most innocent Man, thus treated, from any Remedy (even the recovery of his Cost) by only certifying that in his Opinion there was a probable Cause of Complaint; and thus to make the property of the Subject, in a matter which may reduce him from Opulence to Indigence, depend upon a word before an unknown in the Language & Style of Laws! Are these among the Instances that call for our Expression of "filial Gratitude to our Parent-Country?" These things did not altogether depend upon the Stamp-Act, and therefore are not repealed with it. Can the Foundations of the State be saved, & the Body of the People remain unaffected? Are the Inhabitants of Great Britain absolutely certain that, in the Ministry or Parliament of a future Day, such Incroachments will not be urged as Precedents against themselves? . . .

America has always acknowledged her Dependence upon Great Britain. It is her Interest, it is her Inclination to depend upon Great Britain. We readily own that these Colonys were first setled, not at the Expence, but under the Protection of the English Government; which Protection it has continued to afford them; and we own too, that Protection & Allegiance are reciprocal Dutys. If it is asked at whose Expence they were setled? The Answer is obvious at the Expence of the private Adventurers our Ancestors; the Fruit of whose Toil and Danger we now enjoy.

We claim Nothing but the Liberty & Privileges of Englishmen, in the same Degree, as if we had still continued among our Brethren in Great Britain: these Rights have not been forfeited by any Act of ours, we can not be deprived of them without our Consent, but by Violence & Injustice; We have received them from our Ancestors and, with God's Leave, we will transmit them, unimpaired to our Posterity. Can those, who have hitherto acted as our Friends, endeavour now, insidiously, to draw from Us Concessions destructive to what we hold far dearer than Life!

> —If I cou'd find Example Of thousands, that by base Submission had Preserv'd their Freedom, I'd not do't; but since Nor Brass, nor Stone, nor Parchment bears not one; Let Cowardice itself forswear it.—

Our Laws, our Language, our Principles of Government, our Intermarriages, & other Connections, our constant Intercourse, and above all our Interest, are so many Bands which hold us to Great Britain, not to be broken, but by Tyranny and Oppression. Strange, that among the late Ministry, there shou'd not be found a Man of common Sense & common Honesty, to improve & strengthen these natural Tyes by a mild & just Government, instead of weakening, & almost dissolving them by Partiality & Injustice! But I will not open the wounds which have been so lately bound up, and which still require a skilful & a gentle Hand to heal them. . . .

I am, Gentlemen, Your most obdt. Servt.

A Virginia Planter.

DOCUMENT 5.5

Pitt's Speech on the Stamp Act

William Pitt

Gentlemen, Sir, I have been charged with giving birth to sedition in America. They have spoken their sentiments with freedom against this unhappy act, and that freedom has become their crime. Sorry I am to hear the liberty of speech in this house, imputed as a crime. No gentleman ought to be afraid to exercise it. It is a liberty by which the gentleman who calumniates it might have profited, by which he ought to have profited. He ought to have desisted from this project. The gentleman tells us, America is obstinate; America is almost in open rebellion. I rejoice that America has resisted. Three million of people so dead to all feelings of liberty, as voluntarily to submit to be slaves, would have been fit instruments to make slaves of the rest. . . .

With the enemy at their back, with our bayonets at their breasts, in the day of their distress, perhaps the Americans would have submitted to the imposition: but it would have been taking an ungenerous and unjust advantage. The gentleman boasts of his bounties to America. Are not those bounties intended finally for the benefit of this kingdom? If they are not, he has misapplied the national treasures. I am no courtier of America; I stand up for this kingdom. I maintain, that the parliament has a right to bind, to restrain America. Our legislative power over the colonies is sovereign and supreme. When it ceases to be sovereign and supreme, I would advise every gentleman to sell his lands, if he can, and embark for that country. When two countries are connected together, like England and her colonies, without being incorporated, the one must necessarily

Source: From William Pitt's speech to Parliament, delivered January 14, 1766, urging repeal of the Stamp Act. Available at odur.let.rug.nl/~usa/D/1751-1775/stampact/sapitt.htm.

govern; the greater must rule the less; but so rule it, as not to contradict the fundamental principles that are common to both. . . .

The gentleman asks, when were the colonies emancipated? But I desire to know, when were they made slaves. But I dwell not upon words. When I had the honour of serving his Majesty, I availed myself of the means of information which I derived from my office: I speak, therefore, from knowledge. My materials were good; I was at pains to collect, to digest, to consider them; and I will be bold to affirm, that the profits to Great Britain from the trade of the colonies, through all its branches, is two millions a year. This is the fund that carried you triumphantly through the last war. . . . You owe this to America: this is the price America pays you for her protection.

The Americans have not acted in all things with prudence and temper. They have been wronged. They have been driven to madness by injustice. Will you punish them for the madness you have occasioned? Rather let prudence and temper come first from this side. I will undertake for America, that she will follow the example. There are two lines in a ballad of Prior's, of a man's behaviour to his wife, so applicable to you and your colonies, that I cannot help repeating them:

> "Be to her faults a little blind
> Be to her virtues very kind."

Upon the whole, I will beg leave to tell the House what is really my opinion. It is, that the Stamp Act be repealed absolutely, totally, and immediately; that the reason for the repeal should be assigned, because it was founded on an erroneous principle. At the same time, let the sovereign authority of this country over the colonies be asserted in as strong terms as can be devised, and be made to extend every point of legislation whatsoever: that we may bind their trade, confine their manufactures, and exercise every power whatsoever—except that of taking money out of their pockets without their consent.

DOCUMENT 5.6

John Adams Defends Captain Preston

March 5, 1773, the Third Anniversary of the Boston Massacre
John Adams

I . . . devoted myself to endless labour and Anxiety if not to infamy and death, and that for nothing, except, what indeed was and ought to be all in all, a sense of duty. In the Evening I expressed to Mrs. Adams all my Apprehensions: That excellent Lady, who has always encouraged me, burst into a flood of Tears, but said she was very sensible of all the Danger to her and to our Children as well

Source: From John Adams, *Diary and Autobiography of John Adams*, ed. L. H. Butterfield (Cambridge, MA: Belknap Press of Harvard University Press, 1961). Available at www.law.umkc.edu/faculty/-projects/ftrials/bostonmassacre/diaryentries.html.

as to me, but she thought I had done as I ought, she was very willing to share in all that was to come and place her trust in Providence.

Before or after the Tryal, Preston sent me ten Guineas and at the Tryal of the Soldiers afterwards Eight Guineas more, which were . . . all the pecuniary Reward I ever had for fourteen or fifteen days labour, in the most exhausting and fatiguing Causes I ever tried: for hazarding a Popularity very general and very hardly earned: and for incurring a Clamour and popular Suspicions and prejudices, which are not yet worn out and never will be forgotten as long as History of this Period is read. . . . It was immediately bruited abroad that I had engaged for Preston and the Soldiers, and occasioned a great clamour. . . .

The Part I took in Defence of Cptn. Preston and the Soldiers, procured me Anxiety, and Obloquy enough. It was, however, one of the most gallant, generous, manly and disinterested Actions of my whole Life, and one of the best Pieces of Service I ever rendered my Country. Judgment of Death against those Soldiers would have been as foul a Stain upon this Country as the Executions of the Quakers or Witches, anciently. As the Evidence was, the Verdict of the Jury was exactly right.

This however is no Reason why the Town should not call the Action of that Night a Massacre, nor is it any Argument in favour of the Governor or Minister, who caused them to be sent here. But it is the strongest Proofs of the Danger of Standing Armies.

6

Patriots

The American Revolution and the events leading up to it have played a major role in the shaping of American national character. The key players have taken on heroic stature; the major events and documents have become the cause for national celebrations. The image of the minuteman represented in the statue of John Parker at Lexington Green was produced well after the Revolutionary War, but it illustrates salient features of Americans' perception of power and legitimacy. A citizen soldier ready at any minute to take up arms to preserve and protect freedom is a powerful American icon. It represents distaste for formal military strength and power and a faith in the common person. Perhaps it also represents an attitude that the average person knows what is worth fighting for and is sufficiently politically aware to know when to leave the plow and take up the musket.

George Washington, well experienced in warfare, knew that organizing a war for independence was a daunting task. The posters advertising rewards for the apprehension of deserters further illustrate the problems of assembling and maintaining a force sufficient to prevail in the war with England. The trials and tribulations of soldiers and reasons why they might desert are discussed from the perspective of a soldier who made his appeal to the people of America.

There were those, of course, who interpreted their patriotic duty to be to serve the Crown, as illustrated in the advertisement for enlistments in the British army. The forces that Britain assembled to pursue the battle against the colonists represented both the best and the worst of British imperial policies and relationships. As illustrated in the next document, British soldiers were not always humane in their treatment of colonists in the heat of battle.

Finally, the American Revolution became a civil war for Native Americans as well. Both the British and the colonists sought allies among the native peoples, and there were those on both sides who saw the war as an opportunity to attack and eliminate native groups that might stand in the way of further Anglo expansion into the interior.

DOCUMENT 6.1

Statue of John Parker

DOCUMENT 6.2

George Washington on Raising an Army

Letter to the New Hampshire Convention, January 16, 1776
George Washington

Cambridge, January 16, 1776.

The alarming and almost defenceless state of our Lines, occasioned by the slow progress of raising recruits for the New Army and the departure of a great number of the Militia, which had been called in for their Support, till the 15th Instant, from this and New Hampshire Governments; rendered it necessary for

Source: George Washington, "George Washington to New Hampshire Convention, January 16, 1776," *The Writings of George Washington from the Original Manuscript Sources, 1745–1799*, ed. John C. Fitzpatrick (Westport, CT: Greenwood Press, 1970). Available at memory.loc.gov/cgi-bin/query/r?ammem/mgw:@field(DOCID+@lit(gw040223)).

me to Summon the General Officers in Council, to determine on proper measures to be adopted for their maintenance and preservation.

For this purpose, they met at Head Quarters yesterday and to day and finding that it was with the utmost difficulty and persuasion that such part of the latter, as are now here, had been prevailed on to continue till the last of the Month; after which there is not the remotest probability of their staying one moment; they have judged it expedient and absolutely necessary, that thirteen Regiments should be forthwith raised, equal to those of the New Establishment, to be officered according to the usual mode of their respective Governments, which are to repair to this Camp by the last Instant, if possible, to be in readiness to act in such manner and till the 1st of April, as circumstances may require; of this Number they apprehend the Massachusetts should furnish seven, Connecticut four, and your Government two, being agreeable to the proportion settled by Congress.

In order that each Regiment may consist of a proper number of officers and men, I herewith send you a list for their regulation, as also of the Continental Pay.

I must earnestly solicit your regard to Arms, Amunition, Blankets, Clothing and Kettles, that they may come as well provided with these necessary Articles as they can, particularly the first; of which I find, to my great surprize and concern, there is an amazing deficiency; notwithstanding, I have used every precaution my judgment could point out, to procure them.

The great and constant attention Sir, which you have shewn upon all occasions to promote the public cause, affords me the strongest assurance, that your every exertion and Interest will be employed, to comply with these several requisitions. I am Sir &c.

DOCUMENT 6.3

Deserters

DESERTED from the public Service, on the 28th of April last *William Burt*, who ately inlisted into my Company, Col. *Benjamin Tupper's* Regiment —He is about 23 years of Age, 5 Feet 10 Inches high, much pock-broken ; had on when he went away, a light-coloured Coat, green Facings, green Waistcoat and Breeches. Whoever will take up said Deserter, and convey him to his Regiment, or confine him in Goal, so that he may be brought to Justice, shall have FIVE DOLLARS Reward, and all necessary Charges, paid by
BENJAMIN FARNUM, Capt.
Andover, May 11, 1778.

TEN DOLLARS REWARD.
DESERTED from my company, in Maj. Ebenezer Steven's corps of Artillery, *John Flinn*, about five feet seven inches high, short hair, speaks broad : — *Joseph Mooney*, about five feet three inches high, long black hair, is very slow in speech — also *John Rods*, five feet nine inches high, short light hair ; all had on their regimentals when they went off. Any person who will apprehend said deserters, and deliver them to Lieut. *M'Lane*, in *Boston*, or to me in camp, shall receive the above Reward for each, and all necessary charges paid by me,
JOHN WINSLOW, Capt. *of Artillery*.
Boston, *June* 15, 1778.

DOCUMENT 6.4

To the People of America

I have served in your army from the beginning of the war, and now, while I am indulging the pleasing thought of our having nearly compleated the salvation of our country, I hear a clamour that all is going to ruin. I therefore beg leave to speak a few words. It is agreed, I think by all our talkers and writers, that the depreciation of our money and morals, is the only dangerous symptom in our nation. And shall we, like dastard fouls, think this difficulty insurmountable? And after bearing millstones, sink under the weight of a feather? Let us not stain our glory by ranking this among *difficulties*.—It is even infamous in us, who are honored by Heaven to defend the rights of mankind and posterity, who

Source: Massachusetts newspaper, the *Independent Ledger and the American Advertiser*, July 5, 1779. Document available at home.ptd.net/%7Erevwar/njgaz.html; the War for American Independence Website, owned by Alan Shields.

are pursuing national salvation and solid glory, to hesitate and say, *"There is a Lion in the way."*—When our General leads us on to attack the enemy, we don't pause and ask if there are not difficulties to encounter—we know that nothing glorious can be done without labor, hazard or expence.—In like manner, the people must follow and put into execution the orders of our Supreme Council. Let Congress direct the means and mode of redress for the depreciation of our currency, and let the people set about it instantly, and pursue it with vigor, and the mighty difficulty so much talked about will soon vanish. There is nothing to oppose it but a *rascally* (pardon the expression) love of *self*. And shall this dirty grovelling passion for *earth*, bury all our glorious designs for the happiness of living millions and unborn ages!—Then witness against us, ye beings who people other worlds—and let us sink (like Satan in *Milton*) "nine times the space that measures day and night," nor any longer stain the annals of the world.

The depreciation of morals is an evil big with ruin, but like the other, admits a cure. Vices, like noxious weeds, commonly have a small beginning; but if suffered to take root and spread, they destroy the beauty and happiness of creation. A great deal has been said and written against profane swearing, but what avails a clamour? A remedy must be applied that will make men *feel;* for if there was not a defect in their *mentality*, they would not practice a vice as destitute of honor, pleasure or profit, as *Satan* is of beauty or virtue—vice which is the *filth* of conversation, disgusting to the virtuous and wise, and condemned by the wisdom of the whole universe. Therefore, they must *feel* before they reform. The remedy is with the PEOPLE, they must never dishonor themselves by chusing men to represent them who dishonor God or their country. Let no man be exalted to a seat in Congress, who has not a soul too great to countenance *any* vice; and when none but the virtuous and wise sit in Congress, you will see wisdom and virtue prevailing in every inferior station. I believe there is as much patriotism and wisdom in Congress as in any political body on earth, but it wounds my feelings when I hear of some in that august Council who set examples unworthy of imitation: I hope they are few, very few in number. And that State should blush which sends a *blemished* character to sit in that Council, which ought to be entirely composed of wisdom and virtue. There is nothing wanting to remove all our national difficulties, and to complete the happiness of America, but a noble exertion of those means which God hath put into our hands. Then let us make this exertion, and our Independence will be secure and our fame immortal.

A SOLDIER.

P.S. *Many have endeavored to rouse their countrymen to exertions by painting the wickedness of our enemies, and the horrors of tyranny; as they are both too black for description, I will not attempt it. But the horrid murder of hundreds and thousands of our brethren in the gaols and dungeons of the British* Monsters, *ought to be ever fresh in our minds! And while we contemplate the numberless tortures inflicted on our brave and virtuous citizens, we shall naturally consider what our portion would be, should Heaven in wrath permit the accursed foe to prevail over us.*

Were there not many innocent persons in Britain who might suffer by the continuance of the war, I query whether it would not be an offence to Heaven to make any peace with the tyrant, until we had scourged him off the face of the earth.

DOCUMENT 6.5

Recruiting Loyalist Troops

EMMERICK's CHASSEURS,

To all Gentlemen Volunteers,

BY Virtue of a Warrant from his Excellency Sir HENRY CLINTON, K. B. and Commander in Chief of all his Majesty's Forces in North-America, bearing Date the 30th of April, 1778,

Lieut. Col. Commandant EMMERICK,

Is now raising Six Companies of Foot, to consist of 360 Rank and File, and Two Troops of Light Dragoons, to consist of 100 Men, who will receive immediately their Bounty before attested; their Pay, Provision, and Cloathing regular, and agreeable to the King's Allowance, without clipping or deduction. To any that bring Horses fit for the Service, the Price will be paid immediately. ------- For which Purpose proper Officers will be stationed in New-York, on Long-Island, Staten-Island, Philadelphia, and elsewhere. The Refugees who are single Young Men, and out of Employ, should particularly manifest their Zeal on this Occasion, and shew that they are in Reality Friends to his Majesty.

Whoever knows EMMERICK, knows that his Soldiers live like Gentlemen, and that all such as behave well, he treats like a Brother.

God Save the King.

Source: Andreas Emmerick, Printed Proclamation to Raise Loyalist Troops, April 30, 1778, from memory.loc.gov/mss/mgw/mgw4/050/0600/0655.jpg.

DOCUMENT 6.6

Retribution in War

Continental Congress, September 27, 1781

The committee on the motion of Mr. [John] Mathews, together with the letters from Governor Trumbull and General Greene relative to the burning of New London and Georgetown, delivered in their respective reports.

That the United States in Congress assembled did on the [date missing] day of October A.D. 1778, resolve, "that if our enemies persist in their present career of barbarity we will take such exemplary Vengeance as shall deter others from a like conduct." "We appeal to that God who searches the hearts of men for the rectitude of our intentions, and in his holy presence declare, that we are not moved by any light and hasty suggestions of anger or revenge, so through every possible change of fortune we will adhere to this our determination." The conduct of Britons alone could have produced such a determination, and their persisting in the most savage and barbarous acts impel the United States to execute this Resolution. The flourishing villages of Charlestown and Falmouth in Massachusetts, in the year 1775, Norfolk in Virginia in 1776, Kingston in New York in 1777, Bristol in Rhode Island and Bedford in Massachusetts in 1778, Fairfield and Norwalk in Connecticut in 1779, Springfield and Connecticut Farms in New Jersey 1780, and Georgetown in South Carolina and New London and Groton in Connecticut in 1781, have been consigned by these enemies of Mankind to wanton conflagrations! The ties of relatives have been dissolved by deliberate murder while the most sacred conditions have only tended to enhance Barbarity! The nations of the earth render to bravery the tribute of honor and esteem, while Britons murder the Brave; when captives in their power! Justice has been delayed; but the most solemn of oaths joined to invincible necessity, demand retaliation.

The United States in Congress assembled do therefore resolve, that the War and Marine Departments take order for the demolition of cities and villages in the Kingdom of Great Britain so as fully to retaliate for the destruction of the towns and villages before mentioned.

Resolved, That unless satisfaction be immediately made for the inhuman murder of the brave garrison of Fort Grinnell in the State of Connecticut, after surrendering prisoners of war on the 6th Instant either by consigning to public execution the principal officers concerned in that bloody massacre, or in such other way as shall fully appertain to justice, retaliation shall be had by the execution of an adequate number of British officers and soldiers.

Resolved, If the British Army and Navy continue their present system of inhumanity in burning defenceless villages, or houses, or in murdering inoffensive citizens or prisoners of war, that the War and Marine Departments cause all persons taken in such acts of burning to be immediately consigned to the flames, or afterwards if captivated to be put to death.

Source: Journals of the Continental Congress, Thursday, September 27, 1781, American Memory, Library of Congress, memory.loc.gov/cgi-bin/query/D?hlaw:13:./temp/~ammem_1Hvg:.

DOCUMENT 6.7

Mary Jemison Remembers

Mary Jemison

Chapter 7

After the conclusion of the French war, our tribe had nothing to do till the com-
mencement of the American Revolution. For twelve or fifteen years, the use of
the implements of war was not known, nor the war whoop heard, save on days
of festivity, when the achievements of former times were commemorated in a
kind of mimic warfare, in which the chiefs, and warriors displayed their
prowess, and illustrated their former adroitness, by laying the ambuscade, surprising their enemies, and performing many accurate maneuvers with the tom-
ahawk and scalping knife; thereby preserving, and banding to their children, the
theory of Indian warfare. During that period they also pertinaciously observed
the religious rites of their progenitors, by attending with the most scrupulous ex-
actness, and a great degree of enthusiasm, to the sacrifices, at particular times, to
appease the anger of the Evil Deity; or to excite the commiseration of the Great
Good Spirit, whom they adored with reverence, as the author, governor, sup-
porter, and disposer of every good thing of which they participated.

They also practiced in various athletic games, such as running, wrestling,
leaping, and playing ball, with a view that their bodies might be more supple—
or, rather, that they might not become enervated, and that they might be enabled to make a proper selection of chiefs for the councils of the nation, and
leaders for war.

While the Indians were thus engaged in their round of traditional perfor-
mances, with the addition of hunting, their women attended to agriculture,
their families, and a few domestic concerns of small consequence and attended
with but little labor.

No people can live more happy than the Indians did in times of peace, before the introduction of spiritous liquors among them. Their lives were a continual round of pleasures. Their wants were few, and easily satisfied, and their cares
were only for today—the bounds of their calculation for future comfort not extending to the incalculable uncertainties of tomorrow. If peace ever dwelt with
men, it was in former times, in the recess from war, among what are now termed
barbarians. The moral character of the Indians was (if I may be allowed the expression) uncontaminated. Their fidelity was perfect, and became proverbial.
They were strictly honest; they despised deception and falsehood; and chastity
was held in high veneration, and a violation of it was considered sacrilege. They
were temperate in their desires, moderate in their passions, and candid and honorable in the expression of their sentiments, on every subject of importance.

Source: Excerpted from James E. Seaver, *The Life of Mary Jemison: The White Woman of the Gene-
see* (1824; 5th ed., New York, 1877). Available at personal.pitnet.net/primarysources/jemison.html.

Thus, at peace among themselves and with the neighboring whites—though there were none at that time very near—our Indians lived quietly and peaceably at home, till a little before the breaking out of the Revolutionary War.

* * *

Chapter 9

Soon after the close of the Revolutionary War, my Indian brother, Kau-jises-tau-ge-au, (which being interpreted signifies Black Coals,) offered me my liberty, and told me that if it was my choice I might go to my friends.

My son Thomas was anxious that I should go; and offered to go with me, and assist me on the journey, by taking care of the younger children, and providing food as we traveled through the wilderness. But the chiefs of our tribe, suspecting, from his appearance, actions, and a few warlike exploits, that Thomas would be a great warrior, or a good counselor, refused to let him leave them on any account whatever.

To go myself, and leave him, was more than I felt able to do; for he had been kind to me, and was one on whom I placed great dependence. The chiefs refusing to let him go was one reason for my resolving to stay; but another, more powerful if possible, was, that I had got a large family of Indian children that I must take with me; and that, if I should be so fortunate as to find my relatives, they would despise them, if not myself, and treat us as enemies, or, at least, with a degree of cold indifference, which I thought I could not endure.

Accordingly, after I had duly considered the matter, I told my brother that it was my choice to stay and spend the remainder of my days with my Indian friends, and live with my family as I hitherto had done. He appeared well pleased with my resolution, and informed me that, as that was my choice, I should have a piece of land that I could call my own, where I could live unmolested, and have something at my decease to leave for the benefit of my children.

7

Confederacy

With peace won, the task for the victors was to consolidate the victory and fashion a viable confederacy of states. Initially, the democratic sentiments and the fear of centralized government may have influenced state governments and local political leaders to seek to keep the democratic machinery of independence close to the people in local structures. There were also those who sought to craft something more unified and identifiable as the United States of America. The original design of the Great Seal of the United States was filled with symbolism that might contribute to a shared sense of destiny.

From a practical point of view, the political system had to devise a way of dealing with both the western land claims of the original states and the western lands that did not fit into any one state's claims or aspirations. In addressing the issue of western lands and possible future growth, an ingenious mechanism was devised. The North West Ordinances of the 1780s created a process by which western territories would become part of the national domain, the land surveyed and mapped, and sold at increasingly affordable prices to citizens seeking self-sustaining farms and homesteads. Moreover, when the population of a region reached a certain level, the people in that territory could begin the process of organizing a territorial government and begin the steps to statehood. The truly brilliant aspect of this process was that a system was devised by which democracy would grow and expand and that subsequent states would enter the union with all the same rights, privileges, and powers of the original thirteen states. As with Britain, all other nations had systems of expanding and acquiring more land and territory. But nowhere else in the world were the colonial areas embraced as equals with the mother country.

On the road to properly balancing the power of local and state governments with the federal and central government, there were tensions and conflicts that illustrated the need for stable and reliable authority structures. Daniel Shays, in service to the very freedoms and values he believed he had fought for during the American Revolution, illustrated with his rebellion the tension between human *rights and property rights. Thomas Jefferson thought that it was good for patriots to shake up existing governmental systems from time to time to assure responsiveness to the needs and aspirations of the people. During Shays's Rebellion, James Bowdoin, as governor of Massachusetts, was entrusted with preserving the state's economic and legal systems while being sensitive to the needs of citizens. His report to the people illustrates that even though he took the necessary steps to thwart Shays's movement, he also sought remedies to the cause of discontent in western Massachusetts.*

Having established policies that solved the legal and political issues of westward migration, the young nation continued to face problems with native populations in the west. Native Americans sought to preserve their worlds, as well as accommodations they had learned to expect from Europeans. Native Americans might well have preferred to continue living under the authority and protection of a political system that sought primarily to trade with them rather than a system that sought to dispossess them of their land and territory, but there were ample opportunities for clever manipulators on both sides. After one of the worst defeats of American forces at the hands of Native Americans, General Anthony Wayne was commissioned to pacify the Native Americans and secure their land for white settlement. Organizing his campaign also forced him to come to terms with the abilities and capabilities of those under his command.

Finally, as the two political cartoons from different eras represent, a recurring theme through this period was unity and how to achieve it. The first cartoon was published in the 1750s by Benjamin Franklin to garner support for his Albany Plan of Union, proposed, in part, to strengthen colonial defenses against Native American warriors. The second cartoon was published to support the ratification of the Constitution, the new plan of government designed to address the needs of unity and stability in a national government that could inspire faith among its citizens and gain the respect of its foes.

DOCUMENT 7.1

Original Design of the Great Seal of the United States, 1782

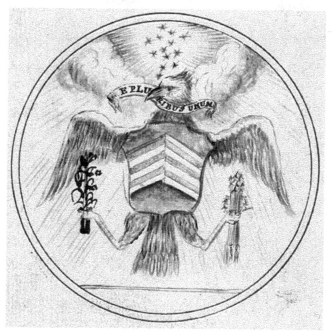

DOCUMENT 7.2

The North West Ordinance, 1787

... And, for extending the fundamental principles of civil and religious liberty, which form the basis whereon these republics, their laws and constitutions are erected; to fix and establish those principles as the basis of all laws, constitutions, and governments, which forever hereafter shall be formed in the said territory: to provide also for the establishment of States, and permanent government therein, and for their admission to a share in the federal councils on an equal footing with the original States, at as early periods as may be consistent with the general interest:

Source: Original design of the Great Seal of the United States, 1782, available at www.ourdocuments .gov/content.php?page=zoom&doc=5.
Source: North West Ordinance, approved by Congress, July 13, 1787. Available at odur.let.rug.nl/~usa/D/1776-1800/ohio/norwes.htm.

It is hereby ordained and declared by the authority aforesaid, That the following articles shall be considered as articles of compact between the original States and the people and States in the said territory and forever remain unalterable, unless by common consent, to wit:

Article 1. No person, demeaning himself in a peaceable and orderly manner, shall ever be molested on account of his mode of worship or religious sentiments, in the said territory.

Article 2. The inhabitants of the said territory shall always be entitled to the benefits of the writ of habeas corpus, and of the trial by jury; of a proportionate representation of the people in the legislature; and of judicial proceedings according to the course of the common law. All persons shall be bailable, unless for capital offenses, where the proof shall be evident or the presumption great. All fines shall be moderate; and no cruel or unusual punishments shall be inflicted. No man shall be deprived of his liberty or property, but by the judgment of his peers or the law of the land; and, should the public exigencies make it necessary, for the common preservation, to take any person's property, or to demand his particular services, full compensation shall be made for the same. And, in the just preservation of rights and property, it is understood and declared, that no law ought ever to be made, or have force in the said territory, that shall, in any manner whatever, interfere with or affect private contracts or engagements, bona fide, and without fraud, previously formed.

Article 3. Religion, morality, and knowledge, being necessary to good government and the happiness of mankind, schools and the means of education shall forever be encouraged. The utmost good faith shall always be observed towards the Indians; their lands and property shall never be taken from them without their consent; and, in their property, rights, and liberty, they shall never be invaded or disturbed, unless in just and lawful wars authorized by Congress; but laws founded in justice and humanity, shall from time to time be made for preventing wrongs being done to them, and for preserving peace and friendship with them.

Article 4. The said territory, and the States which may be formed therein, shall forever remain a part of this Confederacy of the United States of America, subject to the Articles of Confederation, and to such alterations therein as shall be constitutionally made; and to all the acts and ordinances of the United States in Congress assembled, conformable thereto. The inhabitants and settlers in the said territory shall be subject to pay a part of the federal debts contracted or to be contracted, and a proportional part of the expenses of government, to be apportioned on them by Congress according to the same common rule and measure by which apportionments thereof shall be made on the other States; and the taxes for paying their proportion shall be laid and levied by the authority and direction of the legislatures of the district or districts, or new States, as in the original States, within the time agreed upon by the United States in Congress assembled.

The legislatures of those districts or new States, shall never interfere with the primary disposal of the soil by the United States in Congress assembled, nor with any regulations Congress may find necessary for securing the title in such soil to the bona fide purchasers. No tax shall be imposed on lands the property of the United States; and, in no case, shall nonresident proprietors be taxed higher than residents. The navigable waters leading into the Mississippi and St. Lawrence, and the carrying places between the same, shall be common highways and forever free, as well to the inhabitants of the said territory as to the citizens of the United States, and those of any other States that may be admitted into the confederacy, without any tax, impost, or duty therefor.

Article 5. There shall be formed in the said territory, not less than three nor more than five States; and the boundaries of the States, as soon as Virginia shall alter her act of cession, and consent to the same, shall become fixed and established as follows, to wit: The western State in the said territory, shall be bounded by the Mississippi, the Ohio, and Wabash Rivers; a direct line drawn from the Wabash and Post Vincents, due North, to the territorial line between the United States and Canada; and, by the said territorial line, to the Lake of the Woods and Mississippi. The middle State shall be bounded by the said direct line, the Wabash from Post Vincents to the Ohio, by the Ohio, by a direct line, drawn due north from the mouth of the Great Miami, to the said territorial line, and by the said territorial line. The eastern State shall be bounded by the last mentioned direct line, the Ohio, Pennsylvania, and the said territorial line: Provided, however, and it is further understood and declared, that the boundaries of these three States shall be subject so far to be altered, that, if Congress shall hereafter find it expedient, they shall have authority to form one or two States in that part of the said territory which lies north of an east and west line drawn through the southerly bend or extreme of Lake Michigan. And, whenever any of the said States shall have sixty thousand free inhabitants therein, such State shall be admitted, by its delegates, into the Congress of the United States, on an equal footing with the original States in all respects whatever, and shall be at liberty to form a permanent constitution and State government: Provided, the constitution and government so to be formed, shall be republican, and in conformity to the principles contained in these articles; and, so far as it can be consistent with the general interest of the confederacy, such admission shall be allowed at an earlier period, and when there may be a less number of free inhabitants in the State than sixty thousand.

Article 6. There shall be neither slavery nor involuntary servitude in the said territory, otherwise than in the punishment of crimes whereof the party shall have been duly convicted: Provided, always, That any person escaping into the same, from whom labor or service is lawfully claimed in any one of the original States, such fugitive may be lawfully reclaimed and conveyed to the person claiming his or her labor or service as aforesaid.

DOCUMENT 7.3

A Little Rebellion Now and Then

A Letter from Thomas Jefferson to James Madison
Thomas Jefferson

Paris, January 30th, 1787

Dear Sir,

My last to you was of the 16th of December; since which, I have received yours of November 25 and December 4, which afforded me, as your letters always do, a treat on matters public, individual, and economical. I am impatient to learn your sentiments on the late troubles in the Eastern states. So far as I have yet seen, they do not appear to threaten serious consequences. Those states have suffered by the stoppage of the channels of their commerce, which have not yet found other issues. This must render money scarce and make the people uneasy. This uneasiness has produced acts absolutely unjustifiable; but I hope they will provoke no severities from their governments. A consciousness of those in power that their administration of the public affairs has been honest may, perhaps, produce too great a degree of indignation; and those characters, wherein fear predominates over hope, may apprehend too much from these instances of irregularity. They may conclude too hastily that nature has formed man insusceptible of any other government than that of force, a conclusion not founded in truth or experience.

Societies exist under three forms, sufficiently distinguishable: (1) without government, as among our Indians; (2) under governments, wherein the will of everyone has a just influence, as is the case in England, in a slight degree, and in our states, in a great one; (3) under governments of force, as is the case in all other monarchies, and in most of the other republics.

To have an idea of the curse of existence under these last, they must be seen. It is a government of wolves over sheep. It is a problem, not clear in my mind, that the first condition is not the best. But I believe it to be inconsistent with any great degree of population. The second state has a great deal of good in it. The mass of mankind under that enjoys a precious degree of liberty and happiness. It has its evils, too, the principal of which is the turbulence to which it is subject. But weigh this against the oppressions of monarchy, and it becomes nothing. Malo periculosam libertatem quam quietam servitutem. Even this evil is productive of good. It prevents the degeneracy of government and nourishes a general attention to the public affairs.

I hold it that a little rebellion now and then is a good thing, and as necessary in the political world as storms in the physical. Unsuccessful rebellions, indeed, generally establish the encroachments on the rights of the people which have produced them. An observation of this truth should render honest republican governors so mild in their punishment of rebellions as not to discourage them too much. It is a medicine necessary for the sound health of government.

Source: Letter from Thomas Jefferson to James Madison, January 30, 1787, earlyamerica.com/review/summer/letter.html.

If these transactions give me no uneasiness, I feel very differently at another piece of intelligence, to wit, the possibility that the navigation of the Mississippi may be abandoned to Spain. I never had any interest westward of the Allegheny; and I will never have any. But I have had great opportunities of knowing the character of the people who inhabit that country; and I will venture to say that the act which abandons the navigation of the Mississippi is an act of separation between the Eastern and Western country. It is a relinquishment of five parts out of eight of the territory of the United States; an abandonment of the fairest subject for the payment of our public debts, and the chaining those debts on our own necks, in perpetuum.

I have the utmost confidence in the honest intentions of those who concur in this measure; but I lament their want of acquaintance with the character and physical advantages of the people, who, right or wrong, will suppose their interests sacrificed on this occasion to the contrary interests of that part of the confederacy in possession of present power. If they declare themselves a separate people, we are incapable of a single effort to retain them. Our citizens can never be induced, either as militia or as soldiers, to go there to cut the throats of their own brothers and sons, or rather, to be themselves the subjects instead of the perpetrators of the parricide.

Nor would that country quit the cost of being retained against the will of its inhabitants, could it be done. But it cannot be done. They are able already to rescue the navigation of the Mississippi out of the hands of Spain, and to add New Orleans to their own territory. They will be joined by the inhabitants of Louisiana. This will bring on a war between them and Spain; and that will produce the question with us, whether it will not be worth our while to become parties with them in the war in order to reunite them with us and thus correct our error. And were I to permit my forebodings to go one step further, I should predict that the inhabitants of the United States would force their rulers to take the affirmative of that question. I wish I may be mistaken in all these opinions.

Yours affectionately,
Th. Jefferson

DOCUMENT 7.4

James Bowdoin on Shays's Rebellion

An Address, to the Good People of the Commonwealth
James Bowdoin, Governor of the Commonwealth of Massachusetts

A Spirit of discontent, originating in supposed grievances, having, in the course of the last fall, stimulated many of the citizens in several of the Counties of this Commonwealth, to the commission of acts subversive of government, and of the peace and security derived from it, I thought it expedient to assemble, and

Source: James Bowdoin, "An Address, to the Good People of the Commonwealth," broadside (Boston: Adams & Nourse, 1787). Available at memory.loc.gov/cgi-bin/query/r?ammem/rbpe:@field(DOCID+ (rbpe04300600)).

accordingly did assemble, the General Court for the special purpose of considering those grievances, and all complaints whatever, and if possible, removing the causes of them. A patient and candid attention was paid to the business of the Session, and every relief given, consistent with the existence of government, and the principles of equal justice. These the Legislature could not infringe, without bringing upon themselves the detestation of mankind, and the frowns of Heaven.

But relief was not the only object, upon which the General court bestowed their attention. In tenderness to the misguided, and in hopes of reclaiming the obstinate, an Act of Indemnity was passed for all the outrages, which had been committed against law, and the officers of it, upon this mild condition alone, that the perpetrators should return to a due submission to lawful authority; and, as a test of their sincerity, should, before the first day of January following, take and subscribe the oaths of allegiance, required by the Constitution.

In addition to these measures, the state of the Treasury, the expenditure of monies received, the situation of our foreign and domestic debt, and other important matters, were, in particular detail, communicated to the people, by an address from the Legislature. In that address they were also informed, of the dangerous and destructive tendency of popular insurrections; and the Insurgents were conjured, in the most serious and persuasive manner, to desist from their lawless conduct, lest they should involve themselves and their country in ruin. But, what have been the consequences?—The measures intended for giving them satisfaction and indemnity have been spurned at: And since the publication of those measures, the same Insurgents have frequently embodied, and with a military force, repeatedly interrupted the Judicial Courts in the Counties of Hampshire and Worcester: which demonstrates, that the Government is held by them at open defiance; and that the laws are, in those Counties, laid prostrate.

By a resolve of the 24th of October, the Legislature expressed their full confidence, that the Governour would persevere in the exercise of the powers, vested in him by the Constitution, for enforcing due obedience to the authority and laws of government; and for preventing any attempts to interrupt the administration of law and justice; upon which the peace and safety of the Commonwealth so essentially depend.

In the present dangerous and critical situation of affairs, I feel myself constrained, by the most sacred obligations of duty, and for the purposes intended by the Legislature, to call those powers into immediate exercise, for the protection of the Commonwealth, against the attempts of all persons who shall enterprize its destruction, invasion, detriment or annoyance: And I have accordingly, pursuant to my own ideas of duty, as well as the expectations of the General Court, ordered a part of the Militia to assemble in arms, for the purpose of protecting the Judicial Courts next to be holden in the County of Worcester; of aiding the Civil Magistrate to execute the laws; of repelling all Insurgents against the Government; and of apprehending all disturbers of the public peace. It is now become evident, that the object of the Insurgents is to annihilate our present happy constitution, or to force the General Court into measures repugnant to every idea of justice, good faith, and national policy.

And those who encourage, or in any way assist them, either individually, or in a corporate capacity, do partake of their guilt; and will be legally responsible for it. Success, on the part of the Insurgents, in either of those views, must be destructive of civil liberty, and of the important blessings derived from it: and as it would be the result of force, undirected by any moral principle, it must finally terminate in despotism—despotism in the worst of its forms.

Is then the goodly fabric of freedom, which cost us so much blood and treasure, so soon to be thrown into ruins?—Is it to stand but just long enough, and for no other purpose than, to flatter the tyrants of the earth in their darling maxim, that mankind are not made to be free?

The present is certainly a most interesting period; and if we wish to support that goodly fabric, and to avoid domestick slavery, men of principle, the friends of justice and the Constitution, must now take their stations, and unite under the Government in every effort for suppressing the present commotions and all insurrections whatever, or be infamously accessory to their own and their country's ruin. But in such an union, should they prove as firm in the support of justice and the Constitution, as the Insurgents have been obstinate in trampling them under their feet, the force of government will have so decided a superiority as to put an end to the present convulsions, and restore a regular administration of law, without the horrors of bloodshed, and a civil war: which I most ardently deprecate; and will strenuously [sic] endeavor to prevent.

But unless such a force appears, those, which indeed are the greatest of national evils, seem inevitable.

If the Constitution is to be destroyed, and insurrection stalk unopposed by authority, individuals, as they regard their own happiness and freedom, will, from necessity, combine for defence, and meet force with force: or voluntarily and ingloriously relinquish the blessings, without which life would cease to be desirable; and which, by the laws of God and Nature ought never to be tamely surrendered.

What would be the end of such events, is known only to Him, who can open the volume and read the pages of futurity.

Strongly impressed with the truth of these ideas, I must conjure the good people of the Commonwealth, as they value life and the enjoyments of it, as they regard their own characters, and the dignity of human nature, to summon up every virtuous principle within them, and to co-operate with Government in every necessary exertion, for restoring to the Commonwealth that order, harmony and peace, upon which its happiness and character do essentially depend.

Given at the Council-Chamber, in Boston, the 12th day of January, 1787; and in the eleventh year of the Independence of the Confederated States of America.

James Bowdoin.

DOCUMENT 7.5

Promises to Native Americans

A Letter from Six Northern Tribes, 1793

To Mr. Don Trudeau, Lieutenant Governor at Saint Louis.

MY FATHER: We, your children, the Loups, Miamis, Ottawas, Potawatomis, Peorias, and Shawnees, beg you to listen to our words today.

In the past, we used to be with our first father, the Frenchman, whom we always recognized as our real father during the time we were under his domination, and whom we have had the misfortune to lose. However, upon leaving us, he gave us proof that he was a good father by saying to us: "My children, you see the misfortune which is happening to me in losing the country, and you, my children. But I leave you one recourse, which is to go and join your father the Spaniard, who is your father, as I have been yours. Follow my advice; go to him and you will be well received, because I and the Spaniard are allies, and consequently he is your father like myself."

We followed this good advice, but we delayed a few years, upon the pleas of the English who were telling us to stay quietly on our lands, and that they would uphold us and be our fathers. We remained as a result of those offers, but have always looked upon the Englishman as a borrowed father, seeing that he made no alliance with our first father, the Frenchman, nor with our Spanish father. We have perceived that his offers were motivated by the needs he had of us, so that, instead of aiding us and saving our lands, he is letting us lose them, as well as several of our village and war chiefs and a number of our young men who have been killed. We noticed our losses, too late. The desire to retain the lands where we were born and where the bones of our fathers rest, had forced this delay in following the advice of our first father. The Americans have also fooled us with peace treaties which have been neither stable nor sincere on their part, since they usually resumed the war immediately.

We therefore believe, my father, that you are good; we are even sure of it, since you receive us with an open heart and extend to us your beneficent hands. We are coming then to lock ourselves in your bosom; receive use [sic] like your own children.

When we arrived upon your lands, our father (Mr. Cruzat) received us with open arms, saying to us: "My children, hunt and sow in order to feed and clothe your families; settle on my lands and remain at peace with all the nations that are my children; do not disturb them and do not get mixed up in bad transactions. If someone comes to trouble you, complain to me and I shall give you justice." We hunted peacefully to sustain our families without disturbing anybody all the time that our father (Mr. Cruzat) remained here. He treated us like his

Source: "Northern Indians to Trudeau," 1793, *Spain in the Mississippi Valley, 1765–1794,* ed. Lawrence Kinnaird (Washington, DC: Government Printing Office, 1949), part 3, pp. 110–11. Available at www.gbl.indiana.edu/archives/dockett_317/317_8d.html#110.

real children. We never have had to complain to him for nobody disturbed us; but as soon as he had left us and our father (Mr. Perez) had taken his place, we were assaulted on all sides by the Osages who murdered us, stole our horses, and we remembered what our father (Mr. Cruzat) has said about coming to complain to him.

Last year, when our father (Mr. Perez) sent for us in connection with the unfortunate business which happened in St. Louis, we complained to him. He said to us, upon decorating our chief with a medal, that it was an image of our father (the King), and that the flag that he was giving us was to clean and chase away the foul air which might arise on our path; and he also said that he would send no merchandise to the Osages, that he would summon them and that he would let us know when they were at his house, in order to speak to them in our presence. Those are the things he told us before several Frenchmen, our fathers, who had accompanied us.

All the promises which our father (Mr. Perez) made to us have not been fulfilled. The roads which he claimed would be white, are strewn with our bones; the Osages have come to him, and he has not warned us of it; on the contrary, their arrival was hidden from us and we did not get the satisfaction of talking to them. You see, my father, that we have not been the aggressors as regards the Osages. We have not sought revenge for all the bad they have done to us without cause. We come to you, my father, to accomplish it, and we ask you to restrain them and prevent them from killing our horses which are our sole resourse for the maintenance of our families. Examine carefully our sad situation, my father, and render us the right and justice which is due us. May the Master of Life grant you happy days and endow you with a watchful eye to watch over the conduct and the happiness of your children, the Loups, Miamis, Ottawas, Potawatomis, Shawnees, and Peorias.

DOCUMENT 7.6

Defeating the Indians

Letter from Anthony Wayne to Charles Scott, September 26, 1793
Anthony Wayne

Dear Sir,

I have to acknowledge the receipt of your letters . . . and am truly astonished at the reluctance discovered by too many of the mounted volunteers to meet the common Enemy, in order to save the effusion of much innocent blood, as well as difficulty and danger in future.

This is not a common, or little predatory war, made by a few tribes of Indians: it is a confederated war, forming a chain of circumvallation round the frontiers of America, from Canada to East Florida—and unless the fire kindled at

Source: Letter from Anthony Wayne to Charles Scott, September 26, 1793. Image of original available at American Memory, Library of Congress, memory.loc.gov.

the *Miami of the Lake* is extinguished by the blood of the *Hydra* (now a little way in our front) it will inevitably spread along the frontiers of Pennsylvania, Virginia, Kentucky, the Territory S.W. of the Ohio, South Carolina & Georgia inclusive.

One united & gallant effort of the Legion and mounted volunteers will save the lives of many, very many thousands of helpless women & children.

You will therefore immediately advance with every man you may have collected or that you can collect by the 1st of October; leaving a sufficient number of officers to bring forward the Drafts that are to be made agreeably to the enclosed copy of a letter to his Excellency Gov. Shelby for that purpose.

Wishing you Life and happiness
I am with Sincere Esteem
your most obedient
humble Servant

Anthony Wayne

The Hon.
Major General C. Scott

DOCUMENT 7.7

Political Cartoons

8

A More Perfect Union

Having forged the Constitution, the supporters of the new federalism had to build a new government from the ground up. They had already accepted the value of the concept of separation of powers; the creation of an independent federal judiciary was a logical next step. Defining the national territory and establishing the appropriate relationship between the people within those borders and those on their edges was another necessary task. But regardless of how blessed with liberty or how wise the country's leadership, the realities of life still prevailed as Philip Freneau illustrates in his poem about an epidemic that raged through Philadelphia.

It was widely accepted that an educated citizenry was the soul of American democracy and perhaps its most reliable defense mechanism. Education, however, meant different things to different people, as is illustrated in the discussion of the education of women.

Freedom from outside rule brought with it a host of economic opportunities as well. To encourage the inventiveness of Americans and to stimulate the creation of useful machines, the nation developed patent laws, which protected and assured remuneration for innovation and creativity. Eli Whitney, more than once, secured the exclusive rights to profits derived from inventions he patented. One such machine was the cotton gin, which had a profound effect on the entire country as it reestablished the profitability of southern agriculture and revitalized what some had hoped was a dying labor system—slavery.

Throughout the early years, the Washington and Adams administrations sought to navigate the United States through a series of firsts, ranging from a first President and Congress to first encounters with complicated and dangerous foreign relations that might have drawn the fledgling and barely solvent United States into foreign wars and schemes. In so doing, they also laid the foundation for the first political parties and the first partisan elections. In this context, the Adams administration sought to protect itself from criticism and intimidate those portions of the press that favored the Jeffersonians. One result was the Sedition Act, which to many seemed to be a step back in time to attitudes and jurisprudence prior to the Zenger case. Ironically, the Democratic-Republican press was more invigorated by the challenge of the Sedition Act than intimidated by it. There were more anti-Adams newspapers after the passage of the act than before it. Those newspapers contributed to a lively political debate that secured the presidency for Thomas Jefferson in what many have called the "Revolution of 1800." That the national government could be changed peacefully through ballots instead of bullets was perhaps the greatest confirmation of the success of the new government under the Constitution.

While heralding the success of the American democratic experiment, the election of 1800 also revealed that experience could and would reveal problems or potential problems with the system. An ambitious Aaron Burr sought to manipulate the procedures established for presidential and vice presidential ballots to win the presidency for himself. To fix this problem, the Twelfth Amendment was passed and ratified to clarify the selection process, though the Electoral College was retained as a protection against direct democracy.

DOCUMENT 8.1

The Federal Judiciary Act of 1789

Chap. XX. *An Act to establish the Judicial Courts of the United States.*

Section 1. *Be it enacted by the Senate and House of Representatives of the United States of America in Congress assembled,* That the supreme court of the United States shall consist of a chief justice and five associate justices, any four of whom shall be a quorum, and shall hold annually at the seat of government two sessions, the one commencing the first Monday of February, and the other the first Monday of August. That the associate justices shall have precedence according to the date of their commissions, or when the commissions of two or more of them bear date on the same day, according to their respective ages.

Section 2. *And be it further enacted,* That the United States shall be, and they hereby are divided into thirteen districts, . . .

Section 3. *And be it further enacted,* That there be a court called a District Court, in each of the aforementioned districts, to consist of one judge, who shall reside in the district for which he is appointed, and shall be called a District Judge, and shall hold annually four sessions, . . .

Source: Excerpted from the *Judiciary Act of 1789,* September 24, 1789, chap. 20, 1 Stat. 73. Available at air.fjc.gov/history/landmark/02b.html.

Section 4. *And be it further enacted,* That the before mentioned districts, except those of Maine and Kentucky, shall be divided into three circuits, and be called the eastern, the middle, and the southern circuit. . . .

* * *

Section 13. *And be it further enacted,* That the Supreme Court shall have exclusive jurisdiction of all controversies of a civil nature, where a state is a party, except between a state and its citizens; and except also between a state and citizens of other states, or aliens, in which latter case it shall have original but not exclusive jurisdiction. And shall have exclusively all such jurisdiction of suits or proceedings against ambassadors, or other public ministers, or their domestics, or domestic servants, as a court of law can have or exercise consistently with the law of nations; and original, but not exclusive jurisdiction of all suits brought by ambassadors, or other public ministers, or in which a consul, or vice consul, shall be a party. And the trial of issues in fact in the Supreme Court, in all actions at law against citizens of the United States, shall be by jury. The Supreme Court shall also have appellate jurisdiction from the circuit courts and courts of the several states, in the cases herein after specially provided for; and shall have power to issue writs of prohibition to the district courts, when proceeding as courts of admiralty and maritime jurisdiction, and writs of *mandamus,* in cases warranted by the principles and usages of law, to any courts appointed, or persons holding office, under the authority of the United States.

* * *

Section 25. *And be it further enacted,* That a final judgment or decree in any suit, in the highest court of law or equity of a State in which a decision in the suit could be had, where is drawn in question the validity of a treaty or statute of, or an authority exercised under the United States, and the decision is against their validity; or where is drawn in question the validity of a statute of, or an authority exercised under any State, on the ground of their being repugnant to the constitution, treaties or laws of the United States, and the decision is in favour of such their validity, or where is drawn in question the construction of any clause of the constitution, or of a treaty, or statute of, or commission held under the United States, and the decision is against the title, right, privilege or exemption specially set up or claimed by either party, under such clause of the said Constitution, treaty, statute or commission, may be re-examined and reversed or affirmed in the Supreme Court of the United States upon a writ of error, . . .

* * *

Section 34. *And be it further enacted,* That the laws of the several states, except where the constitution, treaties or statutes of the United States shall otherwise require or provide, shall be regarded as rules of decision in trials at common law in the courts of the United States in cases where they apply.

Approved, September 24, 1789.

DOCUMENT 8.2

The Treaty of Holston, July 1791

Article 1. There shall be perpetual peace and friendship between all the citizens of the United States of America, and all the individuals composing the whole Cherokee Nation of Indians.

Article 2. The undersigned Chiefs and Warriors for themselves and all parts of the Cherokee Nation, do acknowledge themselves and the said Cherokee Nation to be under the protection of the United States of America, and of no other sovereign whosoever; and they also stipulate that the said Cherokee Nation will not hold any treaty with any foreign power, individual State, or with individuals of any State.

Article 3. The Cherokee Nation shall deliver to the Governor of the Territory of the United States of America south of the river Ohio, on or before the first day of April next at this place all persons who are now prisoners captured by them from any part of the United States: And the United States shall on or before the same day and at the same place restore to the Cherokees all the prisoners now in captivity which the citizens of the United States have captured from them.

Article 4. . . . . And in order to preclude forever all disputes relative to the said boundary the same shall be ascertained and marked plainly by three persons appointed on the part of the United States and three Cherokees on the part of their nation.

And in order to extinguish forever all claims of the Cherokee Nation or any part thereof to any of the land lying to the right of the line above described, beginning as aforesaid at the Currahee mountain, it is hereby agreed that in addition to the consideration heretofore made for the said land the United States will cause certain valuable goods to be immediately delivered to the undersigned Chiefs and Warriors for the use of their nation, and the said United States will also cause the sum of one thousand Dollars to be paid annually to the said Cherokee Nation—And the undersigned Chiefs and Warriors do hereby for themselves and the whole Cherokee Nation their heirs and descendants for the considerations abovementioned Release quit claim relinquish and cede all the land to the right of the line described and beginning as aforesaid.

* * *

Article 11. If any citizen or inhabitant of the United States or of either of the territorial Districts of the United States, shall go into any town settlement or territory belonging to the Cherokees, and shall there commit any crime upon, or trespass against the person or property of any peaceable and friendly indian or indians, which if committed within the jurisdiction of any State, or within the

Source: Excerpted from the Treaty of Holston, July 1791, *The Territorial Papers of the United States,* vol. 4: *The Territory South of the River Ohio, 1790–1796* (Washington, DC: GPO, 1936), pp. 60–65.

jurisdiction of either of the said districts, against a citizen or white inhabitant thereof, would be punishable by the laws of such State or district—such offender or offenders shall be subject to the same punishment, and shall be proceeded against in the same manner as if the offence had been committed within the jurisdiction of the state or district to which he or they may belong, against a citizen or white inhabitant thereof.

Article 12. In case of violence on the persons or property of the individuals of either party—neither retaliation or reprisal shall be committed by the other—until satisfaction shall have been demanded of the party of which the aggressor is, and shall have been refused.

Article 13. The Cherokees shall give notice to the citizens of the United States, of any designs which they may know, or suspect to be formed in any neighbouring tribe, or by any person whatever, against the peace and interest of the United States.

Article 14. That the Cherokee nation may be led to a greater degree of civilization, and to become Herdsmen and cultivators, instead of remaining in a state of hunters the United States will from time to time furnish gratuitously the said nation with useful implements of husbandry. And further to assist the said nation in so desirable a pursuit, and at the same time to establish a certain mode of communication, the United States will send such and so many persons to reside in said nation as they may judge proper not exceeding four in number, who shall qualify themselves to act as interpreters—These persons shall have lands assigned by the Cherokees for cultivation for themselves and their successors in office. But they shall be precluded exercising any kind of Traffic.

Article 15. All animosities for past grievances shall henceforth cease, and the contracting parties will carry the foregoing treaty into full execution with all good faith and sincerity.

DOCUMENT 8.3

Pestilence in Philadelphia

Philip Freneau

PESTILENCE

Written During the Prevalence of a Yellow Fever

Hot, dry winds forever blowing,
Dead men to the grave-yards going:
    Constant hearses,
    Funeral verses;
Oh! what plagues—there is no knowing!

Source: Philip Freneau, "Pestilence" (Philadelphia, 1793). Available at the website *Writing the Fever,* xroads.virginia.edu/~MA96/forrest/WW/feverlit.html.

Priests retreating from their pulpits!—
Some in hot, and some in cold fits
    In bad temper,
    Off they scamper,
Leaving us—unhappy culprits!

Doctors raving and disputing,
Death's pale army still recruiting—
    What a pother
    One with t'other!
Some a-writing, some a-shooting.

Nature's poisons here collected,
Water, earth, and air infected—
    O, what a pity,
    Such a City,
Was in such a place erected!

DOCUMENT 8.4

The Education of Women

Rev. Doctor Sproat

The Ladies' Academy, is a new institution in this city. And I cannot but hope, that the plan of female education, now adopted and prosecuted in this excellent seminary, will merit the approbation and patronage of all who wish well to the learning, virtue and piety of the rising fair of this metropolis. The proficiency these delicate pupils have made, in several branches of useful literature, not only displays the fertility of their blooming geniuses, but reflects honor on the abilities, and praise to the attention of their worthy Preceptor and his assistants in their instruction. Accuracy in orthography, a very necessary part of an early education—reading with propriety their native language—an acquaintance with English grammar—writing a neat and beautiful character—a knowledge of figures, with many of their valuable uses—a general knowledge of the different parts of the terraqueous globe—its divisions, inhabitants, and productions—such knowledge of the planets that compose the solar system, and their periodical motions—together with such a sketch of history, as to remark the rise, progress, declension, and final extinction of the most remarkable states, kingdoms and empires—the virtues which contributed to their greatness, and the vices which were productive of their ruin—these are such valuable branches of literature, as are not only ornamental, but in many respects exceedingly advantageous to the rising generation of the fair sex. Let it suffice to say, that such academical improvements, tend to molify the temper, refine the manners, amuse the fancy, improve the understanding, and strengthen virtue—to lay a

Source: From Gerda Lerner, *The Female Experience: An American Documentary* (Indianapolis: Bobbs-Merrill, 1977), pp. 210–11.

foundation for a life of usefulness and happiness here, and if rightly improved, for a blessed immortality hereafter.

DOCUMENT 8.5

Patent for the Cotton Gin, 1794

Eli Whitney

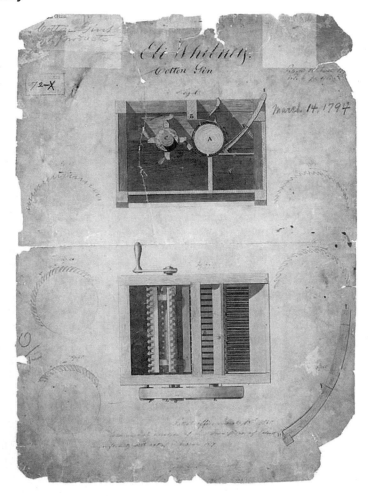

Source: Illustration from Eli Whitney's patent for the cotton gin, 1794. Available from the *Our Documents* website at www.ourdocuments.gov/content.php?page=zoom&doc=14.

DOCUMENT 8.6

The Sedition Act

An Act in Addition to the Act, Entitled "An Act for the Punishment of Certain Crimes Against the United States"

Section 1. *Be it enacted by the Senate and House of Representatives of the United States of America, in Congress assembled,* That if any persons shall unlawfully combine or conspire together, with intent to oppose any measure or measures of the government of the United States, which are or shall be directed by proper authority, or to impede the operation of any law of the United States, or to intimidate or prevent any person holding a place or office in or under the government of the United States, from undertaking, performing or executing his trust or duty, and if any person or persons, with intent as aforesaid, shall counsel, advise or attempt to procure any insurrection, riot, unlawful assembly, or combination, whether such conspiracy, threatening, counsel, advice, or attempt shall have the proposed effect or not, he or they shall be deemed guilty of a high misdemeanor, and on conviction, before any court of the United States having jurisdiction thereof, shall be punished by a fine not exceeding five thousand dollars, and by imprisonment during a term not less than six months nor exceeding five years; and further, at the discretion of the court may be holden to find sureties for his good behaviour in such sum, and for such time, as the said court may direct.

Section 2. *And be it farther enacted,* That if any person shall write, print, utter or publish, or shall cause or procure to be written, printed, uttered or published, or shall knowingly and willingly assist or aid in writing, printing, uttering or publishing any false, scandalous and malicious writing or writings against the government of the United States, or either house of the Congress of the United States, or the President of the United States, with intent to defame the said government, or either house of the said Congress, or the said President, or to bring them, or either of them, into contempt or disrepute; or to excite against them, or either or any of them, the hatred of the good people of the United States, or to stir up sedition within the United States, or to excite any unlawful combinations therein, for opposing or resisting any law of the United States, or any act of the President of the United States, done in pursuance of any such law, or of the powers in him vested by the constitution of the United States, or to resist, oppose, or defeat any such law or act, or to aid, encourage or abet any hostile designs of any foreign nation against United States, their people or government, then such person, being thereof convicted before any court of the United States having jurisdiction thereof, shall be punished by a fine not exceeding two thousand dollars, and by imprisonment not exceeding two years.

Section 3. *And be it further enacted and declared,* That if any person shall be prosecuted under this act, for the writing or publishing any libel aforesaid, it shall be lawful for the defendant, upon the trial of the cause, to give in evidence in his defence, the truth of the matter contained in Republication charged as a

Source: The Sedition Act, July 14, 1798. Available at www.yale.edu/lawweb/avalon/statutes/sedact.htm.

libel. And the jury who shall try the cause, shall have a right to determine the law and the fact, under the direction of the court, as in other cases.

Section 4. *And be it further enacted,* That this act shall continue and be in force until the third day of March, one thousand eight hundred and one, and no longer: Provided, that the expiration of the act shall not prevent or defeat a prosecution and punishment of any offence against the law, during the time it shall be in force.

Approved, July 14, 1798.

DOCUMENT 8.7

Amendment XII

The electors shall meet in their respective states, and vote by ballot for President and Vice President, one of whom, at least, shall not be an inhabitant of the same state with themselves; they shall name in their ballots the person voted for as President, and in distinct ballots the person voted for as Vice President, and they shall make distinct lists of all persons voted for as President, and of all persons voted for as Vice President, and of the number of votes for each, which lists they shall sign and certify, and transmit sealed to the seat of the government of the United States, directed to the President of the Senate; the President of the Senate shall, in the presence of the Senate and House of Representatives, open all the certificates and the votes shall then be counted; the person having the greatest number of votes for President, shall be the President, if such number be a majority of the whole number of electors appointed; and if no person have such majority, then from the persons having the highest numbers not exceeding three on the list of those voted for as President, the House of Representatives shall choose immediately, by ballot, the President. But in choosing the President, the votes shall be taken by states, the representation from each State having one vote; a quorum for this purpose shall consist of a member or members from two thirds of the states, and a majority of all the states shall be necessary to a choice. And if the House of Representatives shall not choose a President whenever the right of choice shall devolve upon them, before the fourth day of March next following, then the Vice President shall act as President, as in the case of the death or other constitutional disability of the President. The person having the greatest number of votes as Vice President, shall be the Vice President, if such number be a majority of the whole number of electors appointed, and if no person have a majority, then from the two highest numbers on the list, the Senate shall choose the Vice President; a quorum for the purpose shall consist of two thirds of the whole number of Senators, and a majority of the whole number shall be necessary to a choice. But no person constitutionally ineligible to the office of President shall be eligible to that of Vice President of the United States.

[The proposed amendment was sent to the states December 12, 1803, by the Eighth Congress. It was ratified July 27, 1804.]

Source: Twelfth Amendment to the Constitution of the United States. Available at www.infoplease.com/ipa/A0749825.html.

9

The Empire of Liberty and the Liberty for Empires

The Naturalization Act of 1795 began a process of establishing rules for membership in the American democratic experiment. That people could choose to change their citizenship and allegiance was a novel concept in the 18th century. The founding fathers decided that only people capable of democracy ought to be permitted citizenship and that the best citizens would be people who were fundamentally similar to the existing citizenry. It should not be surprising, therefore, that only whites could qualify for naturalization, a limitation that remained law well into the 20th century.

Thomas Jefferson believed that the United States should and would establish an Empire of Liberty on the American continent. To expand the national boundaries, he secured one of the best land deals in world history—the Louisiana Purchase. Though he had previously secretly arranged with Congress an exploration of the western portion of the continent, the acquisition of Louisiana provided him the opportunity to publicly dispatch the Lewis and Clark expedition to reconnoiter and explore not only the Louisiana Purchase but also to seek the fabled all-water route to Asia through the American continent. Gathering information about the native peoples that occupied the space between the Mississippi and the Pacific Ocean was yet another goal and objective of the expedition. In Jefferson's mind, Native Americans were welcome in the Empire of Liberty if they achieved the desired goal and expectation of "sameness." It was widely assumed by national leaders that Native Americans bore the responsibility for acculturating themselves for living appropriately among the whites.

Acquiring the Louisiana Territory added different cultural ingredients to the increasingly varied American world. The city of New Orleans, the object of Jefferson's original diplomacy, offered an entry port and trade center linking America's greatest waterway, the Mississippi River, with oceanic transportation via the Gulf of Mexico. As such, it was a prime target for British assault during the War of 1812. General Andrew Jackson's overwhelming victory in *defending the city not only secured the city and the region, as well as signifi-cant swaths of Indian Territory that Jackson fought his way through en route to New Orleans, but also psychologically secured a victory in America's "Second War for Independence."*

Eventually, the lands within the Louisiana Territory would go through the apprenticeship of liberty mapped out in the North West Ordinances and pre-sent themselves for candidacy for statehood in the American republic. Throughout the "Era of Good Feelings" after the War of 1812, territories be-came states, enlarging the Union. By design and happenstance, a balance was achieved between free and slave states. The Missouri Compromise illustrates how important that balance came to be and how the competing political aspi-rations of both slave and free states threatened to disrupt the American re-public.

There were those who witnessed the revolutionary movements of Latin and South America and hoped for those sister republics the same opportunities to devise genuine and productive democratic systems out of the ashes of the old Spanish Empire as had been achieved in North America. President Monroe took a bold step diplomatically to signal to the world the special relationship the United States of America had with the countries south of our border. In enunciating the Monroe Doctrine, he simultaneously gave voice to recurring ideals of democracy and less-than-noble self-interest.

DOCUMENT 9.1

The Naturalization Act of 1795

An Act to establish an uniform Rule of Naturalization; and to repeal the Act heretofore passed on that Subject. For carrying into complete effect the power given by the constitution, to establish an uniform rule of naturalization throughout the United States;

Section 1. BE it enacted by the Senate and House of Representatives of the United States of America, in Congress assembled, that any alien, being a free white person, may be admitted to become a citizen of the United States, or any of them, on the following conditions, and not otherwise. First, he shall have de-clared, on oath or affirmation, before the Supreme, Superior, District, or Circuit Court of some one of the states, or of the territories northwest or south of the Ohio River, or a Circuit or District Court of the United States, three years at least before his admission, that it was, bona fide, his intention to become a citizen of the United States, and to renounce forever all allegiance and fidelity to any for-eign prince, potentate, state, or sovereignty whereof such alien may at that time

Source: From the *Naturalization Act of 1795*, January 29, 1795. Available at www.earlyamerica.com/earlyamerica/milestones/naturalization/naturalization_text.html.

be a citizen or subject. Secondly. He shall, at the time of his application to be admitted, declare on oath or affirmation before some one of the courts aforesaid that he has resided within the United States five years at least, and within the state or territory where such court is at the time held, one year at least; that he will support the Constitution of the United States; and that he does absolutely and entirely renounce and abjure all allegiance and fidelity to any foreign prince, potentate, state, or sovereignty whatever and particularly by name the prince, potentate, state, or sovereignty whereof he was before a citizen or subject; which proceedings shall be recorded by the clerk of the court. Thirdly. The court admitting such alien shall be satisfied that he has resided within the limits and under the jurisdiction of the United States five years. It shall further appear to their satisfaction that during that time he has behaved as a man of a good moral character, attached to the principles of the Constitution of the United States, and well-disposed to the good order and happiness of the same. Fourthly. In case the alien applying to be admitted to citizenship shall have borne any hereditary title, or been of any of the orders of nobility, in the kingdom or state from which he came, he shall, in addition to the above requisites, make an express renunciation of his title or order of nobility in the court to which his application shall be made; which renunciation shall be recorded in the said court.

Section 2. Provided always, and be it further enacted, That any alien now residing within the limits and under the jurisdiction of the United States may be admitted to become a citizen on his declaring, on oath or affirmation, in some one of the courts aforesaid, that he has resided two years, at least, within and under the jurisdiction of the same, and one year, at least, within the state or territory where such court is at the time held; that he will support the Constitution of the United States; and that he does absolutely and entirely renounce and abjure all allegiance and fidelity to any foreign prince, potentate, state, or sovereignty whatever, and particularly by name the prince, potentate, state, or sovereignty whereof he was before a citizen or subject. Moreover, on its appearing to the satisfaction of the court that, during the said term of two years, he has behaved as a man of good moral character, attached to the Constitution of the United States, and well-disposed to the good order and happiness of the same; and when the alien applying for admission to citizenship shall have borne any hereditary title, or been of any of the orders of nobility in the kingdom or state from which he came, on his, moreover, making in the court an express renunciation of his title or order of nobility, before he shall be entitled to such admission; all of which proceedings, required in this proviso to be performed in the court, shall be recorded by the clerk thereof. . . .

Frederick Augustus Muhlenberg, Speaker of the House of Representatives.
John Adams, Vice-President of the United States, And President of the Senate.
Approved, January the 29th, 1795:
George Washington, President of the United States.

DOCUMENT 9.2

Jefferson's Secret Message to Congress Regarding Exploration of the West

Thomas Jefferson

Confidential

Gentlemen of the Senate, and of the House of Representatives:

. . . The Indian tribes residing within the limits of the United States, have, for a considerable time, been growing more and more uneasy at the constant diminution of the territory they occupy, although effected by their own voluntary sales: and the policy has long been gaining strength with them, of refusing absolutely all further sale, on any conditions; insomuch that, at this time, it hazards their friendship, and excites dangerous jealousies and perturbations in their minds to make any overture for the purchase of the smallest portions of their land. A very few tribes only are not yet obstinately in these dispositions. In order peaceably to counteract this policy of theirs, and to provide an extension of territory which the rapid increase of our numbers will call for, two measures are deemed expedient. First: to encourage them to abandon hunting, to apply to the raising stock, to agriculture and domestic manufacture, and thereby prove to themselves that less land and labor will maintain them in this, better than in their former mode of living The extensive forests necessary in the hunting life, will then become useless, and they will see advantage in exchanging them for the means of improving their farms, and of increasing their domestic comforts. Secondly: to multiply trading houses among them, and place within their reach those things which will contribute more to their domestic comfort, than the possession of extensive, but uncultivated wilds. Experience and reflection will develop to them the wisdom of exchanging what they can spare and we want, for what we can spare and they want. In leading them to agriculture, to manufactures, and civilization; in bringing together their and our settlements, and in preparing them ultimately to participate in the benefits of our governments, I trust and believe we are acting for their greatest good. At these trading houses we have pursued the principles of the act of Congress, which directs that the commerce shall be carried on liberally, and requires only that the capital stock shall not be diminished. We consequently undersell private traders, foreign and domestic, drive them from the competition; and thus, with the good will of the Indians, rid ourselves of a description of men who are constantly endeavoring to excite in the Indian mind suspicions, fears, and irritations towards us.

Source: From "Jefferson's Secret Message to Congress Regarding the Lewis & Clark Expedition (1803)," *Our Documents* website, www.ourdocuments.gov/content.php?page=transcript&doc=17.

DOCUMENT 9.3

Jefferson's Recommendation to Native Americans

Thomas Jefferson to Captain Hendrick, December 21, 1808
Thomas Jefferson

Washington, December 21, 1808.

To Captain Hendrick, the Delawares, Mohicans, and Munries:

. . . I learn with pleasure that the Miamis and Powtawatamies have given you some of their lands on the White River to live on, and that you propose to gather there your scattered tribes, and to dwell on it all your days.

The picture which you have drawn, my son, of the increase of our numbers and the decrease of yours is just, the causes are very plain, and the remedy depends on yourselves alone. You have lived by hunting the deer and buffalo—all these have been driven westward; you have sold out on the sea-board and moved westwardly in pursuit of them. As they became scarce there, your food has failed you; you have been a part of every year without food, except the roots and other unwholesome things you could find in the forest. Scanty and unwholesome food produce diseases and death among your children, and hence you have raised few and your numbers have decreased. Frequent wars, too, and the abuse of spirituous liquors, have assisted in lessening your numbers. The whites, on the other hand, are in the habit of cultivating the earth, of raising stocks of cattle, hogs, and other domestic animals, in much greater numbers than they could kill of deer and buffalo. Having always a plenty of food and clothing they raise abundance of children, they double their numbers every twenty years, the new swarms are continually advancing upon the country like flocks of pigeons, and so they will continue to do. Now, my children, if we wanted to diminish our numbers, we would give up the culture of the earth, pursue the deer and buffalo, and be always at war; this would soon reduce us to be as few as you are, and if you wish to increase your numbers you must give up the deer and buffalo, live in peace, and cultivate the earth. You see then, my children, that it depends on yourselves alone to become a numerous and great people. Let me entreat you, therefore, on the lands now given you to begin to give every man a farm; let him enclose it, cultivate it, build a warm house on it, and when he dies, let it belong to his wife and children after him. Nothing is so easy as to learn to cultivate the earth; all your women understand it, and to make it easier, we are always ready to teach you how to make ploughs, hoes, and necessary utensils. If the men will take the labor of the earth from the women they will learn to spin and weave and to clothe their families. In this way you will also raise many children, you will double your numbers every twenty years, and soon fill the land your friends have given you, and your children will never be tempted to sell the spot on which they have been born,

Source: Thomas Jefferson to Captain Hendrick, December 21, 1808, *The Writings of Thomas Jefferson*, vol. 16, ed. Albert Ellery Bergh (Washington, DC, 1853).

raised, have labored and called their own. When once you have property, you will want laws and magistrates to protect your property and persons, and to punish those among you who commit crimes. You will find that our laws are good for this purpose; you will wish to live under them, you will unite yourselves with us, join in our Great Councils and form one people with us, and we shall all be Americans; you will mix with us by marriage, your blood will run in our veins, and will spread with us over this great island. Instead, then, my children, of the gloomy prospect you have drawn of your total disappearance from the face of the earth, which is true, if you continue to hunt the deer and buffalo and go to war, you see what a brilliant aspect is offered to your future history, if you give up war and hunting. Adopt the culture of the earth and raise domestic animals; you see how from a small family you may become a great nation by adopting the course which from the small beginning you describe has made us a great nation.

DOCUMENT 9.4

The Battle of New Orleans

Source: The Battle of New Orleans. January 1815. Copy of engraving by H.B. Hall after W. Momberger. Found at: Images of American Political History, http://teachpol.tcnj.edu/amer_pol_hist/fi/00000072.htm

DOCUMENT 9.5

The Missouri Compromise

Be it enacted by the Senate and House of Representatives of the United States of America, in Congress assembled, That the inhabitants of that portion of the Missouri territory included within the boundaries hereinafter designated, be, and they are hereby, authorized to form for themselves a constitution and state government, and to assume such name as they shall deem proper; and the said state, when formed, shall be admitted into the Union, upon an equal footing with the original states, in all respects whatsoever.

* * *

Section 7. *And be it further enacted,* That in case a constitution and state government shall be formed for the people of the said territory of Missouri, the said convention or representatives, as soon thereafter as may be, shall cause a true and attested copy of such constitution, or frame of state government, as shall be formed or provided, to be transmitted to Congress.

Section 8. *And be it further enacted,* That in all that territory ceded by France to the United States, under the name of Louisiana, which lies north of thirty-six degrees and thirty minutes north latitude, not included within the limits of the state, contemplated by this act, slavery and involuntary servitude, otherwise than in the punishment of crimes, whereof the parties shall have been duly convicted, shall be, and is hereby, forever prohibited: *Provided always,* That any person escaping into the same, from whom labour or service is lawfully claimed, in any state or territory of the United States, such fugitive may be lawfully reclaimed and conveyed to the person claiming his or her labour or service as aforesaid.

Approved, March 6, 1820.

DOCUMENT 9.6

The Monroe Doctrine

James Monroe

In the wars of the European powers in matters relating to themselves we have never taken any part, nor does it comport with our policy so to do. It is only when our rights are invaded or seriously menaced that we resent injuries or make preparation for our defense. With the movements in this hemisphere we are of necessity more immediately connected, and by causes which must be obvious to all enlightened and impartial observers. The political system of the

---

Source: Excerpted from the *Missouri Compromise*, March 6, 1820, chap. 22, 3 Stat. 545.
Source: Excerpted from the Monroe Doctrine, *A Compilation of the Messages and Papers of the Presidents, 1789–1897,* ed. James D. Richardson (U.S. Congress, 1899), pp. 218–19.

allied powers is essentially different in this respect from that of America. This difference proceeds from that which exists in their respective Governments; and to the defense of our own, which has been achieved by the loss of so much blood and treasure, and matured by the wisdom of their most enlightened citizens, and under which we have enjoyed unexampled felicity, this whole nation is devoted. We owe it, therefore, to candor and to the amicable relations existing between the United States and those powers to declare that we should consider any attempt on their part to extend their system to any portion of this hemisphere as dangerous to our peace and safety. With the existing colonies or dependencies of any European power we have not interfered and shall not interfere. But with the Governments who have declared their independence and maintained it, and whose independence we have, on great consideration and on just principles, acknowledged, we could not view any interposition for the purpose of oppressing them, or controlling in any other manner their destiny, by any European power in any other light than as the manifestation of an unfriendly disposition toward the United States. In the war between those new Governments and Spain we declared our neutrality at the time of their recognition, and to this we have adhered, and shall continue to adhere, provided no change shall occur which, in the judgment of the competent authorities of this Government, shall make a corresponding change on the part of the United States indispensable to their security.

The late events in Spain and Portugal shew that Europe is still unsettled. Of this important fact no stronger proof can be adduced than that the allied powers should have thought it proper, on any principle satisfactory to themselves, to have interposed by force in the internal concerns of Spain. To what extent such interposition may be carried, on the same principle, is a question in which all independent powers whose governments differ from theirs are interested, even those most remote, and surely none more so than the United States. Our policy in regard to Europe, which was adopted at an early stage of the wars which have so long agitated that quarter of the globe, nevertheless remains the same, which is, not to interfere in the internal concerns of any of its powers; to consider the government *de facto* as the legitimate government for us; to cultivate friendly relations with it, and to preserve those relations by a frank, firm, and manly policy, meeting in all instances the just claims of every power, submitting to injuries from none. But in regard to those continents circumstances are eminently and conspicuously different. It is impossible that the allied powers should extend their political system to any portion of either continent without endangering our peace and happiness; nor can anyone believe that our southern brethren, if left to themselves, would adopt it of their own accord. It is equally impossible, therefore, that we should behold such interposition in any form with indifference. If we look to the comparative strength and resources of Spain and those new Governments, and their distance from each other, it must be obvious that she can never subdue them. It is still the true policy of the United States to leave the parties to themselves, in the hope that other powers will pursue the same course.

10

Pathways to Progress

Having laid claim to much of the North American continent, it became neces-
sary to knit the nation together through reliable and efficient travel routes. In
the first decades of the 19th century, a transportation revolution took place.
Part of what triggered the revolution and gave it momentum was the evolution
of a body of laws and state and federal court decisions that facilitated the cre-
ation of large corporations with the capacity to take on extensive, multistate
projects necessary for a national transportation infrastructure. The rights of in-
dividuals, states, and corporations were the focus of various Supreme Court
decisions of the era that consistently favored the interests of and affirmed the
legality of the behavior of entrepreneurs. Although supplanted by "the pursuit
of happiness," in the Declaration of Independence, the protection of property
rights emerged increasingly secure, and that security unleashed a burst of
economic activity and development.

The canal boom, which simultaneously illustrates the evolution of corpora-
tions and the development of a national transportation system that contributed
to a regional and national market revolution, created the first "boom" towns
since colonial days. Rochester, New York, lay along the Erie Canal, the single
most successful canal of its day, the results of which are illustrated in the
growth of Rochester's population. Canals became a means not only for the
movement of goods and materials around the country, but for the transporta-
tion of people as well. For many years, canal trips became part and parcel of
the American human and cultural landscape, as illustrated in George William
Bagby's reminiscences of his canal travels.

The transportation revolution fueled the market revolution. The market rev-
olution spurred the growth of American businesses and industries. Perhaps
the most famous early American industrial enterprise was the textile industry
in Lowell, Massachusetts. One of the founders of the Lowell textile works had
once toured Robert Owen's operation at New Lanark, England, for ideas to

organize his endeavor. Charles Dickens returned the favor after Lowell became famous.

Canals increased the flow of goods and services through the country, though few canal companies made profits doing so. They also unleashed the American quest for faster and better ways of conveying material and people. Railroads eventually entered the competition to become America's premier transportation system.

Not all innovations, however, were destined for success and glory. At times Americans confronted geographical barriers and other realities too difficult to overcome. As Secretary of War, Jefferson Davis helped launch the U.S. Army's experimental Camel Corps in the American southwest. Part of his motivation was to secure better communications through the deserts between San Diego and El Paso, Texas, further illustrating the appetite Americans had for laying claim to the entire continent.

DOCUMENT 10.1

Laws of Commerce: *Gibbons v. Ogden*

But it has been urged with great earnestness that, although the power of Congress to regulate commerce with foreign nations and among the several states be coextensive with the subject itself, and have no other limits than are prescribed in the Constitution, yet the states may severally exercise the same power within their respective jurisdictions. In support of this argument, it is said that they possessed it as an inseparable attribute of sovereignty before the formation of the Constitution, and still retain it, except so far as they have surrendered it by that instrument; that this principle results from the nature of the government, and is secured by the Tenth Amendment; that an affirmative grant of power is not exclusive, unless in its own nature it be such that the continued exercise of it by the former possessor is inconsistent with the grant, and that this is not of that description. . . .

In discussing the question, whether this power is still in the states, in the case under consideration, we may dismiss from it the inquiry, whether it is surrendered by the mere grant to Congress, or is retained until Congress shall exercise the power. We may dismiss that inquiry because it has been exercised, and the regulations which Congress deemed it proper to make are now in full operation. The sole question is—Can a state regulate commerce with foreign nations and among the states while Congress is regulating it?. . .

Source: Gibbons v. Ogden, 22 U.S. 1 (1824). Available at www.ourdocuments.gov/content.php? page=transcript&doc=24.

Since, however, in exercising the power of regulating their own purely internal affairs, whether of trading or police, the states may sometimes enact laws, the validity of which depends on their interfering with, and being contrary to, an act of Congress passed in pursuance of the Constitution, the court will enter upon the inquiry, whether the laws of New York, as expounded by the highest tribunal of that state, have, in their application to this case, come into collision with an act of Congress, and deprived a citizen of a right to which that act entitles him. Should this collision exist, it will be immaterial whether those laws were passed in virtue of a concurrent power *to regulate commerce with foreign nations and among the several states,* or in virtue of a power to regulate their domestic trade and police.

In one case and the other the acts of New York must yield to the law of Congress; and the decision sustaining the privilege they confer against a right given by a law of the Union must be erroneous. This opinion has been frequently expressed in this court, and is founded as well on the nature of the government as on the words of the Constitution. In argument, however, it has been contended that, if a law passed by a state in the exercise of its acknowledged sovereignty comes into conflict with a law passed by Congress in pursuance of the Constitution, they affect the subject and each other like equal opposing powers.

But the framers of our Constitution foresaw this state of things and provided for it by declaring the supremacy not only of itself but of the laws made in pursuance of it. The nullity of any act inconsistent with the Constitution is produced by the declaration that the Constitution is supreme law. The appropriate application of that part of the clause which confers the same supremacy on laws and treaties is to such acts of the state legislatures as do not transcend their powers, but though enacted in the execution of acknowledged state powers, interfere with, or are contrary to, the laws of Congress, made in pursuance of the Constitution or some treaty made under the authority of the United States. In every such case, the act of Congress or the treaty is supreme; and the law of the state, though enacted in the exercise of powers not controverted, must yield to it.

Decree

This court is of opinion that so much of the several laws of the state of New York as prohibits vessels, licensed according to the laws of the United States, from navigating the waters of the state of New York, by means of fire or steam, is repugnant to the said Constitution and void. This court is, therefore, of opinion that the decree of the court of New York for the trial of impeachments and the correction of errors, affirming the decree of the chancellor of that state is erroneous and ought to be reversed, and the same is hereby reversed and annulled. And this court doth further direct, order, and decree that the bill of the said Aaron Ogden be dismissed, and the same is hereby dismissed accordingly.

DOCUMENT 10.2

Rochester Population, 1812–1865

Year	Total	Census
1812	15	Local
1815 December	331	Local
1818 September	1,049	Local
1820 August	1,502	Federal
1822 September	2,700	Local
	3,130	Including laborers on public works (i.e., Erie Canal)
1825 February	4,274	Local
1825 August	5,273	State
1826 December	7,669	Local
1830	9,207	Federal
1834	12,252	Local
1835	14,404	State
1836	17,160	Local
1838	19,061	Local
1840	20,191	Federal
1844	23,553	Local
1845	26,965	State
1850	36,403	Federal
1855	43,877	State
1860	48,204	Federal
1865	50,940	State

Source: University of Rochester Department of History, "History of the Erie Canal," www.history.rochester.edu/canal/rochpop.htm.

DOCUMENT 10.3

Canal Reminiscences

Recollections of Travel in the Old Days on the James River and Kanawha Canal

George William Bagby

Fleets of these *batteaux* used to be moored on the river bank near where the depot of the Virginia and Tennessee Railroad now stands; and many years after the "Jeems and Kanawha" was finished, one of them used to haunt the mouth of Blackwater creek above the toll-bridge, a relic of departed glory. For if ever man gloried in his calling,—the negro batteau-man was that man. His was a hardy calling, demanding skill, courage and strength in a high degree. I can see him now striding the plank that ran along the gunwale to afford him footing, his long iron-shod pole trailing in the water behind him. Now he turns, and after one or two ineffectual efforts to get his pole fixed in the rocky bottom of the river, secures his purchase, adjusts the upper part of the pole to the pad at his shoulder, bends to his task, and the long, but not ungraceful bark mounts the rapids like a sea-bird breasting the storm. His companion on the other side plies the pole with equal ardor, and between the two the boat bravely surmounts every obstacle, be it rocks, rapids, quicksands, hammocks, what not. A third negro at the stern held the mighty oar that served as a rudder. A stalwart, jolly, courageous set they were, plying the pole all day, hauling in to shore at night under the friendly shade of a mighty sycamore, to rest, to eat, to play the banjo, and to snatch a few hours of profound, blissful sleep.

The up-cargo, consisting of sacks of salt, bags of coffee, barrels of sugar, molasses and whiskey, afforded good pickings. These sturdy fellows lived well, I promise you, and if they stole a little, why, what was their petty thieving compared to the enormous pillage of the modern sugar refiner and the crooked-whiskey distiller? They lived well. Their cook's galley was a little dirt thrown between the ribs of the boat at the stern, with an awning on occasion to keep off the rain, and what they didn't eat wasn't worth eating. Fish of the very best, both salt and fresh, chickens, eggs, mill: and the invincible, never-satisfying ash-cake and fried bacon. I see the frying-pan, I smell the meat, the fish, the Rio coffee!—I want the *batteau* back again, aye! and the brave, light-hearted slave to boot. What did he know about the State debt? There was no State debt to speak of. Greenbacks? Bless, you! the Farmers Bank of Virginia was living and breathing, and its money was good enough for a king. Re-adjustment, funding bill, tax-receivable coupons—where were all these worries then? I think if we had known they were coming, we would have stuck to the batteaux and never dammed the river. Why, shad used to run to Lynchburg! The world was merry, butter-milk was abundant; Lynchburg a lad, Richmond a mere youth, and the great "Jeems and Kanawha canell" was going to—oh! it was going to do everything. . . .

The perfect cultivation, the abundance, the elegance the ducal splendor, one might almost say, of the great estates that lay along the canal in the old days have passed away in a great measure. Here were gentlemen, not merely refined and educated, fitted to display a royal hospitality and to devote their leisure to the study of the art and practice of government, but they were great and greatly successful farmers as well. The land teemed with all manner of products, cereals, fruits, what not! Negroes by the hundreds and the thousands, under wise direction, gentle but firm control, plied the hoe to good purpose.

There was enough and to spare for all—to spare? aye! to bestow with glad and lavish hospitality. A mighty change has been wrought. What that change is in all of its effects mine eyes have happily been spared the seeing; but well I remember—I can never forget—how from time to time the boat would stop at one of these estates, and the planter, his wife, his daughters, and the guests that were going home with him, would be met by those who had remained behind, and how joyous the greetings were! It was a bright and happy scene, and it continually repeated itself as we went onward.

In fine summer weather, the passengers, male and female, stayed most of the time on deck, where there was a great deal to interest, and naught to mar the happiness, except the oft-repeated warning, *"braidge!" "low braidge!"* No well-regulated packet-hand was ever allowed to say plain "bridge;" that was an etymological crime in canal ethics. . . .

There is a point at which the passengers would get off, and taking a near cut across the hills, would stretch their legs with a mile or two of walking. It was unmanly, I held, to miss that. Apropos of scenery, I must not forget the haunted house near Manchester, which was pointed out soon after we left Richmond, and filled me with awe; for though I said I did not believe in ghosts, I did. The ruined mill, a mile or two further on was always an object of melancholy interest to me; and of all the locks from Lynchburg down, the Three-Mile Locks pleased me most. It is a pretty place, as every one will own on seeing it. It was so clean and green, and white and thrifty-looking. To me it was simply beautiful. I wanted to live there; I ought to have lived there. I was built for a lock-keeper—have that exact moral and mental shape. Ah! to own your own negro, who would do all the drudgery of opening the gates. Occasionally you would go through the form of putting your shoulder to the huge wooden levers, if that is what they call them, by which the gates are opened: to own your own negro and live and die calmly at a lock! What more could the soul ask! I do think that the finest picture extant of peace and contentment—a little abnormal, perhaps, in the position of the animal—is that of a sick mule looking out of the window of a canal freight-boat. And that you could see every day from the porch of your cottage, if you lived at a lock, owned your own negro, and there was no great rush of business on the canal, (and there seldom was) on the "Jeems and Kanawhy," as old Capt. Sam Wyatt always called it, leaving out the word "canal," for that was understood. Yes, one ought to live as a pure and resigned lock-keeper, if one would be blest, really blest.

DOCUMENT 10.4

Charles Dickens Visits Lowell, Massachusetts

Charles Dickens

There are several factories in Lowell, each of which belongs to what we should term a Company of Proprietors, but what they call in America a Corporation. I went over several of these; such as a woollen factory, a carpet factory, and a cotton factory: examined them in every part; and saw them in their ordinary working aspect, with no preparation of any kind, or departure from their ordinary everyday proceedings. I may add that I am well acquainted with our

Source: Excerpted from Charles Dickens, *American Notes and Pictures from Italy* (London: Oxford University Press, 1966), pp. 65–70.

manufacturing towns in England, and have visited many mills in Manchester and elsewhere in the same manner.

I happened to arrive at the first factory just as the dinner hour was over, and the girls were returning to their work; indeed the stairs of the mill were thronged with them as I ascended. They were all well dressed, but not to my thinking above their condition; for I like to see the humbler classes of society careful of their dress and appearance, and even, if they please, decorated with such little trinkets as come within the compass of their means. . . .

They had serviceable bonnets, good warm cloaks, and shawls; and were not above clogs and pattens. Moreover, there were places in the mill in which they could deposit these things without injury; and there were conveniences for washing. They were healthy in appearance, many of them remarkably so, and had the manners and deportment of young women. . . .

The rooms in which they worked, were as well ordered as themselves. In the windows of some, there were green plants, which were trained to shade the glass; in all, there was as much fresh air, cleanliness, and comfort, as the nature of the occupation would possibly admit of. Out of so large a number of females, many of whom were only then just verging upon womanhood, it may be reasonably supposed that some were delicate and fragile in appearance: no doubt there were. But I solemnly declare, that from all the crowd I saw in the different factories that day, I cannot recall or separate one young face that gave me a painful impression. . . .

They reside in various boarding-houses near at hand. The owners of the mills are particularly careful to allow no persons to enter upon the possession of these houses, whose characters have not undergone the most searching and thorough inquiry. Any complaint that is made against them, by the boarders, or by any one else, is fully investigated; and if good ground of complaint be shown to exist against them, they are removed, and their occupation is handed over to some more deserving person. There are a few children employed in these factories, but not many. The laws of the State forbid their working more than nine months in the year, and require that they be educated during the other three. For this purpose there are schools in Lowell; and there are churches and chapels of various persuasions, in which the young women may observe that form of worship in which they have been educated.

At some distance from the factories, and on the highest and pleasantest ground in the neighbourhood, stands their hospital, or boarding-house for the sick: it is the best house in those parts, and was built by an eminent merchant for his own residence. Like that institution at Boston, which I have before described, it is not parcelled out into wards, but is divided into convenient chambers, each of which has all the comforts of a very comfortable home. The principal medical attendant resides under the same roof; and were the patients members of his own family, they could not be better cared for, or attended with greater gentleness and consideration. The weekly charge in this establishment for each female patient is three dollars, or twelve shillings English; but no girl employed by any of the corporations is ever excluded for want of the means of payment. That they do not very often want the means, may be gathered from the fact, that in July, 1841, no fewer than nine hundred and seventy-eight of these girls were depositors in the Lowell Savings Bank: the amount of whose joint savings was estimated at one hundred thousand dollars, or twenty thousand English pounds. . . .

In this brief account of Lowell, and inadequate expression of the gratification it yielded me, and cannot fail to afford to any foreigner to whom the condition of such people at home is a subject of interest and anxious speculation, I have carefully abstained from drawing a comparison between these factories and those of our own land. Many of the circumstances whose strong influence has been at work for years in our manufacturing towns have not arisen here; and there is no manufacturing population in Lowell, so to speak: for these girls (often the daughters of small farmers) come from other States, remain a few years in the mills, and then go home for good.

DOCUMENT 10.5

Pittsburgh, Fort Wayne, and Chicago Railroad

Source: "Pittsburgh, Ft. Wayne, and Chicago R. R. Advertisement," image available from American Memory, Library of Congress, memory.loc.gov.

DOCUMENT 10.6

The Camel Corps

Jefferson Davis

This amendment is to introduce fifty camels and dromedaries, and ten Arabs, with their equipage, pay their expenses for one year, and then pay the expense of sending them home. [Laughter.]

I am sorry that any of my friends should laugh at this proposition. This animal, though associated with man from his earliest history, so far back that we cannot tell when the camel existed in the wild state, is little known in our country. It has even been a matter of dispute among anatomists as to its anatomical organization. But I think if Senators were aware of the extent to which this animal is used, they would be seriously inclined to adopt this proposition. It is truly, as figuratively, the "ship of the desert." It now conveys a great trade between China and St. Petersburg, and Moscow. It is kept in Circassia. It is used by the English army in the East Indies in transportation, and even carrying light guns on their backs. It was used by Napoleon in his Egyptian campaign. He understood the value of a dromedary corps in dealing with the race to which our wild Apaches and Camanches bear a close resemblance. If gentlemen knew how great is the embarrassment, especially in a cavalry corps, in waiting for a great train of mules to draw the guns with which they are incumbered, I do not think the proposition would excite a laugh. Nor would gentlemen smile at the proposed introduction of camels, if they knew how essential they were in the pursuit of the wild Indians, who now escape our cavalry in nearly every pursuit which is made. But recently, under an officer who has been well tried as a commander, a band of Apaches came upon his soldiers, dashed through his camp, got some seven or eight horses, loosened his horse from the picket, and ran off with them. In a still more striking case, as some soldiers were playing cards upon a blanket, seeing the Apaches coming, they sprang to their feet. An Apache caught the blanket upon his lance and galloped off with it. Pursuit was made, but it was unavailing. These dromedaries, who drink enough water before they start to last a hundred miles, traveling continually without rest at the rate of fifteen or twenty miles an hour, would overtake these bands of Indians. This the cavalry cannot do. They would have the advantage of generally being able to capture them in one day. They would certainly overtake them very soon.

There is another advantage. A man who rides a dromedary can take an infantry man behind him, and carry him to the place to which he is to go. The weight is scarcely felt. Small cannon, if it is necessary, can be mounted upon them, and carried over mountains and deserts and plains, where horses cannot draw them. The efficiency of these dromedaries and camels is so great that if they will bear our climate and the food of our country, I believe that it will be

Source: Jefferson Davis, 3 March 1851, *The Papers of Jefferson Davis*, vol. 4: *1849–1852*, ed. Lynda Lasswell Crist, Mary Seaton Cis, and Richard E. Beringer (Baton Rouge: Louisiana State University Press, 1983), pp. 168–69.

the greatest stroke of economy which has ever been made in regard to transportation. This is an experiment which ought to be tried; but when we remember that they are used in the same parallel of latitude, and are accustomed to eat the hardest shrubs, to drink the same brackish water which is said to exist in some portions of our western desert, we may expect they will soon be capable of doing here all that they are capable of doing in the East.

11

Popularizing Democracy

A major contributor to the rapid expansion of the United States was a concerted policy of the federal government to offer land for sale at affordable, if not bargain, prices. To be able to purchase land at $1.20 an acre meant that a large number of people and families could realistically aspire to owning their own farm. By so doing, they could become their own masters, thus contributing to the furtherance and management of American democracy. It was the addition of western states that set in motion reforms that extended to more people than ever before the right and ability to participate in self-government.

Public education became another way that benefits of democracy were shared with larger constituencies. Increasingly, the public education system became a free public education system that sought to achieve a minimal standard of literacy and common civic experiences for people regardless of whether they owned property or not.

The growth of the electorate meant that the political system had to adapt. The election of John Quincy Adams revealed some of the developments in the expansion of democratic activity. Yet that election revealed also that popular elections were only popular up to a point, that there remained structural mechanisms that mitigated against pure, direct democracy. Andrew Jackson's ascension to the White House, upon the defeat of John Quincy Adams in 1828, was deemed the beginning of the era of the "common man." As popular as Jackson was in the early days of his presidency, however, his behavior and bold use of power resulted in the formation of a new party organized around opposition to Jackson and his policies.

Jackson's boldness and willingness to be an active president illustrates both the possibilities and the pitfalls of popular presidents. Encouraged by popular support, Jackson supported policies that pleased his supporters, although some were of questionable legality, such as the removal of Indians from the

Southeast. His behavior and the policies of the federal government created practical, as well as theoretical, challenges for any minority within the nation.

While Native Americans may have had no way of countering removal, the South, led by South Carolina, sought to devise a mechanism by which federal behavior, injurious to some Americans, might be mitigated or nullified. The balance of the rights of individuals and minorities in the pursuit of liberty and happiness has always been a challenge for governments, Jacksonian America included.

DOCUMENT 11.1

Land Law of 1820

An act making further provision for the sale of the public lands.

Be it enacted, That from and after the first day of July next, all the public lands of the United States, the sale of which is, or may be authorized by law, shall, when offered at public sale, to the highest bidder, be offered in half quarter sections; and when offered at private sale, may be purchased, at the option of the purchaser, either in entire sections, half sections, quarter sections, or half quarter sections; . . .

Section 2. That credit shall not be allowed for the purchase money on the sale of any of the public lands which shall be sold after the first day of July next, but every purchaser of land sold at public sale thereafter, shall, on the day of purchase, make complete payment therefor; . . .

Section 3. That from and after the first day of July next, the price at which the public lands shall be offered for sale, shall be one dollar and twenty-five cents an acre; and at every public sale, the highest bidder, who shall make payment as aforesaid, shall be the purchaser; but no land shall be sold, either at public or private sale, for a less price than one dollar and twenty-five cents an acre; and all the public lands which shall have been offered at public sale before the first day of July next, and which shall then remain unsold, as well as the lands that shall thereafter be offered at public sale, according to law, and remain unsold at the close of such public sales, shall be subject to be sold at private sale, by entry at the land office, at one dollar and twenty-five cents an acre, to be paid at the time of making such entry as aforesaid; . . .

Approved, April 24, 1820.

Source: "Land Law of 1820," *Documents of American History*, ed. Henry Steele Commager (New York: Appleton-Century-Crofts, 1963), p. 227.

DOCUMENT 11.2

Massachusetts High School Law, 1827

Be it enacted, That each town or district within this Commonwealth, containing fifty families, or householders, shall be provided with a teacher or teachers, of good morals, to instruct children in orthography, reading, writing, English grammar, geography, arithmetic, and good behavior, for such term of time as shall be equivalent to six months for one school in each year; and every town or district containing one hundred families or householders, shall be provided with such teacher or teachers, for such term of time as shall be equivalent to eighteen months, for one school in each year. In every city, town, or district, containing five hundred families, or householders shall be provided with such teacher or teachers for such term of time as shall be equivalent to twenty-four months, shall also be provided with a master of good morals, competent to instruct, in addition to the branches of learning aforesaid, in the history of the United States, bookkeeping by single entry, geometry, surveying, algebra; and shall employ such master to instruct a school in such city, town, or district, for the benefit of all the inhabitants thereof, at least ten months in each year, exclusive of vacations, in such convenient places, or alternately at such places in such city, town, or district, as said inhabitants, at their meeting in March, or April, annually, shall determine; and in every city, or town, and district, containing four thousand inhabitants, such master shall be competent in addition to all the foregoing branches, to instruct the Latin and Greek languages, history, rhetoric, and logic.

DOCUMENT 11.3

John Quincy Adams Wins the Presidency

John Quincy Adams

May 19.—Mr. Mower, of New York, was here, as I inferred from his conversation, to renew in behalf of De Witt Clinton the attempt to obtain for General Jackson the electoral vote of New York for the Presidency. He told me that he had seen Mr. Clinton, and a particular and intimate friend of his (Ambrose Spencer), who thoroughly approved of all the arrangements of Mower here, and were decidedly of opinion that there was in the Legislature no chance for any person against Mr. Crawford but me. Mr. Clinton was, however, doubtful whether by the purchase of Young, of Peter B. Porter, and with them of Clay's party, Mr. Crawford would not ultimately prevail in the Legislature. But Mr.

Source: "Massachusetts High School Law," *Documents of American History*, ed. Henry Steele Commager (New York: Appleton-Century-Crofts, 1963), p. 247.
Source: John Quincy Adams, *The Diary of John Quincy Adams, 1794–1845*, ed. Allen Nevins (New York: Longmans, 1929), pp. 323–24, 341–42.

Crary and Solomon Van Rensselaer were confident that Crawford could under no circumstances whatever obtain the vote of New York. But Governor Yates had determined to call the Legislature together and recommend to them the passage of an Act giving the choice of electors to the people. The proclamation was already prepared, and would issue immediately after the adjournment of Congress. It would instantly kill two men—William H. Crawford and Henry Clay; and if the election went before the people, no man could stand in competition with General Jackson. The 8th of January and the battle of New Orleans was a thing that every man would understand, and Mr. Clinton had told him that General Jackson would beat him (Clinton himself) before the people of New York by thirty-three and one-third per cent.

Feb. 9.—May the blessing of God rest upon the event of this day!—the second Wednesday in February, when the election of a President of the United States for the term of four years, from the 4th of March next, was consummated. Of the votes in the electoral colleges, there were ninety-nine for Andrew Jackson, of Tennessee; eighty-four for John Quincy Adams, of Massachusetts; forty-one for William Harris Crawford, of Georgia; and thirty-seven for Henry Clay, of Kentucky: in all, two hundred and sixty-one. This result having been announced, on opening and counting the votes in joint meeting of the two Houses, the House of Representatives immediately proceeded to the vote by ballot from the three highest candidates, when John Quincy Adams received the votes of thirteen, Andrew Jackson of seven, and William H. Crawford of four States. The election was thus completed, very unexpectedly, by a single ballot. Alexander H. Everett gave me the first notice, both of the issue of the votes of the electoral colleges as announced in the joint meeting, and of the final vote as declared. Wyer followed him a few minutes afterwards. Mr. Bolton and Mr. Thomas, the Naval Architect, succeeded; and B. W. Crowninshield, calling, on his return from the House to his lodgings, at my house, confirmed the report. Congratulations from several of the officers of the Department of State ensued—from D. Brent, G. Ironside, W. Slade, and Joseas W. King. Those of my wife, children, and family were cordial and affecting, and I received an affectionate note from Mr. Rufus King, of New York, written in the Senate-chamber after the event . . .

After dinner, the Russian Minister, Baron Tuyl, called to congratulate me upon the issue of the election. I attended, with Mrs. Adams, the drawing-room at the President's. It was crowded to overflowing. General Jackson was there, and we shook hands. He was altogether placid and courteous. I received numerous friendly salutations. D. Webster asked me when I could receive the committee of the House to announce to me my election. I appointed to-morrow noon, at my own house.

DOCUMENT 11.4

Electors for Jackson

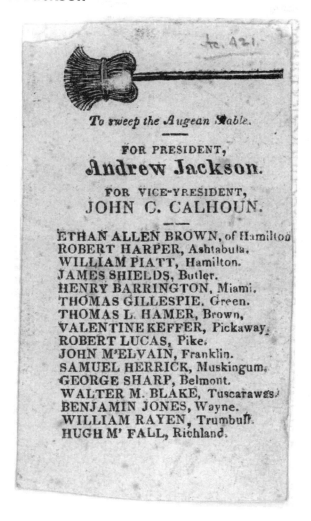

To sweep the Augean Stable.

FOR PRESIDENT,
Andrew Jackson.

FOR VICE-PRESIDENT,
JOHN C. CALHOUN.

ETHAN ALLEN BROWN, of Hamilton
ROBERT HARPER, Ashtabula.
WILLIAM PIATT, Hamilton.
JAMES SHIELDS, Butler.
HENRY BARRINGTON, Miami.
THOMAS GILLESPIE. Green.
THOMAS L. HAMER, Brown,
VALENTINE KEFFER, Pickaway.
ROBERT LUCAS, Pike.
JOHN M'ELVAIN, Franklin.
SAMUEL HERRICK, Muskingum,
GEORGE SHARP, Belmont.
WALTER M. BLAKE, Tuscarawas.
BENJAMIN JONES, Wayne.
WILLIAM RAYEN, Trumbull.
HUGH M' FALL, Richland.

Source: [Cut of broom] To sweep the Augean Stable. For President Andrew Jackson for Vice-President John C. Calhoun, Printed Ephemera Collection; Portfolio 136, Folder 6., rbpe 13600600 http://hdl.loc.gov/loc.rbc/rbpe.13600600, found at: http://memory.loc.gov/ammem/rbpehtml/pehome. html

DOCUMENT 11.5

The Great Whig Meeting

To the People of Waldo.
GREAT WHIG MEETING
In New York.

On the 5th inst. in pursuance of a call of their General Committee, the Whig Young Men of the city of New York assembled in general meeting at Masonic Hall. Upwards of five thousand were in the great Hall and the avenues leading to it; and of this number, at least *one half had been* devoted to the cause of **Jackson!**

The venerable **Erastus Root,** the very corner stone of Democracy in the State—**Ogden Hoffman,** Esq. District Attorney, who in 1823 first hoisted the Jackson flag in Orange county—**John B. Scoles,** heretofore uniformly an adherent of *the* party, and **Isaac R. Van Dusen** of Orange county, the devoted friend of Jackson, who has so long stood in the front rank of the Regency, all addressed the meeting!

After the organization of the meeting, **David Graham,** Jr. Esq. offered a series of resolutions, which he followed by some pertinent and patriotic remarks. The 5th resolution was as follows:

> *Resolved,* That spurning with indignation every attempt to enlist our feelings of state pride, we avow "unqualified and uncompromising opposition to" Martin Van Buren as the successor of General Jackson: *Because* he has always used his influence in his native State for the advancement of his views of *self aggrandisement: Because* we have no confidence in his political integrity: *Because* the measures both of the General and State Administrations which have thus far been pursued so fatally to the interests of our country, are the result of a secret design to perpetuate in his succession to the highest office in our Government, the same system of proscription and corruption which now enslaves us; and because he has uniformly been governed by the policy which *follows* events, instead of *directing* them, and has exhibited the *cunning* of a *demagogue* instead of the *sagacity* of a *statesman.*

* * *

Ogden Hoffman, Esq. District Attorney. When the name of Mr. Hoffman was announced, the cheering from all parts of the Hall became most enthusiastic, and continued so for many minutes. When silence was restored, Mr. Hoffman said—

> . . . I was an early supporter of Andrew Jackson, too early perhaps, for I supported his pretensions at a time when it was as much treason to the party to be

Source: "TO THE PEOPLE OF WALDO. Great Whig Meeting, IN NEW YORK", published 1833, from The Printed Ephemera collection at the Library of Congress, Printed Ephemera Collection; Portfolio 56, Folder 4, **DIGITAL ID** rbpe 05600400 http://hdl.loc.gov/loc.rbc/rbpe.05600400.

his friend as it is now treason to doubt the wisdom of a single measure he had adopted, . . .

But when I saw that in the midst of those demonstrations, and when the gratitude of thousands was as it were, poured like a flood around his course, he had determined to gratify his personal hostility to an institution, by a step in violation of the Constitution;—when I found that a Secretary acting under a conscientious sense of duty, was rudely thrust from office, to make room for a more pliant tool, through whose agency a removal of the public treasury from the hands in which the people had placed it, was effected—seeing all this, I pondered; I could not support him—and so I told my party; and when the memorial approving of the removal of the treasury, came to me from those to whom I owed so much, I told those who presented it, that I owed allegiance to no party who might require me to do what my conscience did not approve, and I believed the removal unwise, unnecessary, and inexpedient—I would not, and I did not sign it. But still I hesitated. I still believed that the groans of a people suffering under the effects of his policy would reach the palace, that Andrew Jackson would discard from his confidence those who had used him for their selfish purposes. Do not mistake me. I felt no sympathy for the Bank, I owned none of its stock, and I wanted and expected nothing from it. I was indeed opposed to all monied monopolies; but when I found that the avowed enemies of the United States Bank were surrounding this State with a cordon of Banks, and the Bank Commissioners were selected for party purposes and with a view to political ends; I inclined to distrust the motives of their avowed hostility. I was opposed to Banks, but not to the good they effected. So far as they were necessary to nerve the arm of enterprise, and contributed to swell the flowing canvass of commerce—so far I was willing to support them, but no farther.

But my feelings were entirely independent of the United States Bank. I looked only to the violated laws of the country, and to the breach of that faith which had been plighted to the Bank at its creation. I thought the Bank entitled to the same justice as the humblest individual prosecuted in your criminal courts—that it should have a fair trial—that the jury should be an impartial one and not packed. When fairly condemned, away with it; but the rights given to it by the people, and identified with the venerable name of Madison, were sacred and should remain untouched.

DOCUMENT 11.6

President Andrew Jackson's Message to Congress "On Indian Removal," 1830

Andrew Jackson

The consequences of a speedy removal will be important to the United States, to individual States, and to the Indians themselves. The pecuniary advantages which it promises to the Government are the least of its recommendations. It

Source: From Andrew Jackson, "President Andrew Jackson's Message to Congress 'On Indian Removal' (1830)," on the website *Our Documents: A National Initiative on American History, Civics, and Service,* www.ourdocuments.gov/content.php?page=transcript&doc=25.

puts an end to all possible danger of collision between the authorities of the General and State Governments on account of the Indians. It will place a dense and civilized population in large tracts of country now occupied by a few savage hunters. By opening the whole territory between Tennessee on the north and Louisiana on the south to the settlement of the whites it will incalculably strengthen the southwestern frontier and render the adjacent States strong enough to repel future invasions without remote aid. It will relieve the whole State of Mississippi and the western part of Alabama of Indian occupancy, and enable those States to advance rapidly in population, wealth, and power. It will separate the Indians from immediate contact with settlements of whites; free them from the power of the States; enable them to pursue happiness in their own way and under their own rude institutions; will retard the progress of decay, which is lessening their numbers, and perhaps cause them gradually, under the protection of the Government and through the influence of good counsels, to cast off their savage habits and become an interesting, civilized, and Christian community.

What good man would prefer a country covered with forests and ranged by a few thousand savages to our extensive Republic, studded with cities, towns, and prosperous farms embellished with all the improvements which art can devise or industry execute, occupied by more than 12,000,000 happy people, and filled with all the blessings of liberty, civilization and religion? . . .

And is it supposed that the wandering savage has a stronger attachment to his home than the settled, civilized Christian? Is it more afflicting to him to leave the graves of his fathers than it is to our brothers and children? Rightly considered, the policy of the General Government toward the red man is not only liberal, but generous. He is unwilling to submit to the laws of the States and mingle with their population. To save him from this alternative, or perhaps utter annihilation, the General Government kindly offers him a new home, and proposes to pay the whole expense of his removal and settlement.

DOCUMENT 11.7

South Carolina Nullification

AN ORDINANCE,

To Nullify an Act of the Congress of the United States, entitled "An Act further to provide for the Collection of Duties on Imports," commonly called the Force Bill.

We, the People of the State of South Carolina, in Convention assembled, do Declare and Ordain, That the Act of the Congress of the United States, entitled "An Act further to provide for the collection of duties on imports," approved the 2d day of March, 1833, is unauthorized by the Constitution of the United States,

Source: From State Papers on Nullification (New York: Da Capo Press, 1970), pp. 373–74.

subversive of that Constitution, and destructive of public liberty; and that the same is, and shall be deemed null and void, within the limits of this State; and it shall be the duty of the Legislature, at such time as they may deem expedient, to adopt such measures and pass such acts as may be necessary to prevent the enforcement thereof, and to inflict proper penalties on any person who shall do any act in execution or enforcement of the same within the limits of this State.

We do further Ordain and Declare, That the allegiance of the citizens of this State, while they continue such, is due to the said State: and that obedience only, and not allegiance, is due by them to any other power or authority, to whom a control over them has been, or may be delegated by the State; and the General Assembly of the said State is hereby empowered from time to time, when they may deem it proper, to provide for the administration to the citizens and officers of the State, or such of the said officers as they may think fit, of suitable oaths or affirmations, binding them to the observance of such allegiance, and abjuring all other allegiance; and, also, to define what shall amount to a violation of their allegiance, and to provide the proper punishment for such violation.

Done in Convention, at Columbia, the eighteenth day of March, in the year of our Lord, one thousand eight hundred and thirty-three, and in the fifty-seventh year of the Sovereignty and Independence of the United States of America.

12

Of Power and Pillars

John C. Calhoun and South Carolina proposed a recipe for protecting liberty in the face of a strong national government. Slavery was a fundamental part of the economy and culture of the American South. The chart portraying the population in 1860 illustrates the interconnection among the different populations of the South. Moreover, the schematic of a southern plantation illustrates the complex and varied, yet obviously commercial, logic of southern agriculture. Farms big and small had to fit themselves into a mosaic of plantations and big producers capable of achieving a competitive advantage over medium and small producers.

John Crawford, once a slave, remembered his wealthy master. Interlaced through Mr. Crawford's reminiscences are numerous examples of paternalism practiced by Southern masters. By assuming the role of father to both free and slaves under their control, the master class could rationalize behaviors that seemed almost familial with people who barely existed in a legal sense in the South.

Frederick Douglass remembers a wide range of experiences from his days as a slave. One particularly significant interlude he remembered was when he was rented out to Mr. Covey, in part to reeducate him about the nature of slavery. The education Douglass received under the tutelage of Mr. Covey, however, was probably not the education the slave system would have wanted him to have. Douglass learned about the importance of struggling to contest and resist inhumane treatment through either appeals to the justice of seemingly thoughtful masters or through one's own clenched fists.

If whites consistently sought life, liberty, and the pursuit of happiness throughout the American experience, then African Americans might have acquired similar hopes and aspirations. John Floyd was governor of Virginia during Nat Turner's revolt, the worst slave insurrection in the history of antebellum slavery. While seeking to thoroughly suppress the insurrection, Floyd wrestled with both the issue of justice for accused slaves and whether his beloved Virginia should continue to burden itself with the problematic system of slavery.

After leaving the presidency, John Quincy Adams returned to Congress and became a vocal opponent of slavery in the House of Representatives. Late in life he became involved in the famous Amistad case as the attorney who argued before the Supreme Court for the freedom of that ship's rebellious cargo. Adams saw that liberty was surely a province that ought to be extended to Africans kidnapped and illegally bought and sold in the Americas.

Finally, southerners themselves varied in the degree to which they supported the repressive codes and legislation the southern states increasingly devised to sustain and maintain slavery. Mrs. Douglass does not necessarily represent opposition to slavery or abolitionism, but she did represent a dangerous logic to southerners. As she sought to educate slave children, if only to extend to them the benefits of the Gospel, she interacted with children in ways that not only verified their humanity, but enabled them to liberate their own hearts and souls through learning and the inspirational catechisms of Christianity.

DOCUMENT 12.1

Southern Population, 1860

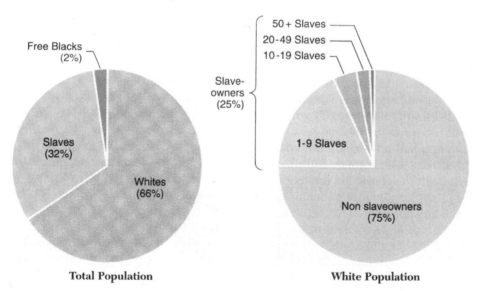

Total Population   White Population

Source: From Davidson, J. W., et al. (2001), Nation of Nations: A Narrative History of the American Republic. New York: McGraw-Hill, p. 398.

DOCUMENT 12.2

A Plantation Layout

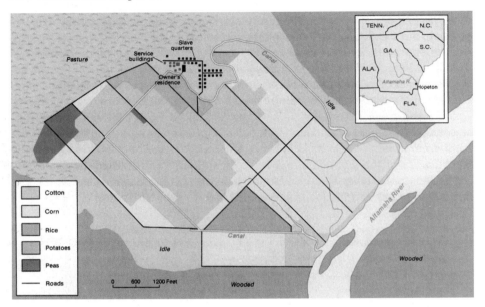

A Plantation Layout Often covering a thousand acres or more, a plantation was laid out like a small village and contained several fields and usually extensive uncleared woods. Somewhere near the master's "big house" were the quarters—slave cabins clustered along one or more streets. Service buildings might include a smokehouse, stables, a gin house (for cotton) or a rice mill, and an overseer's dwelling. Most large plantations produced a considerable amount of foodstuffs and concentrated on a single cash crop.

DOCUMENT 12.3

John Crawford Remembers

John Crawford

When Grandpappy Jake Crawford, my master, come to Mississippi he bought the land, so my pappy tell me, at 14¢ a acre and he bought it by the miles. He

Source: From Davidson, J. W., et al. (2001), *Nation of Nations: A Narrative History of the American Republic.* New York: McGraw-Hill, p. 400.

Source: Excerpted from George P. Rawick, ed., *The American Slave: A Composite Autobiography,* supplement, series 2, vol. 4: *Texas Narratives,* pt. 3 (Westport, CT: Greenwood Press, 1979), pp. 962–66.

was the richest man I ever heared tell of. He was the bestest man too that ever put a shoe on. . . .

When I was a little bitty boy I 'members that Grandpappy used to call all the little niggers up 'round him on the porch and show us how to make shuck dolls and tell us to feel in his pockets for stick candy, rock candy and marbles. He say he like to play with his beard and hair and jest tech him. He used to rub his hand over our head and say, "Grandpappy wouldn't take nothing for his little burr-head niggers."

They jest ain't no tellin' how much land Grandpappy had. But he worked twenty-seven yoke of oxes and mules and horses besides. Enduring the Civil war he sent his mules to work on the government breastworks. He had fifty-two hundred bee hive, nine-hundred head of sheeps, three-hundred head of hogs and lots of cows. He said he wanted nuf milk on his place if he want to swim in it he could.

He had nine-hundred slaves and more sometimes. They went to breakfast at sunup and then to the fields 'til 'leven-thirty when they come back to the house at the ringing of a bell for dinner and then back to the fields at one o'clock and work 'til 'bout five. I always remember seeing the slaves come trooping up to the house for dinner in sech a long line. And it 'pears to me plumb unreasonable for one man to own that many people and keep what they make and sell them off or keep them just as he notions.

My pappy told me that when he was a young man grandpappy sold him off to some folks who took him off to a place called Denver. He said he slipped away from them and was three years getting back to old Grandpappy. He said he walked it barefoot for hundreds of miles and when he come home old Grandpappy cried and swore a swear that he won't sell no more niggers that don't want to go. He said Grandpappy counted out eighteen-hundred dollars to sent the folks to buy him back.

He was mighty good to the niggers. He told them plenty tines, "I ain't a man that cares for wealth. Everything I got you niggers made it out'n you sweat. And I want you to take time to set and enjoy it. I got more things I want to do than set and count money." He never worked us in bad weather or in the cold and when it was hot we didn't work in the middle of the day.

There is only one thing I could say agin' Grandpappy and I hates to say that. But he taught me hissef "Don't tell a lie for credit when you can tell the truth for cash." Grandpappy don't want the niggers to have learnin' out of books and don't want them to pray. He is scared they will pray for freedom. And he b'lieves they will get if they pray. Better not let Grandpappy ketch you prayin. He reads us out'n the Bible every morning and night. He was a powerful Godly man. Sometimes we little nigger plumb thought he was God. Leastways Old Master was so purty like a woman's face with his big tall standing up and shiny black eyes that we thought God look jest like Grandpappy.

DOCUMENT 12.4

Frederick Douglass Awakens

Frederick Douglass

Mr. Covey was at the house, about one hundred yards from the treading-yard where we were fanning. On hearing the fan stop, he left immediately, and came to the spot where we were. He hastily inquired what the matter was. Bill answered that I was sick, and there was no one to bring wheat to the fan. I had by this time crawled away under the side of the post and rail-fence by which the yard was enclosed, hoping to find relief by getting out of the sun. He then asked where I was. He was told by one of the hands. He came to the spot, and, after looking at me awhile, asked me what was the matter. I told him as well as I could, for I scarce had strength to speak. He then gave me a savage kick in the side, and told me to get up. I tried to do so, but fell back in the attempt. He gave me another kick, and again told me to rise. I again tried, and succeeded in gaining my feet; but, stooping to get the tub with which I was feeding the fan, I again staggered and fell. While down in this situation, Mr. Covey took up the hickory slat with which Hughes had been striking off the half-bushel measure, and with it gave me a heavy blow upon the head, making a large wound, and the blood ran freely; and with this again told me to get up. I made no effort to comply, having now made up my mind to let him do his worst. In a short time after receiving this blow, my head grew better. Mr. Covey had now left me to my fate. At this moment I resolved, for the first time, to go to my master, enter a complaint, and ask his protection. In order to [do] this, I must that afternoon walk seven miles; and this, under the circumstances, was truly a severe undertaking. I was exceedingly feeble; made so as much by the kicks and blows which I received, as by the severe fit of sickness to which I had been subjected. I, however, watched my chance, while Covey was looking in an opposite direction, and started for St. Michael's. I succeeded in getting a considerable distance on my way to the woods, when Covey discovered me, and called after me to come back, threatening what he would do if I did not come. I disregarded both his calls and his threats, and made my way to the woods as fast as my feeble state would allow; and thinking I might be overhauled by him if I kept the road, I walked through the woods, keeping far enough from the road to avoid detection, and near enough to prevent losing my way. I had not gone far before my little strength again failed me. I could go no farther. I fell down, and lay for a considerable time. The blood was yet oozing from the wound on my head. For a time I thought I should bleed to death; and think now that I should have done so, but that the blood so matted my hair as to stop the wound. After lying there about three quarters of an hour, I nerved myself up again, and started on my

Source: Excerpted from Frederick Douglass, *Narrative of the Life of Frederick Douglass, an American Slave, Written by Himself*, ed. David W. Blight (Boston: Bedford Books, 1993), pp. 76–79.

way, through bogs and briers, barefooted and bareheaded, tearing my feet sometimes at nearly every step; and after a journey of about seven miles, occupying some five hours to perform it, I arrived at master's store. I then presented an appearance enough to affect any but a heart of iron. From the crown of my head to my feet, I was covered with blood. My hair was all clotted with dust and blood; my shirt was stiff with blood. My legs and feet were torn in sundry places with briers and thorns, and were also covered with blood. I suppose I looked like a man who had escaped a den of wild beasts, and barely escaped them. In this state I appeared before my master, humbly entreating him to interpose his authority for my protection. I told him all the circumstances as well as I could, and it seemed, as I spoke, at times to affect him. He would then walk the floor, and seek to justify Covey by saying he expected I deserved it. He asked me what I wanted. I told him, to let me get a new home; that as sure as I lived with Mr. Covey again, I should live with but to die with him; that Covey would surely kill me; he was in a fair way for it. Master Thomas ridiculed the idea that there was any danger of Mr. Covey's killing me, and said that he knew Mr. Covey; that he was a good man, and that he could not think of taking me from him; that, should he do so, he would lose the whole year's wages; that I belonged to Mr. Covey for one year, and that I must go back to him, come what might; and that I must not trouble him with any more stories, or that he would himself *get hold of me*. After threatening me thus, he gave me a very large dose of salts, telling me that I might remain in St. Michael's that night, (it being quite late,) but that I must be off back to Mr. Covey's early in the morning; and that if I did not, he would *get hold of me*, which meant that he would whip me. I remained all night, and, according to his orders, I started off to Covey's in the morning, (Saturday morning,) wearied in body and broken in spirit. I got no supper that night, or breakfast that morning. I reached Covey's about nine o'clock; and just as I was getting over the fence that divided Mrs. Kemp's fields from ours, out ran Covey with his cowskin, to give me another whipping. Before he could reach me, I succeeded in getting to the cornfield; and as the corn was very high, it afforded me the means of hiding. He seemed very angry, and searched for me a long time. . . .

This was Sunday morning. I immediately started for home; and upon entering the yard gate, out came Mr. Covey on his way to meeting. He spoke to me very kindly, made me drive the pigs from a lot near by, and passed on towards the church. . . .

All went well till Monday morning. On this morning, the virtue of the *root* was fully tested. Long before daylight, I was called to go and rub, curry, and feed, the horses. I obeyed, and was glad to obey. But whilst thus engaged, whilst in the act of throwing down some blades from the loft, Mr. Covey entered the stable with a long rope; and just as I was half out of the loft, he caught hold of my legs, and was about tying me. As soon as I found what he was up to, I gave a sudden spring, and as I did so, he holding to my legs, I was brought sprawling on the stable floor. Mr. Covey seemed now to think he had me, and could do what he pleased; but at this moment—from whence came the spirit I don't know—I resolved to fight; and, suiting my action to the resolution, I seized Covey hard by the throat; and as I did so, I rose. He held on to me, and I to him. My resistance was so entirely unexpected, that Covey seemed taken all aback. He trembled like a leaf. This gave me assurance, and I held him uneasy, causing the blood to run where I touched him with the ends of my fingers. Mr. Covey soon called out to Hughes for help. Hughes came, and, while Covey held me, attempting to tie my right hand. While he was in the act of doing so, I watched my chance, and gave him a heavy kick close under the ribs. This kick fairly sickened Hughes, so that he left me in the hands of Mr. Covey. This kick had the effect of not only weakening Hughes, but Covey also. When he saw Hughes bending over with pain, his courage quailed. He asked me if I meant to persist in my resistance. I told him I did, come what might; that he had used me like a brute for six months, and that I was determined to be used so no longer. With that, he strove to drag me to a stick that was lying just out of the stable door. He meant to knock me down. But just as he was leaning over to get the stick, I seized him with both hands by his collar, and brought him by a sudden snatch to the ground. By this time, Bill came. Covey called upon him for assistance. Bill wanted to know what he could do. Covey said, "Take hold of him, take hold of him!" Bill said his master hired him out to work, and not to help to whip me; so he left Covey and myself to fight our own battle out. We were at it for nearly two hours. Covey at length let me go, puffing and blowing at a great rate, saying that if I had not resisted, he would not have whipped me half so much. The truth was, that he had not whipped me at all. I considered him as getting entirely the worst end of the bargain; for he had drawn no blood from me, but I had from him. The whole six months afterwards, that I spent with Mr. Covey, he never laid the weight of his finger upon me in anger. He would occasionally say, he didn't want to get hold of me again. "No," thought I, "you need not; for you will come off worse than you did before."

This battle with Mr. Covey was the turning-point in my career as a slave. It rekindled the few expiring embers of freedom, and revived within me a sense of my own manhood. It recalled the departed self-confidence, and inspired me again with a determination to be free. The gratification afforded by the triumph was a full compensation for whatever else might follow, even death itself. He only can understand the deep satisfaction which I experienced, who has himself repelled by force the bloody arm of slavery. I felt as I never felt before. It was a glorious resurrection, from the tomb of slavery, to the heaven of freedom. My long-crushed spirit rose, cowardice departed, bold defiance took its place; and I now resolved that, however long I might remain a slave in form, the day had passed forever when I could be a slave in fact. I did not hesitate to let it be known of me, that the white man who expected to succeed in whipping, must also succeed in killing me.

DOCUMENT 12.5

John Floyd and Slavery in Virginia

John Floyd

August, 1831

Twenty-third day. This will be a very noted day in Virginia. At daylight this morning the Mayor of the City put into my hands a notice to the public, written by James Trezvant of Southampton County, stating that an insurrection of the slaves in that county had taken place, that several families had been massacred and that it would take a considerable military force to put them down.

Upon the receipt of this information, I began to consider how to prepare for the crisis. To call out the militia and equip a military force for that service. But according to the forms of this wretched and abominable Constitution, I must first require advice of Council, and then disregard it, if I please. On this occasion there was not one councillor in the city. I went on, made all the arrangements for suppressing the insurrection, having all my orders ready for men, arms, ammunition, etc., when by this time, one of the council came to town, and that vain and foolish ceremony was gone through. In a few hours the troops marched, Captain Randolph with a fine troop of cavalry and Captain John B. Richardson with light artillery, both from this city and two companies of Infantry from Norfolk and Portsmouth. The light Artillery had under their care one thousand stand of arms for Southampton and Sussex, with a good supply of ammunition. All these things were dispatched in a few hours. . . .

Twenty-seventh day. I have received a record of the trial of three slaves, for treason in Southampton. Am recommended to mercy, which I would grant but the forms of our infamous Constitution makes it necessary before the Governor does any act involving discretionary power, first to require advice of Council, and in this case I cannot do so, because there is not one member of the Council of State in Richmond, wherefore the poor wretch must lose his life by their absence from their official duty.

I have received this day another number of the "Liberator," a newspaper printed in Boston, with the express intention of inciting the slaves and free negroes in this and the other States to rebellion and to murder the men, women and children of those states. Yet we are gravely told there is no law to punish such an offence. The amount of it then is this, a man in our States may plot treason in one

Source: Excerpted from "Diary of Governor John Floyd, 1831–1832," in *The Confessions of Nat Turner and Related Documents,* ed., Kenneth S. Greenberg (Boston: Bedford Books, 1996), pp. 104–9.

state against another without fear of punishment, whilst the suffering state has no right to resist by the provisions of the Federal Constitution. If this is not checked it must lead to a separation of these states. If the forms of law will not punish, the law of nature will not permit men to have their families butchered before their eyes by their slaves and not seek by force to punish those who plan and encourage them to perpetrate these deeds. I shall notice this in my next message to the General Assembly of this State. Something must be done and with decision. . . .

December, 1831

Twenty-sixth day. The public business gets on slowly. The question of the gradual abolition of slavery begins to be mooted. The Eastern members, meaning those east of the Blue Ridge Mountains, wish to avoid the discussion, but it must come if I can influence my friends in the Assembly to bring it on. I will not rest until slavery is abolished in Virginia.

January, 1832

Ninth day. Members begin to talk of debating the question of gradually emancipating the Slaves of Virginia. It has been very adroitly brought about. Summers, Faulkner, Preston and Berry, also Campbell and Brook will be fast friends to the measure. They are talented young men and will manage this affair most excellently well.

Tenth day. The slave question increases.

Eleventh day. Hopes are entertained by my young friends that a debate can be had upon the slave question.

Twelfth day. Mr. Goode this day made a motion to discharge the Committee on so much of the Governor's message as relates to free negroes and mulattoes and to which a memorial of sundry citizens of Hanover had been referred with a view to prevent debate upon the Slave question involved in that memorial. The abolition party opposed it and hence the slave party have produced the very debate they wished to avoid, and too, have entered upon it with open doors.

Thirteenth day. The debate in the House of Delegates still continues.

Fifteenth day. The debate in the House continued with great ability by Faulkner. This is a fine talented young gentleman.

Sixteenth day. The debate continues with increased ability. . . .

Nineteenth day. The debate still goes on.

Twentieth day. Nothing now is talked of or creates any interest but the debate on the abolition of slavery. All is well.

Twenty-first day. The debate in the House is growing in interest and I fear engendering bad and party feelings. It must be checked in erratic tendencies.

Twenty-third day. Many speculations are now made upon the result of this debate. We can carry the question, if necessary, by about two votes which will depend upon the views and objects to be developed by the slave part of the state. I think as yet nothing has transpired other than to prove that they must not be hurt, but held in check.

Twenty-fourth day. The debate begins to be carried on in an angry tone. It is not good that it should be so.

Twenty-fifth day. The debate is stopped but the members from the South side of the James River talk of making a proposition to divide the State by the Blue Ridge Mountains sooner than part with their negroes, which is the property of that part of the State.

DOCUMENT 12.6

The *Amistad* and Justice

John Quincy Adams

Feb. 19.—I walked home; and about half-past six, Jeremy Leary died, almost without a groan.

Feb. 20.—The arrangements had been made for the funeral of my poor, humble, but excellent friend Jeremy Leary, at three o'clock this afternoon. I walked to the Capitol this morning, with a spirit humbled to the dust, with a heart melted in sorrow, and a mind agitated and confused. The case of the *Amistad* captives had been fixed to commence in the Supreme Court this morning. . . . I therefore, as soon as the Court was opened and the case was called, requested as a personal favor of the Court to suspend the proceedings in this case from 2 o'clock p.m. today till Monday; to which Chief Justice Taney answered, "Certainly.". . .

March 29.—I am yet to revise for publication my argument in the case of the *Amistad* Africans; and, in merely glancing over the slave-trade papers lent me by Mr. Fox, I find impulses of duty upon my own conscience which I cannot resist, while on the other hand are the magnitude, the danger, the insurmountable burden of labor to be encountered in the undertaking to touch upon the slave-trade. No one else will undertake it; no one but a spirit unconquerable by man, woman or fiend can undertake it but with the heart of martyrdom. The world, the flesh, and all the devils in hell are arrayed against any man who now in this North American Union shall dare to join the standard of Almighty God to put down the African slave-trade; and what can I, upon the verge of my seventy-fourth birthday, with a shaking hand, a darkening eye, a drowsy brain, and with all my faculties dropping from me one by one, as the teeth are dropping from my head—what can I do for the cause of God and man, for the progress of human emancipation, for the suppression of the African slave-trade? Yet my conscience presses me on; let me but die upon the breach.

Source: Excerpted from John Quincy Adams, *The Diary of John Quincy Adams, 1794–1845*, ed. Allen Nevins (New York: Longmans, 1929), pp. 517–19.

DOCUMENT 12.7

Teaching Slave Children to Read

The Trial of Margaret Douglass

[Margaret Douglass.] I am a Southern woman by birth, education and feeling. I have been a slaveholder myself, and I would be again, if I felt so disposed. I am a native of and have always resided in a Southern slave state. The home of my childhood is as dear to me as my life, and I am as deeply interested in the welfare of Virginia, and of the whole united Southern slave states, as I am in the State of South Carolina; yes, and a great deal more so than very many who call themselves men. I am no abolitionist, neither am I a fanatic, and I am by education as strongly opposed as you are to the interference of Northern anti-slavery men with our institutions, although I believe that their principles are based on a religious foundation. I deem it the duty of every Southerner, morally and religiously, to instruct his slaves, that they may know their duties to their masters, and to their common God. Let the masters first do their duty to them, for they are still our slaves and servants, whether bond or free, and can be nothing else in our community. Let us not quarrel with our neighbors, but rather look around us and see what we have ourselves to do that we have left undone so long. I am a strong advocate for the religious and moral instruction of the whole human family. I have always instructed my own slaves, and will continue to do so as long as I remain in a slave state. . . .

Let us look into the situation of our colored population in the city of Norfolk, for they are not dumb brutes. If they were, they would be more carefully considered, and their welfare better provided for. For instance, two or three of these people are not allowed to assemble together by themselves, whether in sickness or in health. There is no provision made for them, whatever the circumstances may be, and such meetings are pronounced unlawful and treasonable. Think you, gentlemen, that there is not misery and distress among these people? Yes, indeed, misery enough, and frequently starvation. Even those that are called free are heavily taxed, and their privileges greatly limited; and when they are sick, or in want, on whom does the duty devolve to seek them out and administer to their necessities? Does it fall upon you, gentlemen? Oh no, it is not expected that gentlemen will take the trouble to seek out a negro hut for the purpose of alleviating the wretchedness he may find within it. Why then persecute your benevolent ladies for doing that which you yourselves have so long neglected? Shall we treat our slaves with less compassion than we do the cattle in our fields?

In my opinion, we have nothing to fear from the true blooded negro. It is the half-breed, or those with more or less white blood in their veins, whom I

Source: Excerpted from John D. Lawson, ed., *American State Trials* (Wilmington, DE: Scholarly Resources, 1972), pp. 53–60.

have always found presumptive, treacherous and revengeful And do you blame them for this? How can you? Ask yourselves the cause. Ask how that white blood got beneath those tawny skins, and let nature herself account for the exhibition of these instincts. Blame the authors of this devilish mischief, but not the innocent victims of it.

As for myself, I shall keep on with my good work; not, however, by continuing to violate what I now know to be your laws, but by endeavoring to teach the colored race humility and a prayerful spirit; how to bear their sufferings as our Savior bore his for us all. I will teach them their duty to their superiors, how to live, and how to die. And now, if ignorance of your peculiar laws is not a sufficient excuse for my violation of the letter of them, surely my good intentions, and the abundant examples set before me by your most worthy and pious citizens, ought to convince you that I was actuated by no improper motives, and had no ulterior designs against the peace and dignity of your Commonwealth. . . .

[Judge.] The law under which you have been tried and found guilty is not to be found among the original enactments of our Legislature. The first legislative provision upon this subject was introduced in the year 1831, immediately succeeding the bloody scenes of the memorable Southampton insurrection; and that law being found not sufficiently penal to check the wrongs complained of, was re-enacted with additional penalties in the year 1848, which last mentioned act, after several years' trial and experience, has been re-affirmed by adoption, and incorporated into our present code. After these several and repeated recognitions of the wisdom and propriety of the said act, it may well be said that bold and open opposition to it is a matter not to be slightly regarded, especially as we have reason to believe that every Southern slave state in our country, as a measure of self-preservation and protection, has deemed it wise and just to adopt laws with similar provisions.

There might have been no occasion for such enactments in Virginia, or elsewhere, on the subject of negro education, but as a matter of self-defense against the schemes of Northern incendiaries, and the outcry against holding our slaves in bondage. Many now living well remember how, and when, and why the anti-slavery fury began, and by what means its manifestations were made public. Our mails were clogged with abolition pamphlets and inflammatory documents, to be distributed among our Southern negroes to induce them to cut our throats. Sometimes, it may be, these libelous documents were distributed by Northern citizens professing Southern feelings, and at other times by Southern people professing Northern feelings. These, however, were not the only means resorted to by the Northern fanatics to stir up insubordination among our slaves. They scattered far and near pocket handkerchiefs, and other similar articles, with frightful engravings, and printed over with anti-slavery nonsense, with the view to work upon the feeling and ignorance of our negroes, who otherwise would have remained comfortable and happy. Under such circumstances there was but one measure of protection for the South, and that was adopted.

13

Lone and Assembled Stars

The search for liberty and happiness also contributed to the expansiveness of the United States. A certain romanticism has evolved regarding the frontier and what used to be referred to as the winning of the West. Oftentimes, migrating westward was less glamorous, however, and more an encounter with work, work, work.

Beyond the seas of grass on the prairie, other Americans expanded their horizons on the high seas. During the middle part of the 19th century the American whaling fleet ventured to many parts of the world and actually contributed to the impetus for expansive endeavors such as the acquisition of California and the diplomatic opening of Japan by Commodore Mathew Perry in 1854. Of course, the movement to obtain California involved the complicated relations among Texas and Mexico and the United States that ultimately resulted in the Mexican-American War (1846–48). The Treaty of Guadalupe Hidalgo ended that war and secured most of the rest of the continent for the United States. It also suggested that the American nation promised to be respectful of other nationalities and cultures by absorbing them.

On the West Coast, communities were forming. Throughout the 1840s, Oregon fever was a compelling force for westward migration, and Sara Sprenger notes what life was like there in the early days. Oregon represented the expectation that Thomas Jefferson and other founding fathers had in establishing the process by which states came into being through the provisions of the Northwest Ordinances. Areas would gradually gain population, farming communities and towns would spring up, a small population would begin to practice democracy in territorial governments, and after a period of years the area would be sufficiently populated and experienced to write a state constitution and secure membership in the Union. It had never been anticipated, however, that a region would almost instantly progress from frontier to candidate for statehood. That proved to be the case for California, which grew at an astounding pace after the Gold Rush of 1848. Faced with a vast increase in population that virtually overran all preexisting institutions, structures, and infrastructure, some sought to establish law and order through vigilantism. Lell Hawley Woolley reveals some of the real wildness of the Wild West.

DOCUMENT 13.1

Report on Fort Atkinson

Colonel George Croghan

St. Louis, October, 1826

Having now completed an inspection of the posts designated in the order of 17th May, 1826, from General Headquarters, I will proceed to make some general remarks which could not have been previously so well introduced. . . .

Fort Atkinson is certainly the weakest . . . work which I have visited. . . . Our frontier posts ought to be viewed as if placed directly upon the lines of a hostile territory and should therefore be prepared for immediate hostilities. The posts should be strong in themselves, the garrison sufficient, well supplied, and throughout that vigilant police observed which would presuppose a state of war. This is far from being the case; it would seem that the purpose was not to operate upon the fears of the Indians by an array of military strength and an appearance of constant watchfulness, but to gain them over by the softer arguments of unreserved intercourse and unsuspecting confidence. I now repeat that which I before asserted, "Our military have lost character among the Indians," and that it can not be recovered under a continuance of the present system of external police. . . .

That the Indians are at peace and that nothing is likely to disturb the present quiet argues not at all against the positive necessity for placing our frontiers in a position the best calculated to invite military criticism. As well might the propriety of entirely disbanding the army be urged upon us for the same reason, and truly, I would advocate the latter, sooner than witness a total annihilation of all military feeling under the operations of the present system, a system which would sink the proud soldier into the menial and reduce him who may have gallantly led in the front of our enemies into the base overseer of a troop of awkward ploughmen. . . .

Look at Fort Atkinson and you will see barn yards that would not disgrace a Pennsylvania farmer, herds of cattle that would do credit to a Potomac grazier, yet where is the gain in this, either to the soldier or to the government? Ask the individual who boastingly shews you all this, why such a provision of hay and corn. His answer will be, to *feed* the *cattle*. But why so many *cattle*? Why—to eat the *hay and corn.*

Source: Excerpted from Francis Paul Prucha, *Army Life on the Western Frontier: Selections from the Official Reports Made between 1826 and 1845 by Colonel George Croghan* (Norman: University of Oklahoma Press, 1958), pp. 4–7.

DOCUMENT 13.2

Being Young in Frontier Iowa

George C. Duffield

We broke twelve acres of land in 1837, and planted it in corn, wheat and pota-toes. By 1838 we had three head of horses, five yoke of cattle and twenty-five hogs. Our neighbors had from a single ox to as much stock as we. The land was open to the Pacific coast. Hundreds of deer visited the salt licks, and the springs and streams of the locality. Deer would leave the finest wild pasture to ravage growing crops. So the first two or three years there was serious danger of crop destruction from the small acreage compared with the number of animals named, and from other enemies such as bears, raccoons, squirrels, blue jays and woodpeckers. From the planting to the gathering time, and even after that, the settler's crop was preyed upon day and night by a horde as hungry as himself.

* * *

After we were settled in our new cabin and had our first crop planted, with my brothers, from almost the smallest to John who was grown, I was put at con-structing a "defense." Not a defense against the Indians who were living all around us, it is true, but against our own stock, and that of the other settlers; from the Indian ponies, the herds of deer, and the elk that remained. And the protection of crops, while a great problem, was not the only one. Acquiring, in-creasing and identifying domestic animals was an immense and important work. A few hogs, for instance, would be brought into this new country and turned out into the open with those of other settlers, where the woods, the streams and annoying enemies encouraged them to shun the settlements; to re-cover these animals was difficult and required a system of identification forever gone from Iowa. The difficulties increased with the population and with the numbers of live stock.

* * *

From 1837 to 1842, it then seemed to me, father's only thoughts were of brush, timber, fence; chop, chop, chop. Laborious, drudging, toilsome youth-time in Iowa!

Source: George C. Duffield, "Youthtime in Frontier Iowa," as excerpted in Catherine Reef, *Working in America: An Eyewitness History* (New York: Facts On File, 2000), p. 15.

DOCUMENT 13.3

Whaling the World

The Cruise of the Dove, A Whalers' Song (ca. 1845)

Ye men of renown who are a-swearing
For some noble deeds your lordships have done
Come listen to me and hear things full as daring
Which we brother spouters think nothing but fun.

It was a fine ship with prime captain and crew,
Surpassed by none and equaled by few,
With courage undaunted by oars and by sail,
So nimble we chased the spermacety whale.

The name of our ship I suppose you'd like to know,
The name of our captain and owners also.
She was called the Dove, you will see in my song,
And nothing I tell you I swear it is wrong.

Our captain's name is Butler, a man fine and bold.
Our owners named Hazzard and Worth, I hear told.
On the Coast of Peru we were destined to cruise,
But if we'd stopped there it would not have been much use.

Then away to the westward in hopes for to find
Some work for all hands, being that way inclined.
Then away to the northward to Japan likewise,
Where the whale both the irons and lances defies.

"There she breathes, there she blows," was the cry heard one day.
The captain looked up and hailed out where away
Right ahead and abeam on each hand them we spy,
Like logs around us so sweetly they lie.

The captain went up and he soon gave the word.
Being his orders by all should be heard.
So back the main yard and stop the ship's way.
Do swing out your boats boys and lower away.

Now, our boats being lowered, there arose a contest
Among the boats' crews to see which should do best.
"Spring on," says the headsman, "don't let them pass by."
When up starts a whale and "lay on" is the cry.

"Stand up" was the next word that I heard him say.
"Into her she's got it. Lay on the other way.
I have got a good iron just over her fin,
So work sharp my boys and pull on her again."

Source: From the *AmDocs* website, www.ku.edu/carrie/docs/texts/whalers.htm.

Now we worked for our lives while each tar done his best.
We brought the school to and had work for the rest.
And while that our whales were bleeding and dying,
The shipkeepers so anxious were to windward ever plying.

Now our whales are turned up, and we prepared for our toil.
We will soon get on board with the blubber to boil.
When it's boiled out and stowed down in the hold,
We'll drink greasy luck to the whalers so bold.

Our ship she is full and home we are bound.
We fill up our glasses and drink all around.
We fill up our glasses and so merry we will be
And drink a good health to the liberty tree.

Now in New York harbor our good ship lies moored
With a hold full of oil and all hands well on board.
Being paid by our owners, we leave captain and mate.
We're bound for the park boys to blow us out straight.

DOCUMENT 13.4

Treaty of Guadalupe Hidalgo, 1848

ARTICLE VIII

Mexicans now established in territories previously belonging to Mexico, and which remain for the future within the limits of the United States, as defined by the present treaty, shall be free to continue where they now reside, or to remove at any time to the Mexican Republic, retaining the property which they possess in the said territories, or disposing thereof, and removing the proceeds wherever they please, without their being subjected, on this account, to any contribution, tax, or charge whatever.

Those who shall prefer to remain in the said territories may either retain the title and rights of Mexican citizens, or acquire those of citizens of the United States. But they shall be under the obligation to make their election within one year from the date of the exchange of ratifications of this treaty; and those who shall remain in the said territories after the expiration of that year, without having declared their intention to retain the character of Mexicans, shall be considered to have elected to become citizens of the United States.

In the said territories, property of every kind, now belonging to Mexicans not established there, shall be inviolably respected. The present owners, the heirs of these, and all Mexicans who may hereafter acquire said property by contract, shall enjoy with respect to it guarantes equally ample as if the same belonged to citizens of the United States.

Source: Excerpted from the Treaty of Guadalupe Hidalgo, as made available on the *Our Documents* website, www.ourdocuments.gov/content.php?page=transcript&doc=26.

ARTICLE IX

The Mexicans who, in the territories aforesaid, shall not preserve the character of citizens of the Mexican Republic, conformably with what is stipulated in the preceding article, shall be incorporated into the Union of the United States, and be admitted at the proper time (to be judged of by the Congress of the United States) to the enjoyment of all the rights of citizens of the United States, according to the principles of the Constitution; and in the mean time, shall be maintained and protected in the free enjoyment of their liberty and property, and secured in the free exercise of their religion without restriction.

DOCUMENT 13.5

Sarah Sprenger Remembers Oregon, 1852

Sarah Sprenger

Along the trail, we saw buffaloes wallowing in their mudholes, and many antelope. Once in a while the boys would kill an antelope, which made delicious meat. We found that buffalo meat was too coarse, and bear meat too greasy to eat much, but that prairie hens were a real delicacy.

Father always rode ahead to hunt good camping grounds with plenty of water, grass, and wood—at least water and grass for the cattle. Often we had to cook with grease wood or sagebrush. We had iron pots and teakettles for cooking, and did our baking in a Dutch oven with coals under it and over it. It was difficult for my Mother and sisters to work and cook this way, as we had been used to a large house, a cook stove and brick oven, and maid to do the hard work. When our cow gave plenty of milk, we put the milk in a large, tin can and hung this can on the wagon, where the jolting would churn the milk to butter. But most of the time, since the cow didn't get the right kind of food, it took all her milk for my little brother Tommy. Besides, a number of the cattle died before we reached Oregon, and we had to be frugal with the milk we could get.

One night, my oldest sister and I were going from one wagon to another one and a big wolf came up. We didn't stay to see what he wanted!

We saw Indians often. Once when we were in Nez Perce country, a chief came and offered my brother a lot of horses in trade for my sister Maria, a beautiful girl with black hair and snapping black eyes. My brother jokingly agreed, and the next day the chief came with his ponies, looking for Maria. Father hid my sister in one of the wagons, and after several days managed to persuade the chief that my brother had been in fun.

There was a great deal of cholera that year. So many people had started without any tools to do anything with, and without enough food to eat. The night before we came to Old Fort Kearney, my sister Abbie was taken sick.

Source: From "Reminiscence of Sarah Sprenger: Ohio to Oregon—1852," at www.endoftheoregontrail.org/sprenger.html.

Father went to the Fort when we got near to get help. As he was a Presbyterian and a Mason, they allowed him within the grounds, but not in the Fort itself. The doctor and his wife came down and sat up that night with Father and Mother caring for Abbie, but she died. They gave us the best coffin they had— a plain board one—and they allowed us to bury her in their cemetery. The doctor and his wife promised to care for her grave as long as they were there, but it was heart-breaking for Father and Mother to have to leave her.

While we were traveling along the South Platte, Father also contracted cholera. That night we had a terrible hail and rainstorm, and to keep Father from getting wet, Mother put the feather bed and boards over him. Thanks to this sweating, and the medicine, Father recovered. During the hail storm, the cattle became frightened and ran off and swam over to an island. The next day, when it had cleared, the boys had to swim over and drive them back so that we could travel on.

Maria got the cholera, too, but Mother cared for her as she had cared for Father, and she too recovered.

As we traveled, we met a great many people who were sick and dying. Often there was nothing to dig a grave with, and the dead had to be wrapped in quilts and blankets, and laid on the ground with stones piled over them. In spite of these precautions we saw many graves that had been invaded by wolves. . . .

We arrived in Oregon City on October 26, 1852. My brother had found a house for us; it had only four rooms and no plaster, and was not very comfortable, but it did have a cookstove, and was the best that we could get at the time. At that time, flour sold at $5.00 a sack, butter at $1.00 a pound, apples 25 cents apiece, cabbage 25 cents for a little head, and potatoes about the size of walnuts were all prices. All the big potatoes were sent to California.

One day a man came and begged Mother to care for his three little girls, as his wife had died on the plains. He wanted to get work and would come for them in a couple of weeks, he said. They were awfully dirty, but Mother and my sisters took care of them for about two months without pay of any kind from their father.

While in Oregon City we met again Walter McFarland, his father who had crossed the plains in 1849, and his stepmother and sister and brother. We met also Captain Cochran who, with my brother, was running the hotel named Oregon House. And we met Judge Waite, who became much in love with my sister Mary Ann, as Captain Cochran was with my sister Maria.

My sisters sewed to help us along until my Father and the boys could get a farm. It was in Linn county on the Calapooia River, eleven miles south of Albany. The family stayed in Oregon City until the first of February, when we moved to the farm.

Our home on the farm had three rooms at first, the center room of logs, and on each side a room of shakes, with puncheon floors. Our fireplace was made of sticks and mud, as there were no bricks available there at that time. There were little sternwheel steamboats running up the Willamette River to Albany and Corvallis in winter, and as long as they could in the summer. As soon as possible, Father added two more rooms, and an attic where we could sleep. One of the new rooms was a good sized kitchen where we cooked and ate, and the other was part storeroom and part curtained off for sleeping.

When spring came, the prairies were covered with lovely flowers and delicious wild strawberries. We would go out with wash tubs and buckets and fill them with these delicious strawberries, as large as most cultivated berries and much sweeter. We ate all we could and Mother made jam of the rest. We also had many blackberries in their season, and in a few years plenty of fruit of all kinds that our family had planted.

My sisters were a wonder to some people who had been in the wilds for several years. One day a woman came to our house and asked Mother if the girls could cook and wash and make soap and such things. Mother told her that the girls were proficient in all home making, as even when they had had plenty of help, she had insisted that her daughters learn how to do everything. The woman said that her son John thought if they could keep house and sew he would like to marry one of them. Mother told her that it would not be necessary for John to come and see them as they both were to be married in May.

DOCUMENT 13.6

The Wild West: Vigilantes in San Francisco

Lell Hawley Woolley

On the 2nd of June, 1856, the city was in great excitement at an attempt by David S. Terry to stab Sterling A. Hopkins, a member of the Committee. Terry was one of the judges of the Supreme Court. Hopkins and a posse were arresting one Rube Maloney when set upon by Terry. Hopkins was taken to Engine House No. 12 where Dr. R. Beverly Cole examined and cared for his wound which was four inches deep and caused considerable hemorrhage. The blade struck Hopkins near the collar bone and severed parts of the left carotid artery and penetrated the gullet. Terry and Maloney at once fled to the armory of the "Law and Order Party" on the corner of Jackson and Dupont streets. The alarm was at once sounded on the bell at Fort Gunnybags and in less than fifteen minutes armed details were dispatched to and surrounded the headquarters of the "Law and Order Party" where Terry had taken refuge, and in less than half an hour had complete control of the situation, and by 4:15 o'clock in the afternoon Terry and Maloney and the others found there had been taken to the Committee rooms as well as the arms (a stand of 300 muskets) and ammunition. About 150 "Law and Order" men together with about 250 muskets were also taken from the California Exchange. Several other places were raided and stripped of their stands of arms.

Terry was held by the Vigilance Committee until August 7th and charged with attempt to murder. Mr. Hopkins recovered and Terry, after a fair and impartial trial, was discharged from custody, though many were dissatisfied at his

Source: "Lell Hawley Woolley Remembers 'Frontier' San Francisco," on the website of the Museum of the City of San Francisco, www.sfmuseum.org/hist6/woolley.html.

dismissal and claimed that he should have been held. Terry was requested to re-sign and resigned his position as judge of the Supreme Court.

In 1859 Judge Terry had an altercation with United States Senator David C. Broderick which caused the former to challenge the latter to a duel. This duel which was with pistols was fought September 13, 1859, near Lake Merced, near the present site of the Ocean House. It resulted in Broderick's death, whose last words were, "They killed me because I was opposed to a corrupt administration, and the extension of slavery." Terry was indicted for his duel with Broderick, as it came in conflict with the State laws. The case was transferred to another county, Marin, and there dismissed. During the Civil War Terry joined the Confederate forces, attained the rank of Brigadier-General, and was wounded at the Battle of Chickamauga. At the close of the conflict he repaired to California and in 1869 located at Stockton and resumed the practice of the legal profession. Some years later he became advocate for a lady [Sarah Althea Hill Sharon] who was one of the principals in a noted divorce suit. Subsequently she became his wife. Legal contention arising from the first marriage caused her to appear before the Circuit Court held in Oakland, over which Stephen J. Field, Associate Justice of the United States Supreme Court, presided.

14

Purity

Having secured a degree of happiness in the form of material prosperity, it occurred to many Americans that it was necessary to continue to tinker with and strive to perfect the realities of life, liberty, and other avenues to happiness through a host of reform movements that had been emerging since the days of Andrew Jackson. Part of the energy for these reforms was derived from a renewed sense of spirituality emanating from the Second Great Awakening. Even more so than the First Great Awakening that took place in 18th-century colonial America, the Second Great Awakening utilized the revival as a way of reaching out to sinners and inspiring people to greater commitments to religion.

If democracy was to be extended to the common man, the question soon arose for many whether it ought not be extended to the common woman as well. Some assumed that women were indeed full-fledged partners in the American experiment and, properly educated, could function in a broader range of capacities fully equal to men. Indeed, the women's rights movement was born in the 1840s and reached one of its early high-water marks with the Seneca Falls Convention of 1848. After producing a document that was patently fashioned after the American Declaration of Independence, the convention delegates began to append other desires, wants, and resolutions according to their needs. This produced a degree of hesitancy on some issues for fear they were being too radical or premature.

An increase in spirituality and a broadening of the definition of the proper behavior of citizens also caused the issue of slavery to emerge again, a perpetually open wound for some as they pondered liberty. Many people thought about the elimination of slavery, and some contemplated what ought to be the state of America if and when slavery was abolished. One program that was initiated by a combination of former slaves, free blacks, and white supporters was that of colonization, or the remigration of African Americans to Africa. This proposal was controversial in both black and white circles, and for many appeared a confession of the failure of democracy to solve its problems and extend itself to all peoples regardless of race or place of origin.

Envisioning a perfect existence has long been an American pastime. From John Winthrop and his efforts to construct a city upon a hill to Joseph Smith and the founding of the Mormon faith and the emergence of numerous millennial cults and groups in 19th-century America, there have been those who sought to create their own utopian worlds to secure opportunities for people. One such endeavor by New England intellectuals was Brook Farm. A characteristic trait of Americans is to write a constitution for nearly every association, club, or organization they form. Such was the case with Brook Farm. Its constitution is a blend of utopian aspirations for the welfare of humankind and patently practical legal provisions for property and profits.

If the founders of Brook Farm sought to create a perfect society based on knowledge, the American political system was an open free-for-all for those who desired to perfect America through direct political action. Such was the case with the American Party, more commonly known as the Know-Nothing Party and referred to by the Californios—the original Spanish-Mexican residents of California absorbed into the Union with the Mexican War—as "los ignorantes." The Know-Nothing Party sought to preserve, protect, and perfect America by preventing un-American ideas, influences, and individuals from participating in the common quest for life, liberty, and happiness. Perhaps its ideology was less an endorsement of the universality of the appeal and applicability of democracy and more an indication that some would seek to deal with challenges by ignoring and refusing to accept their existence.

DOCUMENT 14.1

The Second Great Awakening

Rev. Wm. B. Cary

"On the first of April, 1741, the Rev. Mr. Gilbert Tennent preached two excellent sermons in this place,—which were blessed to a great awakening among my people; and two or three were deeply wounded, so that they discovered it in their looks and behavior. The concern spread and increased apace, and persons were solicitous what they should do to be saved. And evening religions [sic] meetings were set up."

On the 14th of April, Mr. Parsons [Rev. Jonathan Parsons] preached in the East Parish, and there it was that the remarkable exhibitions which characterized the revival, were first manifested. "The word fell with great power on Sunday. Some had fits, some fainted. After this, cryings out at the preaching were

Source: Excerpted from Rev. Wm. B. Cary, "Revival Experiences during the Great Awakening in 1741–44, in New London County," *New Englander* vol. 42 (vol. 6, n.s.), issue 177 (November 1883): 733–36; pages available at Cornell University Library's *Making of America* website, cdl.library.cornell.edu/moa/.

frequent. Out-crys, fainting, and fits were oft in the meetings." "Many have had such discoveries of the love of God and Christ, as to be overcome, and to lose their bodily strength thereby; which (latter peculiarity) I think was observed to begin toward the latter end of July, 1741."

. . . "Sometime in this month Mr. Griswold invited me [Rev. Parsons] to preach a lecture for him, and I consented. While I was preaching I observed many of the assembly in tears, and heard many crying out in great bitterness of soul. When sermon was over I could better take notice of the cause; and the language was to this purpose, viz: 'Alas! I'm undone, I'm undone! O my sins! How they prey upon my vitals! What will become of me? How shall I escape the damnation of hell, who have spent away a golden opportunity under gospel light, in vanity?' "

And further on he says of this sermon, "under this sermon many had their countenances changed; their thoughts seemed to trouble them so that the joints of their loins were loosed, and their knees smote one against another. Great numbers cried out aloud in the anguish of their souls; several stout men fell as though a cannon had been discharged, and a ball had made its way through their hearts. Some young women were thrown into hysteric fits. It seemed a little resemblance of what we may imagine will be when the Great Judge pronounces the tremendous sentence of 'Go ye cursed into everlasting fire.' " How quaint is the expression here used to express an almost universal sentiment in favor of short sermons. We do not wonder that the people cried, "When will sermon be over?" after reading one of them that was preached in the Lyme church at that time. . . .

Mr. Griswold expresses the opinion that these exhibitions, though so extravagant, were the legitimate effects of the work of God upon the hearts and souls of listless people. "I have all along taken care," he says however, "to caution persons against laying weight on crying-out, fainting, and fits, as signs or marks of conversion. Conversion may be, and often is without them. True conversion is an inward work of the Spirit of God, turning the sinner from darkness to light, from Satan to God, and from Sin to Holiness: it brings the heart to embrace Jesus Christ; and if these things are not wrought in a person, he is not converted, whatever distress or joy he may have had." Mr. Parsons declared, "I am humbly of opinion, that it is not reasonable for any to conclude persons to be under the influences of the Holy Spirit either in convincing of sin or in sanctifying the soul, merely because they cry out aloud, faint away, or the like. Nay, it is a clear case that persons may be thrown into hysterisms, faintings, outcries, etc., and that under the ministration of truth, by the mere power of imagination, a sudden fright, or bodily disease." And yet, he goes on to say that persons exhibiting these signs are not on that account to be suspected of not having received the Spirit, for these signs *may* accompany his visitation.

"Now I thought the people in great danger, and especially those that were most deeply wounded. I knew, in all probability, that Hell was in an uproar, the Prince of Darkness seeing his kingdom shaking, he being in great danger of losing many of his obedient subjects; so I spent my time abroad among distressed souls, and others that fell in my way that were more lightly touched."

DOCUMENT 14.2

The Best Protector Any Woman Can Have

Elizabeth Cady Stanton

Dear Friends:—. . . The great work before us is the education of those just coming on the stage of action. Begin with the girls of *to-day*, and in twenty years we can revolutionize this nation. The childhood of woman must be free and untrammeled. The girl must be allowed to romp and play, climb, skate, and swim; her clothing must be more like that of the boy—strong, loose-fitting garments, thick boots, etc., that she may be out at all times, and enter freely into all kinds of sports. Teach her to go alone, by night and day, if need be, on the lonely highway, or through the busy streets of the crowded metropolis. The manner in which all courage and self-reliance is educated *out* of the girl, her path portrayed with dangers and difficulties that never exist, is melancholy indeed. Better, far, suffer occasional insults or die outright, than live the life of a *coward*, or never move without a protector. The best protector any woman can have, one that will serve her at all times and in all places, is *courage*; this she must get by her own experience, and experience comes by exposure. Let the girl be thoroughly developed in body and soul, not modeled, like a piece of clay, after some artificial specimen of humanity, with a body like some plate in Godey's book of fashion, and a mind after the type of Father Gregory's pattern daughters, loaded down with the traditions, proprieties, and sentimentalities of generations of silly mothers and grandmothers, but left free to be, to grow to feel, to think, to act. Development is one thing, that system of cramping, restraining, torturing, perverting, and mystifying, called education, is quite another. We have had women enough befooled under the one system, pray let us try the other. The girl must early be impressed with the idea that she is to be "a hand, not a mouth"; a worker, and not a drone, in the great hive of human activity. Like the boy, she must be taught to look forward to a life of self-dependence, and early prepare herself for some trade or profession. Woman has relied heretofore too entirely for her support on the *needle*—that one-eyed demon of destruction that slays its thousands annually; that evil genius of our sex, which, in spite of all our devotion, will never make us healthy, wealthy, or wise.

Teach the girl it is no part of her life to cater to the prejudices of those around her. Make her independent of public sentiment, by showing her how worthless and rotten a thing it is. It is a settled axiom with me, after much examination and reflection, that public sentiment is false on every subject. Yet what a tyrant it is over us all, woman especially, whose very life is to please, whose highest ambition is to be approved. But once outrage this tyrant, place yourself beyond his jurisdiction, taste the joy of free thought and action, and how powerless is his rule over you! his sceptre lies broken at your feet; his very

Source: "Elizabeth Cady Stanton to the Woman's Convention, Held at Akron, Ohio, May 25, 1851," in *The Female Experience: An American Documentary*, ed. Gerda Lerner (Indianapolis: Bobbs-Merrill, 1977), pp. 416–17.

babblings of condemnation are sweet music in your ears; his darkening frown is sunshine to your heart, for they tell of your triumph and his discomfort. Think you, women *thus* educated would long remain the weak, dependent beings we now find them? By no means. Depend upon it, they would soon settle for themselves this whole question of Woman's Rights. As educated capitalists and skilled laborers, they would not be long in finding their true level in political and social life.

DOCUMENT 14.3

Resolutions at Seneca Falls

After much delay, one of the circle took up the Declaration of 1776, and read it aloud with much spirit and emphasis, and it was at once decided to adopt the historic document, with some slight changes such as substituting "all men" for "King George." Knowing that women must have more to complain of than men under any circumstances possibly could, and seeing the Fathers had eighteen grievances, a protracted search was made through statute books, church usages, and the customs of society to find that exact number. Several well-disposed men assisted in collecting the grievances, until, with the announcement of the eighteenth, the women felt they had enough to go before the world with a good case. One youthful lord remarked, "Your grievances must be grievous indeed, when you are obliged to go to books in order to find them out."

The eventful day dawned at last, and crowds in carriages and on foot, wended their way to the Wesleyan church. When those having charge of the Declaration, the resolutions, and several volumes of the Statutes of New York arrived on the scene, lo! the door was locked. However, an embryo Professor of Yale College was lifted through an open window to unbar the door; that done, the church was quickly filled. It had been decided to have no men present, but as they were already on the spot, and as the women who must take the responsibility of organizing the meeting, and leading the discussions, shrank from doing either, it was decided, in a hasty council round the altar, that this was an occasion when men might make themselves pre-eminently useful. It was agreed they should remain, and take the laboring oar through the Convention. . . .

The following resolutions were discussed by Lucretia Mott, Thomas and Mary Ann McClintock, Amy Post, Catharine A. F. Stebbins, and others, and were adopted:

WHEREAS, The great precept of nature is conceded to be, that "man shall pursue his own true and substantial happiness." Blackstone, in his Commentaries remarks, that this law of Nature being coeval with mankind, and dictated by God himself, is of course superior in obligation to any other. It is binding over all the globe, in all countries and at all times; no human laws are of any validity if

Source: Excerpted from Elizabeth Cady Stanton, Susan B. Anthony, and Matilda Joslyn Gage, eds., *History of Woman Suffrage*, vol. 1: *1848–1861* (Rochester, NY: Susan B. Anthony, 1889), pp. 68–73.

contrary to this, and such of them as are valid, derive all their force, and all their validity, and all their authority, mediately and immediately, from this original; therefore,

Resolved, That such laws as conflict, in any way, with the true and substantial happiness of woman, are contrary to the great precept of nature and of no validity, for this is "superior in obligation to any other."

Resolved, That all laws which prevent woman from occupying such a station in society as her conscience shall dictate, or which place her in a position inferior to that of man, are contrary to the great precept of nature, and therefore of no force or authority.

Resolved, That woman is man's equal—was intended to be so by the Creator, and the highest good of the race demands that she should be recognized as such.

Resolved, That the women of this country ought to be enlightened in regard to the laws under which they live; that they may no longer publish their degradation by declaring themselves satisfied with their present position, nor their ignorance, by asserting that they have all the rights they want.

Resolved, That inasmuch as man, while claiming for himself intellectual superiority, does accord to woman moral superiority, it is pre-eminently his duty to encourage her to speak and teach, as she has an opportunity, in all religious assemblies.

Resolved, That the same amount of virtue, delicacy, and refinement of behavior that is required of woman in the social state, should also be required of man, and the same transgressions should be visited with equal severity on both man and woman.

Resolved, That the objection of indelicacy and impropriety, which is so often brought against woman when she addresses a public audience, comes with a very ill-grace from those who encourage, by their attendance, her appearance on the stage, in the concert, or in feats of the circus.

Resolved, That woman has too long rested satisfied in the circumscribed limits which corrupt customs and a perverted application of the Scriptures have marked out for her, and that it is time she should move in the enlarged sphere which her great Creator has assigned her.

Resolved, That it is the duty of the women of this country to secure to themselves their sacred right to the elective franchise.

Resolved, That the equality of human rights results necessarily from the fact of the identity of the race in capabilities and responsibilities.

Resolved, therefore, That, being invested by the Creator with the same capabilities, and the same consciousness of responsibility for their exercise, it is demonstrably the right and duty of woman, equally with man, to promote every righteous cause by every righteous means; and especially in regard to the great subjects of morals and religion, it is self-evidently her right to participate with her brother in teaching them, both in private and in public, by writing and by speaking, by any instrumentalities proper to be used, and in any assemblies proper to be held; and this being a self-evident truth growing out of the divinely implanted principles of human nature, any custom or authority adverse to it, whether modern or wearing the hoary sanction of antiquity, is to be regarded as self-evident falsehood, and at war with mankind.

At the last session Lucretia Mott offered and spoke to the following resolution:

> *Resolved,* That the speedy success of our cause depends upon the zealous and untiring efforts of both men and women, for the overthrow of the monopoly of the pulpit, and for the securing to woman an equal participation with men in the various trades, professions, and commerce.

The only resolution that was not unanimously adopted was the ninth, urging the women of the country to secure to themselves the elective franchise. Those who took part in the debate feared a demand for the right to vote would defeat others they deemed more rational, and make the whole movement ridiculous.

But Mrs. Stanton and Frederick Douglass seeing that the power to choose rulers and make laws, was the right by which all others could be secured, persistently advocated the resolution, and at last carried it by a small majority.

DOCUMENT 14.4

Anti-Colonization

Anti-Slavery Tracts, No. 3: Colonization
Rev. O. B. Frothingham

(Published for gratuitous distribution, at the Office of the American Anti-Slavery Society, *No. 138 Nassau Street, New York. Also to be had at the Anti-Slavery Offices, No. 21 Cornhill, Boston, and No. 31 North Fifth Street, Philadelphia.)*

* * *

5. The Colonization Society *wages war* upon the free blacks. It calls them "notoriously ignorant, degraded, and miserable, mentally diseased, broken spirited; acted upon by no motives to honorable exertion; scarcely reached in their debasement by the heavenly light;" an incubus, a nuisance; "more addicted to crime, and vice, and dissolute manners than any other portion of the people of the United States." And not in pity is this said of them, but in hate, and with the design of awakening against them more hate. What kind of love is it that thus vilifies its objects? What kind of love is it that strives to deepen degradation; that views with "highest gratification" the barbarous edicts of southern legislatures, by which free colored people entering the State (Maryland) must pay twenty dollars, on conviction, for the first offence, and five hundred dollars for the second offence, or be sold to

Source: From Rev. O. B. Frothingham, "Colonization," Anti-Slavery Tracts, no. 3 (New York: American Anti-Slavery Society, 1855). Available at *American Memory*, Library of Congress, memory.loc.gov.

satisfy the demand;[1] are forbidden to attend religious meetings, save when conducted by whites;[2] and may not sell any of the most common articles of traffic among whites, nine in number, without proving by certificate that they came honestly by them? Do they who despise and persecute the blacks here really wish them well any where, even in Liberia? To think so is absurd. Men do not scorn and revile those they love. The free blacks are objects of antipathy; and in banishing them, the slaveholders wish only to protect *themselves*.

6. Finally, the enemies of slavery, with almost unanimous consent, are hostile to the Colonization Society. Repeatedly have the free people of color exposed and protested against it, as in direct opposition to their best hopes, prospects, and rights. As early as 1817, *ere an anti-slavery society was formed*, it was denounced in Virginia, and by public resolves, as *cruel*, and "in direct violation of those principles which have been the boast of the republic." And in 1853 the colored people of Syracuse held a meeting, and unanimously resolved, "That our *abhorrence* of the scheme of African colonization is *not in the slightest degree abated*; that we recognize in it the most *intense hatred* of the colored race, clad in the garb of *pretended* philanthropy." The same estimate of its character was formed and promulgated by such men as Wilberforce, Macaulay, Gurney, Lushington, Buxton, Cropper, and O'Connell. And Thomas Clarkson, in a letter to Mr. Garrison, giving his reasons for first accepting, and afterwards rejecting, the plan, says, "I will only say that I saw the scheme—shall I say the *diabolical* scheme?—with new eyes, and that the new light thrown upon it determined me to wash my hands clean forever of the undertaking." Who are the truest friends of the slave—such persons as these? or the Clays, Stantons, Wises, and Archers, who favor colonization?

We think now we have fairly proved our propositions, that the Colonization Society aims to expatriate the free blacks of the United States, and that in doing this it has in view the security of slavery. Many more evidences might be produced; but let candid men ponder these. Let them consider, moreover, how much respect is fairly due to a society whose agents say one thing at the north, and another at the south; commend slavery in Georgia, and condemn it in Massachusetts; profess themselves the friends of the negro on one side of the line, and the friends of the negro's oppressor on the other side; and use unsuspecting anti-slavery feeling to advance the ends of crafty pro-slavery principles. Let them estimate the feasibility of a scheme so slow that in thirty-six years it transported to Liberia only about two thirds of the annual increase of the free black population, and not one sixth of the annual increase of those in bondage, and so costly that Mr. Webster's famous bid of two hundred million dollars would pay not quite one third of the expense of carrying it out. Let them ask

---

[1]Note: One half the net proceeds of sale goes to the State Colonization Society!
[2]Note: In Baltimore and Annapolis it is only necessary that the meeting should be held "with the written permission of a white licensed ordained preacher."

what kind of civilization is likely to be diffused in Africa by slaves, and how it is possible that a free, enlightened Christian republic can be established by people who are "notoriously ignorant, degraded, and miserable; more addicted to crime, and vice, and dissolute manners than any other portion of the United States." Let them weigh well these facts and reasonings; and if they hear from colonizationists, as they will, sentiments verbally at variance with the propositions maintained above, let them regard such as illustrations of the duplicity, the sublime hypocrisy and treachery, which are not the least remarkable among the peculiarities of this remarkable society.

Protest. (1833.)

We the undersigned, observing with regret that the American Colonization Society appears to be gaining some adherents in this country, are desirous to express our opinions respecting it.

Our motive and excuse for thus coming forward are the claims which the society has put forth to anti-slavery support. These claims are, in our opinion, wholly groundless; and we feel bound to affirm that our deliberate judgment and conviction are, that the professions made by the Colonization Society, of promoting the abolition of slavery, are altogether delusive.

DOCUMENT 14.5

The Brook-Farm Constitution

CONSTITUTION.

In order more effectually to promote the great purposes of human culture; to establish the external relations of life on a basis of wisdom and purity; to apply the principles of justice and love to our social organization in accordance with the laws of Divine Providence; to substitute a system of brotherly cooperation for one of selfish competition; to secure to our children and those who may be entrusted to our care, the benefits of the highest physical, intellectual and moral education, which in the progress of knowledge the resources at our command will permit; to institute an attractive, efficient, and productive system of industry; to prevent the exercise of worldly anxiety, by the competent supply of our necessary wants; to diminish the desire of excessive accumulation, by making the acquisition of individual property subservient to upright and disinterested uses; to guarantee to each other forever the means of physical support, and of spiritual progress; and thus to impart a greater freedom, simplicity, truthfulness, refinement, and moral dignity, to our mode of life;—we the undersigned do unite in a voluntary Association, and adopt and ordain the following articles of agreement, to wit:

Source: From Octavius B. Frothingham, *Transcendentalism in New England: A History* (Boston: American Unitarian Assoc., 1903), pp. 159–61.

Article I.

Name and Membership.

Section 1. The name of this Association shall be "The Brook-Farm Association for Industry and Education." All persons who shall hold one or more shares in its stock, or whose labor and skill shall be considered an equivalent for capital, may be admitted by the vote of two-thirds of the Association, as members thereof.

Section 2. No member of the Association shall ever be subjected to any religious test; nor shall any authority be assumed over individual freedom of opinion by the Association, nor by one member over another; nor shall any one be held accountable to the Association, except for such overt acts, or omissions of duty, as violate the principles of justice, purity, and love, on which it is founded; and in such cases the relation of any member may be suspended or discontinued, at the pleasure of the Association.

Article II.

Capital Stock.

Section 1. The members of this Association shall own and manage such real and personal estate in joint stock proprietorship, divided into shares of one hundred dollars each, as may from time to time be agreed on.

Section 2. No shareholder shall be liable to any assessment whatever on the shares held by him; nor shall he be held responsible individually in his private property on account of the Association; nor shall the Trustees, or any officer or agent of the Association, have any authority to do any thing which shall impose personal responsibility on any shareholder, by making any contracts or incurring any debts for which the shareholders shall be individually or personally responsible.

Section 3. The Association guarantees to each shareholder the interest of five per cent. annually on the amount of stock held by him in the Association, and this interest may be paid in certificates of stock and credited on the books of the Association; provided that each shareholder may draw on the funds of the Association for the amount of interest due at the third annual settlement from the time of investment.

Section 4. The shareholders on their part, for themselves, their heirs and assigns, do renounce all claim on any profits accruing to the Association for the use of their capital invested in the stock of the Association, except five per cent. interest on the amount of stock held by them, payable in the manner described in the preceding section.

Article III.

Guaranties.

Section 1. The Association shall provide such employment for all its members as shall be adapted to their capacities, habits, and tastes; and each member shall select and perform such operations of labor, whether corporal or mental, as shall be deemed best suited to his own endowments and the benefit of the Association.

Section 2. The Association guarantees to all its members, their children and family dependents, house-rent, fuel, food, and clothing, and the other necessaries of life, without charge, not exceeding a certain fixed amount to be decided annually by the Association; no charge shall ever be made for support during inability to labor from sickness or old age, or for medical or nursing attendance, except in case of shareholders, who shall be charged therefor, and also for the food and clothing of children, to an amount not exceeding the interest due to them on settlement; but no charge shall be made to any members for education or the use of library and public rooms.

Section 3. Members may withdraw from labor, under the direction of the Association, and in that case, they shall not be entitled to the benefit of the above guaranties.

Section 4. Children over ten years of age shall be provided with employment in suitable branches of industry; they shall be credited for such portions of each annual dividend, as shall be decided by the Association, and on the completion of their education in the Association at the age of twenty, shall be entitled to a certificate of stock to the amount of credits in their favor, and may be admitted as members of the Association.

DOCUMENT 14.6

The Know-Nothing Platform, 1856

1. An humble acknowledgment to the Supreme Being for His protecting care vouchsafed to our fathers in their successful revolutionary struggle, and hitherto manifested to us, their descendants, in the preservation of the liberties, the independence, and the union of these states.
2. The perpetuation of the federal Union and Constitution as the palladium of our civil and religious liberties, and the only sure bulwark of American independence.
3. Americans must rule America; and to this end native-born citizens should be selected for all state, federal, and municipal government employment, in preference to all others. Nevertheless,
4. Persons born of American parents residing temporarily abroad should be entitled to all the rights of native-born citizens.
5. No person should be selected for political station (whether of native or foreign birth) who recognizes any allegiance or obligation of any description to any foreign prince, potentate or power, or who refuses to recognize the federal and state Constitutions (each within its own sphere) as paramount to all other laws as rules of political action.

Source: From Thomas Hudson McKee, *The National Conventions and Platforms of All Political Parties: 1789 to 1905*, 6th ed. (Baltimore: Friedenwald Co., 1906), pp. 101–2.

6. The unequalled recognition and maintenance of the reserved rights of the several states, and the cultivation of harmony and fraternal good-will between the citizens of the several states, and, to this end, non-interference by Congress with questions appertaining solely to the individual states, and non-intervention by each state with the affairs of any other state.

7. The recognition of the right of native-born and naturalized citizens of the United States, permanently residing in any territory thereof, to frame their constitution and laws, and to regulate their domestic and social affairs in their own mode, subject only to the provisions of the federal Constitution, with the privilege of admission into the Union whenever they have the requisite population for one representative in Congress.

   Provided, That none but those who are citizens of the United States under the Constitution and laws thereof, and who have a fixed residence in any such territory, are to participate in the formation of the constitution or in the enactment of laws for said territory or state.

8. An enforcement of the principles that no state or territory ought to admit others than citizens to the right of suffrage or of holding political offices of the United States.

9. A change in the laws of naturalization, making a continued residence of twenty-one years, of all not heretofore provided for, an indispensable requisite for citizenship hereafter, and excluding all paupers or persons convicted of crime from landing upon our shores; but no interference with the vested rights of foreigners.

10. Opposition to any union between church and state; no interference with religious faith or worship; and no test oaths for office.

11. Free and thorough investigation into any and all alleged abuses of public functionaries, and a strict economy in public expenditures.

12. The maintenance and enforcement of all laws constitutionally enacted, until said laws shall be repealed or shall be declared null and void by competent judicial authority.

13. Opposition to the reckless and unwise policy of the present administration in the general management of our national affairs, and more especially as shown in removing "Americans" (by designation) and conservatives in principle, from office, and placing foreigners and ultraists in their places; as shown in a truckling subserviency to the stronger, and an insolent and cowardly bravado toward the weaker powers; as shown in re-opening sectional agitation, by the repeal of the Missouri Compromise; as shown in granting to unnaturalized foreigners the right of suffrage in Kansas and Nebraska; as shown in its vacillating course on the Kansas and Nebraska question; as shown in the corruptions which pervade some of the departments of the government; as shown in disgracing meritorious naval officers through prejudiced caprice; and as shown in the blundering mismanagement of our foreign relations.

14. Therefore, to remedy existing evils and prevent the disastrous consequences otherwise resulting therefrom, we would build up the "American
Party" upon the principles herein-before stated.
15. That each state council shall have authority to amend their several constitutions, so as to abolish the several degrees and substitute a pledge of
honor, instead of other obligations, for fellowship and admission into the
party.
16. A free and open discussion of all political principles embraced in our
platform.

15

Bleeding Kansas

By the 1850s it was clear to many that two different systems had evolved within the context of American democracy. Enough liberty had existed for the North and the South to take different routes to their respective futures. But it had also become apparent that the desires and rights of both the majority and minorities within the nation were effectively preserved and sustained by the political system of the country. When something arose to disrupt the delicate balance of that political system and tip the scales of politics and justice in one direction or the other, those affected reacted with alarm and zealous defense of their world and views. The admission of California tipped the scales in favor of the free states, and one southern reaction was the Nashville convention. For many southerners it was just a matter of time before the northern states began to interfere again with slavery and the rights of southern states.

There were still vast tracts of land in the West that had not been organized into territories and had not begun the long-established apprenticeship to statehood in the Union. California insisted that once it became a state, a national transportation system was necessary to more effectively connect it with the other states. In order to build railroads that could reach from Chicago to San Francisco, the intervening territory needed to be surveyed, organized, and set on the path toward formal incorporation within the Union. There were already established policies and previous political compromises that had imagined the free or slave status of the territories. Still, there were those who would seek their own desires and impose their own will on the territories even if it meant subverting democratic mechanisms in support of sectional loyalties and programs. The Kansas-Nebraska Act lit a long, slow fuse that eventually produced the Civil War. The nation had found it impossible to continue to compromise over land, liberty, and different definitions of happiness.

During the debates over Kansas and Nebraska and whether Kansas was to be slave or free, our political system witnessed a horrific physical assault by Preston Brooks on Charles Sumner, an abolitionist senator from Massachusetts.

The nation was horrified as blood actually splattered in the Senate chamber as Brooks's cane found its mark on Senator Sumner's skull. But Brooks later defended himself in the House of Representatives, of which he was a member, even against efforts to censure him.

Chief Justice Roger B. Taney, a southerner who owed his position on the Supreme Court to his political support for Andrew Jackson during the national bank controversy, sought to settle the issue of slavery in the territories once and for all by his decision in the Dred Scott Case. If Taney's goal was to settle the issue of slavery, however, he provided more fuel to the firestorm threatening to consume the nation in war. For many southerners, the first salvo of that war was John Brown's raid at Harper's Ferry, Virginia. Literally invading the South and specifically seeking to inspire an armed slave insurrection, Brown was the embodiment of many southerners' worst fears. Failing in his initial purpose, Brown could only hope that he might become a martyr to the greater cause of a free life for African Americans.

DOCUMENT 15.1

Resolutions of the Nashville Convention

1. *Resolved,* that the territories of the United States belong to the people of the several states of the Union as their common property. That the citizens of the several states have equal rights to migrate with their property to these territories, and are equally entitled to the protection of the federal government in the enjoyment of that property so long as the territories remain under the charge of that government.
2. *Resolved,* that Congress has no power to exclude from the territory of the United States any property lawfully held in the states of the Union, and any act which may be passed by Congress to effect this result is a plain violation of the Constitution of the United States.

* * *

5. *Resolved,* that the slaveholding states cannot and will not submit to the enactment by Congress of any law imposing onerous conditions or restraints upon the rights of masters to remove with their property into the territories of the United States, or to any law making discrimination in favor of the proprietors of other property against them.
6. *Resolved,* that it is the duty of the federal government plainly to recognize and firmly to maintain the equal rights of the citizens of the several states in the territories of the United States, and to repudiate the power to make a discrimination between the proprietors of different species of property in federal legislation. The fulfillment of this duty by the federal government

Source: Excerpted from *Resolutions and Address Adopted by the Southern Convention, Held at Nashville, Tennessee, June 3–12, 1850* (Columbia, SC, 1850), pp. 3–9.

would greatly tend to restore the peace of the country and to allay the exasperation and excitement which now exist between the different sections of the Union. For it is the deliberate opinion of this Convention that the tolerance Congress has given to the notion that federal authority might be employed incidentally and indirectly to subvert or weaken the institutions existing in the states confessedly beyond federal jurisdiction and control is a main cause of the discord which menaces the existence of the Union, and which has well-nigh destroyed the efficient action of the federal government itself.

* * *

11. *Resolved*, that in the event a dominant majority shall refuse to recognize the "neat constitutional rights we assert and shall continue to deny the obligations of the federal government to maintain them, it is the sense of this Convention that the territories should be treated as property and divided between the sections of the Union, so that the rights of both sections be adequately secured in their respective shares. That we are aware this course is open to grave objections, but we are ready to acquiesce in the adoption of the line of 36″ 30′ north latitude, extending to the Pacific Ocean, as an extreme concession, upon consideration of what is due to the stability of our institution.

* * *

24. *Resolved*, that slavery exists in the United States independent of the Constitution. That it is recognized by the Constitution in a threefold aspect: first, as property, second, as a domestic relation of service or labor under the law of a state; and, last, as a basis of political power. And, viewed on any or all of these lights, Congress has no power under the Constitution to create or destroy it anywhere; nor can such power be derived from foreign laws, conquest, cession, treaty, or the laws of nations, nor from any other source but an amendment of the Constitution itself.
25. *Resolved*, that the Constitution confers no power upon Congress to regulate or prohibit the sale and transfer of slaves between the states.

DOCUMENT 15.2

Organizing the Territories

That the Constitution, and all laws of the United States which are not locally inapplicable, shall have the same force and effect within the said Territory of Kansas as elsewhere within the United States, except the eighth section of the

Source: From *An Act to Organize the Territories of Nebraska and Kansas,* Thirty-third Congress, Sess. 1, Chap. 59, 1854, p. 289.

act preparatory to the admission of Missouri into the Union, approved March sixth, eighteen hundred and twenty, which, being inconsistent with the principle of non-intervention by Congress with slavery in the States and Territories, as recognized by the legislation of eighteen hundred and fifty, commonly called the Compromise Measures, is hereby declared inoperative and void; it being the true intent and meaning of this act not to legislate slavery into any Territory or State, nor to exclude it therefrom, but to leave the people thereof perfectly free to form and regulate their domestic institutions in their own way, subject only to the Constitution of the United States: *Provided,* That nothing herein contained shall be construed to revive or put in force any law or regulation which may have existed prior to the act of sixth of March, eighteen hundred and twenty, either protecting, establishing, prohibiting, or abolishing slavery.

DOCUMENT 15.3

Bleeding Kansas

I. T. Yunker

Lawrence, K.T. Aug. 23, 1856
J. S. Clarke Esq.
Dubuque, Ia.

Dr Friend
Agreeable to promise I will endeavor to post you as far as I am capable in Kansas affairs. I arrived here on the 9th inst. We had a Very pleasant trip and would have enjoyed it much more had we not been anoyed considerably by pro Slavery passengers on the Boat and others who came aboard along the River to inspect the passengers but we didn't fear the consequences so much as we abhored the necessity of disguising our political sentiments.

    I have engaged to work at House joining—to commence as soon as the excitement abates enough for people to lay aside their arms. As yet I have spent my time loafing and rusticating with the ladies!! Except when I have been in the *battle field* or on drill. I have joined a military company called the "Stubbs" or Company A. We drill twice a day. Yesterday we had a grand battalion drill, the company numbering in all about 400 Infantry and Cavalry headed by two companies of Artillery (12 & 6 pound pieces)—all of which are quartered at Lawrence in expectation of the Town being attacked. Report says 2000 men are forming at Westport for that purpose. The only fear the people here have is that the report is false. They want to get a good body of them together and wipe them out at a stroke (they can do it). I have had the pleasure of being in two battles—and one I wasn't in for the reason that after we had marched about 13 miles to attack a party of 300 Georgians on Washington Creek they got wind of

Source: From the collection *War Letters, "Bleeding Kansas,"* at the Kansas State Historical Society website, www.kshs.org/ms/warletters/yunker.htm.

us and fled, leaving their provisions, arms and other goods which we took possession of and burnt their block House. We then changed our course for Lecompton 12 miles distant for the purpose of rescuing 12 prisoners who we heard were about to be hung. That night about 12 oclock when we were marching on the open Prairie within about 5 miles of Lecompton, we were fired upon by a party of 27 Ruffians who were in the act of stealing horses and sacking the settlers' houses. They were well mounted and seeing the strength of our party they fled pell mell over the Prairie, all but one who fell from his horse and was taken prisoner. We afterwards learned that we wounded one of the company in the leg as we fired upon them as they retreated. We then spread down our blankets and slept directly till morning, when we were called upon just as we were baking our flap jacks for breakfast to move forward notwithstanding we had marched allday the day before and most of the night with nothing but a few dough cakes and bacon to regale our gaunt stomachs. It was necessary in order to save the poor victims from an innocent and shameful death. We reached the block house where Col. Titus and a crew of his men were stationed, and supposing the prisoners were there and wishing to capture the old ring leaders of the Ruffians, we pitched in to their fort. We gave them 9 6-pound balls made of the type of the Free State press that was destroyed at the sacking of Lawrence, during which time we were sending Sharps rifle balls into the windows and doors incessantly. The firing was responded to from the fort & held out about ½ of an hour when the white flag was hoisted from the window. We rushed up and took charge of old Titus and 17 of his men—all that surrendered, 2 being killed and two wounded. Titus himself was wounded twice. Our side had had 10 wounded. Captain Shambree so mortally that he died 30 hours after. His loss is deeply felt and much lament by the free State men. I was a very energetic man in the cause of freedom. Next day Sunday 17 Old Gov. Shanon came over to make a treaty in behalf of the Border Ruffians which resulted in the exchange of prisoners and the proviso on his part to do all that he could to disband the Ruffians and restore peace and harmony. They also gave us a cannon to boot (12 pounder). Lawrence is the only safe place in the territory for a free state individual. We hear of the latter being butchered in the most horrible manner almost daily. One was scalped alive on the road near Leavenworth yesterday morning. I did not hear his name. There is not the slightest danger of Kansas ever being a slave state. These people are so much excited and so eager to avenge the wrongs for their friends who have been slaughtered in cold blood by the lawless devils. They would fight till the last man would drop on the field. But don't fear. If the Missourians or the southern Statesmen attempt to rally again, they wish they never had been such a country as Kansas. You must come here Clarke, as you never can know what a lovely country it is. Please write and excuse my bunglesome style.

Your true friend,

I. T. Yunker

DOCUMENT 15.4

In Defense of Honor

Representative Preston Brooks of South Carolina Defends His Assault on Senator Charles Sumner of Massachusetts, July 14, 1856
Preston S. Brooks

Mr. Speaker:

Some time since, a Senator from Massachusetts allowed himself, in an elaborately prepared speech, to offer a gross insult to my State, and to a venerable friend, who is my State representative, and who was absent at the time.

Not content with that, he published to the world, and circulated extensively, this uncalled for libel on my State and my blood. Whatever insults my State insults me. Her history and character have commanded my pious veneration; and in her defence I hope I shall always be prepared, humbly and modestly, to perform the duty of a son. I should have forfeited my own self-respect, and perhaps the good opinion of my countrymen, if I had failed to resent such an injury by calling the offender in question to a personal account. It was a personal affair, and in taking redress into my own hands I meant no disrespect to the Senate of the United States or to this House. Nor, sir, did I design insult or disrespect to the State of Massachusetts. I was aware of the personal responsibilities I incurred, and was willing to meet them. I knew, too, that I was amenable to the laws of the country, which afford the same protection to all, whether they be members of Congress or private citizens. I did not, and do not now believe, that I could be properly punished, not only in a court of law, but here also, at the pleasure and discretion of the House. I did not then, and do not now, believe that the spirit of American freemen would tolerate slander in high places, and permit a member of Congress to publish and circulate a libel on another, and then call upon either House to protect him against the personal responsibilities which he had thus incurred. But if I had committed a breach of privilege, it was the privilege of the Senate, and not of this House, which was violated. I was answerable there, and not here. They had no right, as it seems to me, to prosecute me in these Halls, nor have you the right in law or under the Constitution, as I respectfully submit, to take jurisdiction over offences committed against them. The Constitution does not justify them in making such a request, nor this House in granting it. If, unhappily, the day should ever come when sectional or party feeling should run so high as to control all other considerations of public duty or justice, how easy it will be to use such precedents for the excuse of arbitrary power, in either House, to expel members of the minority who may have rendered themselves obnoxious to the prevailing spirit in the House to which they belong. . . .

Source: Excerpted from "Preston S. Brooks of South Carolina," at www.iath.virginia.edu/seminar/unit4/brooks.html.

If I desired to kill the Senator, why did not I do it? You all admit that I had him in my power. Let me tell the member from New Jersey that it was expressly to avoid taking life that I used an ordinary cane, presented to me by a friend in Baltimore, nearly three months before its application to the "bare head" of the Massachusetts Senator. I went to work very deliberately, as I am charged and this is admitted and speculated somewhat as to whether I should employ a horsewhip or a cowhide; but knowing that the Senator was my superior in strength, it occurred to me that he might wrest it from my hand, and then for I never attempt any thing I do not perform I might have been compelled to do that which I would have regretted the balance of my natural life.

The question has been asked in certain newspapers, why I did not invite the Senator to personal combat in the mode usually adopted. Well, sir, as I desire the whole truth to be known about the matter, I will for once notice a newspaper article on the floor of the House, and answer here.

My answer is, that the Senator would not accept a message; and having formed the unalterable determination to punish him, I believed that the offence of "sending a hostile message," superadded to the indictment for assault and battery, would subject me to legal penalties more severe than would be imposed for a simple assault and battery. That is my answer.

DOCUMENT 15.5

Dred Scott's Case

ENQUIRER (RICHMOND)

"The *Dred Scott* Case"

March 10, 1857

In anticipation of the definitive decision of the Supreme Court of the United States in the Dred Scott case, some two months or more ago, its adjudication was announced through a respectable proportion of the press, emanating, we do not now recollect precisely, whence or how; but, as the sequel shows, not from mere conjecture, or without reliable data, for it was then stated that seven of the nine judges constituting the court, agreed in the opinion that the Missouri Compromise was unconstitutional, and consequently, that the rights originating in it and under it, were even factitious and ineffective. And it will be seen by the authentic annunciation of the grave and deliberate decision of that august body, in another column, that what was rumor then is reality now.—Thus has a politico-legal question, involving others of deep import, been decided emphatically in favor of the advocates and supporters of the Constitution and the

Source: From Paul Finkelman, *Dred Scott v. Sandford: A Brief History with Documents* (Boston: Bedford/St. Martin's, 1997), pp. 129–30, 147–48.

Union, the equality of the States and the rights of the South, in contradistinction to and in repudiation of the diabolical doctrines inculcated by factionists and fanatics; and that too by a tribunal of jurists, as learned, impartial and unprejudiced as perhaps the world has ever seen. A prize, for which the athletes of the nation have often wrestled in the halls of Congress, has been awarded at last, by the proper umpire, to those who have justly won it. The *nation* has achieved a triumph, *sectionalism* has been rebuked, and abolitionism has been staggered and stunned. Another supporting pillar has been added to our institutions; the assailants of the South and enemies of the Union have been driven from their *point d'appui;* a patriotic principle has been pronounced; a great national, conservative, union saving sentiment has been proclaimed. An adjudication of the constitutionality of the Missouri Compromise, in the *Dred Scott* case, inseparably embraced collateral questions of such character, as also to involve incidental issues, not unfrequently arising in the councils of the country, and which have ever proved, points of irreconcilable antagonism between the friends and enemies of the institutions of the South; all of which, it will be seen, have been unequivocally established in accordance with the sense of the Southern people. And thus it is, that reason and right, justice and truth, always triumph over passion and prejudice, ignorance and envy, when submitted to the deliberations of honest and able men: that the dross and the genuine metal are separated when the ore is accurately assayed.

EVENING POST (NEW YORK)

The Supreme Court of the United States

March 7, 1857

The dangers apprehended from the organic tendencies of the Supreme Court to engross the legislative power of the federal government, which Jefferson foresaw and so often warned his countrymen against, are no longer imaginary. They are upon us. The decision rendered by that body yesterday, in the case of a Missouri negro who had appealed to it for assistance in asserting his right to share the promises of the Declaration of Independence, has struck at the very roots of the past legislative policy of this country in reference to slavery. It has changed the very blood of the constitution, from which we derive our political existence, and has given to our government a direction and a purpose as novel as it is barbarous and humiliating.

In the first place, it has annihilated at a single blow the citizenship of the entire colored population of the country, and with it all laws and constitutional provisions of the different states for the protection of those rights.

In the next place, it has stripped Congress of a power to exclude slavery from the territories, which has been exercised by every President of the United States from Washington down to Fillmore, and which has had an effect in shaping the political and domestic institutions of more than half the territory of the United States. The [Northwest] ordinance of 1787, with the passage or defence of which the names of the most eminent American statesman have been imperishably associated, is not only pronounced unconstitutional, but the power to enact any laws which contemplate a restriction upon the right to buy, hold and sell slaves in our territories is distinctly denied.

Nor is this all. The doctrine which has been recognized wherever the common law prevails, since the days of Lord Mansfield, that when a slave is taken by his master into the jurisdiction of a state which prohibits slavery, he is from that moment free, is not only set aside, but the power is denied to the states of this Union to prohibit masters bringing slaves within their jurisdiction, provided that they do not enter it with the intention of establishing a permanent residence there.

All of these positions are new in the juridical history of the country; the law in reference to all of them was settled by a long line of judicial decisions by the highest tribunals of the several states, and until within the last twelve years was regarded as much beyond the reach of controversy as the right of the people of the United States to a republican form of government. If precedent, usage, public acquiescence could hallow any doctrines of constitutional interpretation, then were those doctrines hallowed which have been ruthlessly subverted by the Supreme Court.

It is with feelings of more than ordinary solemnity that we record this decision, for its consequences are beyond the reach of human calculation. We are not so much concerned at the invasion of the laws and constitution of the country, both of which accomplishes—for the American people, we have no doubt, will take care of their rights in spite of the Supreme Court—as we are, in being forced to the melancholy conviction that the moral authority and consequen[t] usefulness of that tribunal, under its present organization, is seriously impaired, if not destroyed.

DOCUMENT 15.6

John Brown's Final Address to the Court

November 2, 1859

I have, may it please the court, a few words to say.

In the first place, I deny everything but what I have all along admitted: of a design on my part to free slaves. I intended certainly to have made a clean thing of that matter, as I did last winter, when I went into Missouri and there took slaves without the snapping of a gun on either side, moving them through the country, and finally leaving them in Canada. I designed to have done the same thing again on a larger scale. That was all I intended. I never did intend murder, or treason, or the destruction of property, or to excite or incite slaves to rebellion, or to make insurrection.

Source: John Brown, "John Brown's Final Address to the Court," November 2, 1859. Available at members.aol.com/jfepperson/brown.html.

I have another objection, and that is that it is unjust that I should suffer such a penalty. Had I interfered in the manner which I admit, and which I admit has been fairly proved—for I admire the truthfulness and candor of the greater portion of the witnesses who have testified in this case—had I so interfered in behalf of the rich, the powerful, the intelligent, the so-called great, or in the behalf of any of their friends, either father, mother, brother, sister, wife, or children, or any of that class, and suffered and sacrificed what I have in this interference, it would have been all right. Every man in this court would have deemed it an act worthy of reward rather than punishment.

This court acknowledges, too, as I suppose, the validity of the law of God. I see a book kissed, which I suppose to be the Bible, or at least the New Testament, which teaches me that all things whatsoever I would that men should do to me, I should do even so to them. It teaches me, further, to remember them that are in bonds as bound with them. I endeavored to act up to the instruction. I say I am yet too young to understand that God is any respecter of persons. I believe that to have interfered as I have done, as I have always freely admitted I have done, in behalf of his despised poor, I did not wrong but right. Now, if it is deemed necessary that I should forfeit my life for the furtherance of the ends of justice, and mingle my blood further with the blood of my children and with the blood of millions in this slave country whose rights are disregarded by wicked, cruel, and unjust enactments, I say let it be done.

Let me say one word further. I feel entirely satisfied with the treatment I have received on my trial. Considering all the circumstances, it has been more generous than I expected. But I feel no consciousness of guilt. I have stated from the first what was my intention, and what was not. I never had any design against the liberty of any person, nor any disposition to commit treason or incite slaves to rebel or make any general insurrection. I never encouraged any man to do so, but always discouraged any idea of that kind.

Let me say, also, in regard to the statements made by some of those who were connected with me, I hear it has been stated by some of them that I have induced them to join me. But the contrary is true. I do not say this to injure them, but as regretting their weakness. Not one but joined me of his own accord, and the greater part at his own expense. A number of them I never saw, and never had a word of conversation with, till the day they came to me, and that was for the purpose I have stated.

Now I have done.

16

His Terrible Swift Sword— the Civil War

Southerners eventually reached the point that they could no longer endure what seemed to many a betrayal of their rights, as well as political compromises that had been accepted in order to secure the adoption of the Constitution. The Constitution had specifically secured and protected substantial state's rights. It had accepted the institution of slavery, though never mentioning it specifically. By 1860, however, a new political and cultural majority sought to use their rights and their liberties to change and alter the system and those original political compromises. Therefore, southern states sought to exercise the ultimate state's right. The states had assembled to create the Union in the first place; it should be possible for states to subsequently unmake the Union and create a different association and combination of states should they so desire.

President Lincoln had a different interpretation. Once created, the Union was a living organism that could not be uncreated by any of its constituent parts without causing the death of the Union and the American democratic experiment. From the perspective of both southerners and Lincoln himself, those days in April 1861 were the days during which decisions were made, large and small, that set the nation on the course toward its worst and most painful conflict, the American Civil War.

Men had to be recruited to wage the battles. Both sides had to assemble armies and devise strategies for attacks and defenses that might secure the goals and objectives of the war. Caught in the middle were slaves, who quickly understood the possible, practical implications of the appearance of Union armies. The Union forces might indeed mean their liberation and freedom, and, acting upon that, they flocked to the Union lines. General Grant found the presence of slaves seeking freedom to be a logistical problem that threatened to interfere with his ability to prosecute the war and to defeat southern armies.

President Lincoln came to realize that the war was having a devastating effect on thousands of lives and families. People were sacrificing their lives, their liberties, and their happiness in the struggle to determine the future of the American nation. Lincoln came to realize that one function of his leadership was to give the American people reasons and justifications for their sacrifices and to suggest that those sacrifices would be applied to the creation of yet a better America and future. In building patriotism to causes greater than the base desires of individuals, songs like The Battle Hymn of the Republic *played a role by suggesting the proper alignment between American spirit and aspirations and divine justice.*

Robert E. Lee eventually reached the conclusion that further resistance was futile, and continuing the struggle would represent an unacceptable abuse of the faith and loyalty of southerners. Accordingly, he issued the surrender order to his command and basically brought the war to a close. Certain inconsistencies and dilemmas in the American political, cultural, and even economic equations had been sorted out and solved by the Union victory. As General Lee released the men under his command so that they could return to their homes, he set them, and to some degree the entire nation, back on a path for seeking and securing life, liberty, and happiness.

DOCUMENT 16.1

Declaration of Causes

In the momentous step which our State has taken of dissolving its connection with the government of which we so long formed a part, it is but just that we should declare the prominent reasons which have induced our course.

Our position is thoroughly identified with the institution of slavery—the greatest material interest of the world. Its labor supplies the product which constitutes by far the largest and most important portions of commerce of the earth. These products are peculiar to the climate verging on the tropical regions, and by an imperious law of nature, none but the black race can bear exposure to the tropical sun. These products have become necessities of the world, and a blow at slavery is a blow at commerce and civilization. That blow has been long aimed at the institution, and was at the point of reaching its consummation. There was no choice left us but submission to the mandates of abolition, or a dissolution of the Union, whose principles had been subverted to work out our ruin.

That we do not overstate the dangers to our institution, a reference to a few facts will sufficiently prove.

The hostility to this institution commenced before the adoption of the Constitution, and was manifested in the well-known Ordinance of 1787, in regard to the Northwestern Territory.

Source: From "A Declaration of the Immediate Causes Which Induce and Justify the Secession of the State of Mississippi from the Federal Union," copied by Justin Sanders from *Journal of the State Convention* (Jackson, MS: E. Barksdale, State Printer, 1861), pp. 86–88, at sunsite.utk.edu/civil-war/reasons.html.

The feeling increased, until, in 1819–20, it deprived the South of more than half the vast territory acquired from France.

The same hostility dismembered Texas and seized upon all the territory acquired from Mexico.

It has grown until it denies the right of property in slaves, and refuses protection to that right on the high seas, in the Territories, and wherever the government of the United States had jurisdiction.

It refuses the admission of new slave States into the Union, and seeks to extinguish it by confining it within its present limits, denying the power of expansion.

It tramples the original equality of the South under foot.

It has nullified the Fugitive Slave Law in almost every free State in the Union, and has utterly broken the compact which our fathers pledged their faith to maintain.

It advocates negro equality, socially and politically, and promotes insurrection and incendiarism in our midst.

It has enlisted its press, its pulpit and its schools against us, until the whole popular mind of the North is excited and inflamed with prejudice.

It has made combinations and formed associations to carry out its schemes of emancipation in the States and wherever else slavery exists.

It seeks not to elevate or to support the slave, but to destroy his present condition without providing a better.

It has invaded a State, and invested with the honors of martyrdom the wretch whose purpose was to apply flames to our dwellings, and the weapons of destruction to our lives.

It has broken every compact into which it has entered for our security.

It has given indubitable evidence of its design to ruin our agriculture, to prostrate our industrial pursuits and to destroy our social system.

It knows no relenting or hesitation in its purposes; it stops not in its march of aggression, and leaves us no room to hope for cessation or for pause.

It has recently obtained control of the Government, by the prosecution of its unhallowed schemes, and destroyed the last expectation of living together in friendship and brotherhood.

Utter subjugation awaits us in the Union, if we should consent longer to remain in it. It is not a matter of choice, but of necessity. We must either submit to degradation, and to the loss of property worth four billions of money, or we must secede from the Union framed by our fathers, to secure this as well as every other species of property. For far less cause than this, our fathers separated from the Crown of England.

Our decision is made. We follow their footsteps. We embrace the alternative of separation; and for the reasons here stated, we resolve to maintain our rights with the full consciousness of the justice of our course, and the undoubting belief of our ability to maintain it.

DOCUMENT 16.2

A Diary from Dixie

Mary Boykin Chesnut

March 5th. We stood on the balcony to see our Confederate flag go up. Roars of cannon, etc., etc. Miss Sanders complained (so said Captain Ingraham) of the deadness of the mob. "It was utterly spiritless," she said; "no cheering, or so little, and no enthusiasm." Captain Ingraham suggested that gentlemen "are apt to be quiet," and this was "a thoughtful crowd, the true mob element with us just now is hoeing corn." And yet! It is uncomfortable that the idea has gone abroad that we have no joy, no pride, in this thing. The band was playing "Massa in the cold, cold ground." Miss Tyler, daughter of the former President of the United States, ran up the flag.

Captain Ingraham pulled out of his pocket some verses sent to him by a Boston girl. They were well rhymed and amounted to this: she held a rope ready to hang him, though she shed tears when she remembered his heroic rescue of Koszta. Koszta, the rebel! She calls us rebels, too. So it depends upon whom one rebels against—whether to save or not shall be heroic.

* * *

April 12th. Anderson will not capitulate. Yesterday's was the merriest, maddest dinner we have had yet. Men were audaciously wise and witty. We had an unspoken foreboding that it was to be our last pleasant meeting. Mr. Miles dined with us to-day. Mrs. Henry King rushed in saying, "The news, I come for the latest news. All the men of the King family are on the Island," of which fact she seemed proud.

While she was here our peace negotiator, or envoy, came in—that is, Mr. Chesnut returned. His interview with Colonel Anderson had been deeply interesting, but Mr. Chesnut was not inclined to be communicative. He wanted his dinner. He felt for Anderson and had telegraphed to President Davis for instructions—what answer to give Anderson, etc. He has now gone back to Fort Sumter with additional instructions. When they were about to leave the wharf A. H. Boykin sprang into the boat in great excitement. He thought himself ill-used, with a likelihood of fighting and he to be left behind!

I do not pretend to go to sleep. How can I? If Anderson does not accept terms at four, the orders are, he shall be fired upon. I count four, St. Michael's bells chime out and I begin to hope. At half-past four the heavy booming of a cannon. I sprang out of bed, and on my knees prostrate I prayed as I never prayed before.

There was a sound of stir all over the house, pattering of feet in the corridors. All seemed hurrying one way. I put on my double-gown and a shawl and went, too. It was to the housetop. The shells were bursting. In the dark I heard a man say, "Waste of ammunition." I knew my husband was rowing about in a boat somewhere in that dark bay, and that the shells were roofing it over, bursting toward the fort. If Anderson was obstinate, Colonel Chesnut was to order the fort on one side to open fire. Certainly fire had begun. The regular roar of the cannon, there it was. And who could tell what each volley accomplished of death and destruction?

The women were wild there on the housetop. Prayers came from the women and imprecations from the men. And then a shell would light up the scene. To-night they say the forces are to attempt to land. We watched up there, and everybody wondered that Fort Sumter did not fire a shot. . . .

April 13th. Nobody has been hurt after all. How gay we were last night. Reaction after the dread of all the slaughter we thought those dreadful cannon were making. Not even a battery the worse for wear. Fort Sumter has been on fire. Anderson has not yet silenced any of our guns. So the aides, still with swords and red sashes by way of uniform, tell us. But the sound of those guns makes regular meals impossible. None of us go to table. Tea-trays pervade the corridors going everywhere. Some of the anxious hearts lie on their beds and moan in solitary misery. Mrs. Wigfall and I solace ourselves with tea in my room. These women have all a satisfying faith. "God is on our side," they say. When we are shut in Mrs. Wigfall and I ask "Why?" "Of course, He hates the Yankees, we are told. You'll think that well of Him."

Not by one word or look can we detect any change in the demeanor of these negro servants. Lawrence sits at our door, sleepy and respectful, and profoundly indifferent. So are they all, but they carry it too far. You could not tell that they even heard the awful roar going on in the bay, though it has been dinning in their ears night and day. People talk before them as if they were chairs and tables. They make no sign. Are they stolidly stupid? or wiser than we are; silent and strong, biding their time?

So tea and toast came; also came Colonel Manning, red sash and sword, to announce that he had been under fire, and didn't mind it. He said gaily: "It is one of those things a fellow never knows how he will come out until he has been tried. Now I know I am a worthy descendant of my old Irish hero of an ancestor, who held the British officer before him as a shield in the Revolution, and backed out of danger gracefully." We talked of St. Valentine's eve, or the maid of Perth, and the drop of the white doe's blood that sometimes spoiled all.

* * *

April 15th. I did not know that one could live such days of excitement. Some one called: "Come out! There is a crowd coming." A mob it was, indeed, but it was headed by Colonels Chesnut and Manning. The crowd was shouting and showing these two as messengers of good news. They were escorted to Beauregard's headquarters. Fort Sumter had surrendered! Those upon the housetops shouted to us "The fort is on fire." That had been the story once or twice before.

When we had calmed down, Colonel Chesnut, who had taken it all quietly enough, if anything more unruffled than usual in his serenity, told us how the surrender came about. Wigfall was with them on Morris Island when they saw the fire in the fort; he jumped in a little boat, and with his handkerchief as a white flag, rowed over. Wigfall went in through a porthole. When Colonel Chesnut arrived shortly after, and was received at the regular entrance, Colonel Anderson told him he had need to pick his way warily, for the place was all mined. As far as I can make out the fort surrendered to Wigfall. But it is all confusion. Our flag is flying there. Fire-engines have been sent for to put out the fire. Everybody tells you half of something and then rushes off to tell something else or to hear the last news.

DOCUMENT 16.3

Lincoln's Orders

Abraham Lincoln

May 26, 1862

To the Senate and House of Representatives:

The insurrection which is yet existing in the United States, and aims at the overthrow of the federal Constitution and the Union, was clandestinely prepared during the winter of 1860 and 1861, and assumed an open organization in the form of a treasonable provisional government at Montgomery, in Alabama, on the 18th day of February, 1861. On the 12th day of April, 1861, the insurgents committed the flagrant act of civil war by the bombardment and capture of Fort Sumter, which cut off the hope of immediate conciliation. Immediately afterwards all the roads and avenues to this city were obstructed, and the capital was put into the condition of a siege. The mails in every direction were stopped, and the lines of telegraph cut off by the insurgents, and military and naval forces, which had been called out by the government for the defence of Washington, were prevented from reaching the city by organized and combined treasonable resistance in the State of Maryland. There was no adequate and

Source: Excerpted from Abraham Lincoln, "To the Senate and House of Representatives," May 26, 1862, in *The Collected Works of Abraham Lincoln,* ed. Roy P. Basler (New Brunswick, NJ: Rutgers University Press, 1953), pp. 240–42.

effective organization for the public defence. Congress had indefinitely ad-journed. There was no time to convene them. It became necessary for me to choose whether, using only the existing means, agencies, and processes which Congress had provided, I should let the government fall at once into ruin, or whether, availing myself of the broader powers conferred by the Constitution in cases of insurrection, I would make an effort to save it with all its blessings for the present age and for posterity.

I thereupon summoned my constitutional advisers, the heads of all the departments, to meet on Sunday, the 20th [21st] day of April, 1861, at the office of the Navy Department, and then and there, with their unanimous concurrence, I directed that an armed revenue cutter should proceed to sea, to afford protection to the commercial marine. . . . I also directed the commandant of the navy yard at Boston to purchase or charter, and arm as quickly as possible, five steamships, for purposes of public defence. I directed the commandant of the navy yard at Philadelphia to purchase, or charter and arm, an equal number for the same purpose. I directed the commandant at New York to purchase, or charter and arm, an equal number. I directed Commander Gillis to purchase, or charter and arm, and put to sea two other vessels. Similar directions were given to Commodore DuPont, with a view to the opening of passages by water to and from the capital. . . .

On the same occasion I directed that Governor Morgan and Alexander Cummings, of the city of New York, should be authorized by the Secretary of War, Simon Cameron, to make all necessary arrangements for the transportation of troops and munitions of war, in aid and assistance of the officers of the army of the United States. . . .

On the same occasion I authorized and directed the Secretary of the Treasury to advance, without requiring security, two millions of dollars of public money to John A. Dix, George Opdyke, and Richard M. Blatchford, of New York, to be used by them in meeting such requisitions as should be directly consequent upon the military and naval measures necessary for the defence and support of the government, requiring them only to act without compensation, and to report their transactions when duly called upon.

The several departments of the government at that time contained so large a number of disloyal persons that it would have been impossible to provide safely, through official agents only, for the performance of the duties thus confided to citizens favorably known for their ability, loyalty, and patriotism.

The several orders issued upon these occurrences were transmitted by private messengers, who pursued a circuitous way to the seaboard cities, inland, across the States of Pennsylvania and Ohio and the northern lakes. I believe that by these and other similar measures taken in that crisis, some of which were without any authority of law, the government was saved from overthrow. I am not aware that a dollar of the public funds thus confided without authority of law to unofficial persons was either lost or wasted, although apprehensions of such misdirection occurred to me as objections to those extraordinary proceedings, and were necessarily overruled.

DOCUMENT 16.4

New Jersey Recruitment Poster

DOCUMENT 16.5

General Ulysses S. Grant to President Abraham Lincoln

June 11, 1863

Sir:

Enclosed herewith I send report of Chaplain J. Eaton, Gen. Supt. of Contraband for this Department, embracing a very complete history of what has been done for, and with, this class of people within my command to the present time.

Source: "Wanted: Able-Bodied Recruits," poster (Trenton, NJ: State Gazette, Summer 1863), Civil War Posters collection, PR-055-3-46, New York Historical Society. Image available from American Memory, Library of Congress, memory.loc.gov, digital ID nhnycw/ac ac03046.
Source: From "From Ulysses S. Grant to Abraham Lincoln," June 11, 1863, American Memory, Library of Congress, memory.loc.gov/cgi-bin/query/r?ammem/mal:@field(DOCID+@lit(d23983900)).

Finding that negroes were coming into our lines in great numbers, and receiving kind or abusive treatment according to the peculiar views of the troops they first come in contact with, and not being able to give that personal attention to their care and use the matter demanded I determined to appoint a General Superintendent over the whole subject and give him such Assistants as the duties assigned him might require. Mr. Eaton was selected for this position. I have given him such Aid as was in my power by the publication from time to time of such orders as seemed to be required, and generally at the suggestion of the Supt.

Mr. Eatons labors in his undertaking have been unremitting and skillful and I fear in many instances very trying. That he has been of very great service to the blacks in having them provided for when otherwise they would have been neglected, and to the Government in finding employment for the negro whereby he might earn what he was receiving, the accompanying report will show, and many hundreds of visiters [sic] and officers and soldiers near the different Camps can bear witness to.

I commend the report to your favorable notice and especially that portion of it which would suggest orders regulating the subject of providing for the government of the contraband subject which a Department Commander is not competant [sic] to issue.

I have the honor to be
Very respectfully
your obt. svt.

U. S. Grant
Maj. Gen. Vols.

DOCUMENT 16.6

The Battle Hymn of the Republic

Julia Ward Howe

Mine eyes have seen the glory of the coming of the Lord.
He is trampling out the vintage where the grapes of wrath are stored.
He has loosed the fateful lightening of His terrible swift sword.
His truth is marching on.

Glory! Glory! Hallelujah!
Glory! Glory! Hallelujah!
Glory! Glory! Hallelujah!
His truth is marching on.

I have seen Him in the watch-fires of a hundred circling camps.
They have builded Him an altar in the evening dews and damps.
I can read His righteous sentence by the dim and flaring lamps.
His day is marching on.

Glory! Glory! Hallelujah!
Glory! Glory! Hallelujah!
Glory! Glory! Hallelujah!
His truth is marching on.

I have read a fiery gospel writ in burnish'd rows of steel,
"As ye deal with my contemners, so with you my grace shall deal";
Let the Hero, born of woman, crush the serpent with his heel
Since God is marching on.

Glory! Glory! Hallelujah!
Glory! Glory! Hallelujah!
Glory! Glory! Hallelujah!
His truth is marching on.

He has sounded forth the trumpet that shall never call retreat.
He is sifting out the hearts of men before His judgment-seat.
Oh, be swift, my soul, to answer Him! be jubilant, my feet!
Our God is marching on.

Glory! Glory! Hallelujah!
Glory! Glory! Hallelujah!
Glory! Glory! Hallelujah!
His truth is marching on.

In the beauty of the lilies Christ was born across the sea,
With a glory in His bosom that transfigures you and me:
As He died to make men holy, let us die to make men free,
While God is marching on.

Glory! Glory! Hallelujah!
Glory! Glory! Hallelujah!
Glory! Glory! Hallelujah!
His truth is marching on.

DOCUMENT 16.7

Robert E. Lee, General Order, No. 9

Headquarters, Army of Northern Virginia
April 10, 1865

After four years of arduous service, marked by unsurpassed courage and fortitude, the Army of Northern Virginia has been compelled to yield to overwhelming numbers and resources.

I need not tell the brave survivors of so many hard fought battles, who have remained steadfast to the last, that I have consented to the result from no distrust of them.

Source: Robert E. Lee, "General Order No. 9, April 10, 1865, in *The Wartime Papers of R. E. Lee,* ed. Clifford Dowdey and Louis H. Martin (New York: Bramhall House, 1961), pp. 934–35.

But feeling that valor and devotion could accomplish nothing that would compensate for the loss that must have attended the continuance of the contest, I determined to avoid the useless sacrifice of those whose past services have endeared them to their countrymen.

By the terms of the agreement officers and men can return to their homes and remain until exchanged. You will take with you the satisfaction that proceeds from the consciousness of duty faithfully performed, and I earnestly pray that a Merciful God will extend to you His blessing and protection.

With an increasing admiration of your constancy and devotion to your country, and a grateful remembrance of your kind and generous considerations for myself, I bid you all an affectionate farewell.

R. E. LEE
Genl

17

Binding the Wounds

In the early days of the Civil War there were a few persons so confident of a Union victory they began to consider appropriate policies to deal with rebellious states and citizens. The preservation of life, liberty, and the pursuit of happiness for both the victorious and the vanquished and the entity known as the United States presented problematic issues.

The first document in this chapter suggests there were those inclined to be stern with the rebellious south. The selection from the "Southern Homestead Act" raises issues regarding the extension to the south of previously enacted and applied federal policies, the possible punishment of southern plantation owners, and opportunities for newly freed slaves to acquire land. African Americans received citizenship through the provisions of the 13th and 14th Amendments. It is important to understand that in the early days of the American Republic, Congress passed the first federal naturalization act (1790), which barred non-whites from American citizenship and relegated citizenship policies in general to the individual states. Hence, the 14th Amendment broke tradition in two ways—creating an American citizenship by federal law and central government activity as well as conferring citizenship on non-whites en masse.

Federal land policies had long been based on making relatively cheap land available to farmers as both a positive economic and social benefit. With few exceptions African Americans had been shackled to a tenuous dependent status and excluded from the process or the ability to become landowners. The relationship between land and independence had become so obvious, it was only natural that, in the aftermath of the Civil War, many could embrace the ability to acquire land and become independent farmers as the bridge by which Black Americans could join the American democratic experiment as equal partners. General Rufus Saxton had been assigned responsibilities by General Sherman to find ways of implanting freed slaves on southern soil to empower and sustain themselves as freemen. Could the experiment succeed or was it doomed to failure? Despite the smoothness of Henry W. Grady's

*views for a new southern society, an older south, with deep political, social,
and cultural roots, envisioned a less-than-equal partnership between the new
Southerner and African American citizens.*

DOCUMENT 17.1

What Is to Be Done with the South?

It seems to me in contemplating the past two years history, all the people of our
country north, south, east & west have been undergoing a Salutary Political
Schooling, learning lessons which might have been taught by the History of
other People; but we had all become so wise in our own conceit, that we would
only learn by actual experience of our own.

The people even of small & unimportant localities north as well as south,
had reasoned themselves into the belief that their opinions were superior to the
aggregated interest of the whole nation. Half our territorial nation rebelled on a
doctrine of secession that they themselves now scorn, and a real numerical majority actually believed, that a little state was endowed with such sovereignty,
that it could defeat the Policy of the Great Whole. I think the present war has ex-
ploded that notion, and were this war to cease now, the experience gained
though dear would be worth the expense.

Another Great & important natural Truth is still in contest and can only be
solved by War. Numerical majorities by vote is our Great Arbiter. Heretofore all
have submitted to it in questions left open, but numerical majorities are not necessarily physical majorities. The South though numerically inferior, contend
they can whip the Northern superiority of numbers, and therefore by natural
Law are not bound to submit. This issue is the only real one, and in my judge-
ment all else should be deferred to it. War alone can decide it, and it is the only
question left to us as a People.

Can we whip the South? If we can, our numerical majority has both the natural and constitutional right to govern. If we cannot whip them they contend
for the natural right to Select their own Government, and they have the argument. Our Armies must prevail over theirs, our officers, marshals and courts
must penetrate into the innermost recesses of their Land before we have the
natural right to demand their submission. I would banish all minor questions,
and assert the broad doctrine that as a nation the United States has the Right and
also the Physical Power to penetrate to every part of the National domain, and
that we will do it—that we will do it in our own time and in our own way, that
it makes no difference whether it be in one year, or two, or ten or twenty: that
we will remove & destroy every obstacle, if need be take every life, every acre
of land, every particle of property, every thing that to us seems proper, that we
will not cease till the end is attained, that all who do not aid are enemies, and

Source: Brooks D. Simpson and Jean V. Berlin, eds., *Sherman's Civil War: Selected Correspondence
of William T. Sherman, 1860–1865,* the University of North Carolina Press, Chapel Hill, 1999.

we will not account to them for our acts. If the People of the South oppose they do so at their peril, and if they stand by mere lookers on the domestic tragedy, they have no right to immunity, protection or share in the final Result.

I even believe and contend further, that in the North every member of the Nation is bound by both natural & constitutional Law to "maintain and defend the Government against all its opposers whomsoever." If they fail to do it, they are derelict, and can be punished, or deprived of all advantage arising from the labors of those who do—If any man north or south withholds his share of taxes, or physical assistance in this crisis of our History, he could and should be deprived of all voice in the future Elections of this country and might be banished or reduced to the condition of a Denizen of the Land.

War is upon us. None can deny it. It is not the act of the Government of the United States but of a Faction. The Government was forced to accept the issue or submit to a degradation fatal & disgraceful to all the Inhabitants. In accepting war it should be pure & simple as applied to the Belligerents. I would Keep it so, till all traces of war are effaced, till those who appealed to it are sick & tired of it, and come to the emblem of our Nation and Sue for Peace. I would not coax them, or even meet them halfway, but make them so sick of war that Generations would pass before they would again appeal to it.

I know what I say, when I repeat that the insurgents of the South sneer at all overtures looking to their interest. They Scorn the alliance with Copperheads: they tell me to my face that they respect Grant, McPherson and our brave associates who fight manfully & well for a principle, but despise the Copperheads & sneaks, who profess friendship for the South, and opposition to the War, as mere covers to their Knavery & poltroonery.

God knows that I deplored this fratricidal war as much as any man living, but it is upon us a physical fact; and there is only one honorable issue from it. We must fight it out, army against army, and man against man, and I know and you Know, and civilians begin to realize the fact, that reconciliation and reconstruction will be easier through and by means of strong, well equipped & organised armies than through any species of conventions that can be framed. The issues are made & all discussion is out of place and ridiculous.

The Section of 30 pounder Parrott Rifles now drilling before my tent is a more convincing argument than the largest Democratic or Union meeting the State of New York could assemble at Albany: and a simple order of the War Department to draft enough men to fill our Skeleton Regiments would be more convincing as to our national perpetuity, than an humble pardon to Jeff Davis and all his misled host.

The only Government now needed or deserved by the States of Louisiana, Arkansas and Mississipi now exists in Grants Army. It needs simply enough privates to fill its Ranks, all else will follow in due season. This army has its well defined code of Laws and Practice, and can adapt itself to the wants and necessities of a city, the country, the Rivers, the Sea, indeed to all parts of this Land. It better subserves the interest and Policy of the General Government and the People prefer it to any weak or servile combination, that would at once from force of habit revive & perpetuate local prejudices and passions. The People of this country have forfeited all Right to a voice in the Councils of the Nation. They Know it and feel it, and in after years they will be the better citizens from the dear bought experience of the present Crisis. Let them learn now, and learn it well that good citizens must obey as well as command. Obedience to law, absolute yea even abject is the lesson that this war under Providence will teach the Free & enlightened American Citizen. As a Nation we will be the better for it.

DOCUMENT 17.2

An Act Providing for Southern Homesteads

Be it enacted by the Senate and House of Representatives of the United States of America, in Congress assembled, That from and after the passage of this act all the public lands in the States of Alabama, Mississippi, Louisiana, Arkansas, and Florida shall be disposed of according to the stipulations of the homestead law of twentieth May, eighteen hundred and sixty-two, entitled "An act to secure homesteads to actual settlers on the public domain," and the act supplemental thereto, approved twenty-first of March, eighteen hundred and sixty-four, but with this restriction, that until the expiration of two years from and after the passage of this act, no entry shall be made for more than a half-quarter section, or eighty acres; and in lieu of the sum of ten dollars required to be paid by the second section of said act, there shall be paid the sum of five dollars at the time of the issue of each patent; and that the public lands in said States shall be disposed of in no other manner after the passage of this act: *Provided,* That no distinction or discrimination shall be made in the construction or execution of this act on account of race or color: *And provided further,* That no mineral lands shall be liable to entry and settlement under its provisions.

SEC. 2. *And be it further enacted,* That section second of the above-cited homestead law, entitled " An act to secure homesteads to actual settlers on the public domain," approved May twentieth, eighteen hundred and sixty-two, be so amended as to read as follows: That the person applying for the benefit of this act shall, upon application to the register of the land office in which he or she is about to make such entry, make affidavit before the said register or receiver that he or she is the head of a family, or is twenty-one years or more of age, or shall have performed service in the army or navy of the United States, and that such application is made for his or her exclusive use and benefit, and that said entry is made for the purpose of actual settlement and cultivation, and not either directly or indirectly for the use or benefit of any other person or persons whomsoever; and upon filing the said affidavit with the register or receiver, and on payment of five dollars, when the entry is of not more than eighty acres, he or she shall thereupon be permitted to enter the amount of land specified: *Provided,*

Source: The Southern Homestead Act, Thirty-ninth Congress, Session I, Ch 123, 124, 126, 127, 1866, [U. S. Statutes at Large] "An Act for the Disposal of the Public Lands for Homestead Actual Settlement in the States of Alabama, Mississippi, Louisiana, Arkansas, and Florida," pp. 66–67.

however, That no certificate shall be given, or patent issued therefor, until the expiration of five years from the date of such entry; and if, at the expiration of such entry, or at any time within two years thereafter, the person making such entry, or, if he be dead, his widow; or in case of her death, his heirs or devisee; or in case of a widow making such entry, her heirs or devisee, in case of her death, shall prove by two credible witnesses that he, she, or they have resided upon or cultivated the same for the term of five years immediately succeeding the time of filing the affidavit aforesaid, and shall make affidavit that no part of said land has been alienated, and that he will bear true allegiance to the government of the United States; then, in such case, he, she, or they, if at that time a citizen of the United States, shall be entitled to a patent, as in other cases provided by law: *And provided further,* That in case of the death of both father and mother, leaving an infant child or children under twenty-one years of age, the right and fee shall enure to the benefit of said infant child or children; and the executor, administrator, or guardian may, at any time within two years after the death of the surviving parent, and in accordance with the laws of the State in which such children, for the time being, have their domicile, sell said land for the benefit of said infants, but for no other purpose; and the purchaser shall acquire the absolute title by the purchase, and be entitled to a patent from the United States on the payment of the office fees and sum of money herein specified: *Provided,* That until the first day of January, eighteen hundred and sixty-seven, any person applying for the benefit of this act shall, in addition to the oath, hereinbefore required, also make oath that he has not borne arms against the United States, or given aid and comfort to its enemies.

SEC. 3. *And be it further enacted,* That all the provisions of the said homestead law, and the act amendatory thereof, approved March twenty-first, eighteen hundred and sixty-four, so far as the same may be applicable, except so far as the same are modified by the preceding sections of this act, are applied to and made part of this act as fully as if herein enacted and set forth.

APPROVED, June 21, 1866.

DOCUMENT 17.3

Amendment XIV

Section 1. All persons born or naturalized in the United States, and subject to the jurisdiction thereof, are citizens of the United States and of the state wherein they reside. No state shall make or enforce any law which shall abridge the privileges or immunities of citizens of the United States; nor shall any state deprive any person of life, liberty, or property, without due process of law; nor deny to any person within its jurisdiction the equal protection of the laws.

Section 2. Representatives shall be apportioned among the several states according to their respective numbers, counting the whole number of persons in each state, excluding Indians not taxed. But when the right to vote at any election for the choice of electors for President and Vice President of the United

States, Representatives in Congress, the executive and judicial officers of a state, or the members of the legislature thereof, is denied to any of the male inhabitants of such state, *being twenty-one years of age*, and citizens of the United States, or in any way abridged, except for participation in rebellion, or other crime, the basis of representation therein shall be reduced in the proportion which the number of such male citizens shall bear to the whole number of male citizens twenty-one years of age in such state.

Section 3. No person shall be a Senator or Representative in Congress, or elector of President and Vice President, or hold any office, civil or military, under the United States, or under any state, who, having previously taken an oath, as a member of Congress, or as an officer of the United States, or as a member of any state legislature, or as an executive or judicial officer of any state, to support the Constitution of the United States, shall have engaged in insurrection or rebellion against the same, or given aid or comfort to the enemies thereof. But Congress may by a vote of two-thirds of each House, remove such disability.

Section 4. The validity of the public debt of the United States, authorized by law, including debts incurred for payment of pensions and bounties for services in suppressing insurrection or rebellion, shall not be questioned. But neither the United States nor any state shall assume or pay any debt or obligation incurred in aid of insurrection or rebellion against the United States, or any claim for the loss or emancipation of any slave; but all such debts, obligations and claims shall be held illegal and void.

Section 5. The Congress shall have power to enforce, by appropriate legislation, the provisions of this article.

DOCUMENT 17.4

Rufus Saxton, Testimony Before Congress, 1866

[Question] What is [the freedmen's] disposition in regard to purchasing land, and what is the disposition of the landowners in reference to selling land to Negroes?

[Answer] The object which the freedman has most at heart is the purchase of land. They all desire to get small homesteads and to locate themselves upon them, and there is scarcely any sacrifice too great for them to make to accomplish this object. I believe it is the policy of the majority of the farm owners to prevent Negroes from becoming landholders. They desire to keep the Negroes landless, and as nearly in a condition of slavery as it is possible for them to do. I think that the former slaveholders know really less about the freedmen than any other class of people. The system of slavery has been one of concealment on the part of the Negro of all his feelings and impulses; and that feeling of concealment is so ingrained with the very constitution of the Negro that he

Source: Testimony of Rufus Saxton, *Report of the Joint Committee on Reconstruction* (Washington, 1866). Found at: http://vi.uh.edu/pages/mintz/41.htm.

deceives his former master on almost every point. The freedman has no faith in his former master, nor has his former owner any faith in the capacity of the freedman. A mutual distrust exists between them. But the freedman is ready and willing to contract to work for any northern man. One man from the North, a man of capital, who employed large numbers of freedmen, and paid them regularly, told me, as others have, that he desired no better laborers; that he considered them fully as easy to manage as Irish laborers. That was my own experience in employing several thousands of them in cultivating the soil. I have also had considerable experience in employing white labor, having, as quartermaster, frequently had large numbers of laborers under my control.

[Question] If the Negro is put in possession of all his rights as a man, do you apprehend any danger of insurrection among them?

[Answer] I do not; and I think that is the only thing which will prevent difficulty. I think if the Negro is put in possession of all his rights as a citizen and as a man, he will be peaceful, orderly, and self-sustaining as any other man or class of men, and that he will rapidly advance. . . .

[Question] It has been suggested that, if the Negro is allowed to vote, he will be likely to vote on the side of his former master, and be inveigled in the support of a policy hostile to the government of the United States; do you share in that apprehension?

[Answer] I have positive information from Negroes, from the most intelligent freedmen in those States, those who are leaders among them, that they are thoroughly loyal, and know their friends, and they will never be found voting on the side of oppression. . . . I think it vital to the safety and prosperity of the two races in the south that the Negro should immediately be put in possession of all his rights as a man; and that the word "color" should be left out of all laws, constitutions, and regulations for the people; I think it vital to the safety of the Union that this should be done.

DOCUMENT 17.5

Henry W. Grady, His Life, Writings, and Speeches

What shall the South do to be saved? Through what paths shall she reach the end? Through what travail, or what splendors, shall she give to the Union this section, its wealth garnered, its resources utilized, and its rehabilitation complete—and restore to the world this problem solved in such justice as the finite mind can measure, or finite hands administer?

In dealing with this I shall dwell on two points.

First, the duty of the South in its relation to the race problem.

Second, the duty of the South in relation to its no less unique and important industrial problem.

Source: Joel Chandler Harris, *Life of Henry W. Grady Including his Writings and Speeches, Memorial Volume,* New York: Cassell Publishing Company, 1890.

What of the negro? This of him. I want no better friend than the black boy who was raised by my side, and who is now trudging patiently with downcast eyes and shambling figure through his lowly way in life. I want no sweeter music than the crooning of my old "mammy," now dead and gone to rest, as I heard it when she held me in her loving arms, and bending her old black face above me stole the cares from my brain, and led me smiling into sleep. I want no truer soul than that which moved the trusty slave, who for four years while my father fought with the armies that barred his freedom, slept every night at my mother's chamber door, holding her and her children as safe as if her husband stood guard, and ready to lay down his humble life on her threshold. History has no parallel to the faith kept by the negro in the South during the war. Often five hundred negroes to a single white man, and yet through these dusky throngs the women and children walked in safety, and the unprotected homes rested in peace. Unmarshaled, the black battalions moved patiently to the fields in the morning to feed the armies their idleness would have starved, and at night gathered anxiously at the big house to "hear the news from marster," though conscious that his victory made their chains enduring. Everywhere humble and kindly; the bodyguard of the helpless; the rough companion of the little ones; the observant friend; the silent sentry in his lowly cabin; the shrewd counselor. And when the dead came home, a mourner at the open grave. A thousand torches would have disbanded every Southern army, but not one was lighted. When the master going to a war in which slavery was involved said to his slave, "I leave my home and loved ones in your charge," the tenderness between man and master stood disclosed. And when the slave held that charge sacred through storm and temptation, he gave new meaning to faith and loyalty. I rejoice that when freedom came to him after years of waiting, it was all the sweeter because the black hands from which the shackles fell were stainless of a single crime against the helpless ones confided to his care.

My countrymen, right here the South must make a decision on which very much depends. Many wise men hold that the white vote of the South should divide, the color line be beaten down, and the southern States ranged on economic or moral questions as interest or belief demands. I am compelled, to dissent from this view. The worst thing in my opinion that could happen is that the white people of the South should stand in opposing factions, with the vast mass of ignorant or purchasable negro votes between. Consider such a status. If the negroes were skillfully led,—and leaders would not be lacking,—it would give them the balance of power—a thing not to be considered. If their vote was not compacted, it would invite the debauching bid of factions, and drift surely to that which was the most corrupt and cunning. With the shiftless habit and irresolution of slavery days still possessing him, the negro voter will not in this generation, adrift from war issues, become a steadfast partisan through conscience or conviction. In every community there are colored men who redeem their race from this reproach, and who vote under reason. Perhaps, in time the bulk of this race may thus adjust itself. But, through what long and monstrous periods of political debauchery this status would be reached, no tongue can tell.

The clear and unmistakable domination of the white race, dominating not through violence, not through party alliance, but through the integrity of its own vote and the largeness of its sympathy and justice through which it shall compel the support of the better classes of the colored race,—that is the hope and assurance of the South. Otherwise, the negro would be bandied from one faction to another. His credulity would be played upon, his cupidity tempted, his impulses misdirected, his passions inflamed. He would be forever in alliance with that faction which was most desperate and unscrupulous. Such a state would be worse than reconstruction, for then intelligence was banded, and its speedy triumph assured. But with intelligence and property divided—bidding and overbidding for place and patronage—irritation increasing with each conflict—the bitterness and desperation seizing every heart—political debauchery deepening, as each faction staked its all in the miserable game—there would be no end to this, until our suffrage was hopelessly sullied, our people forever divided, and our most sacred rights surrendered.

This problem is not only enduring, but it is widening. The exclusion of the Chinese is the first step in the revolution that shall save liberty and law and religion to this land, and in peace and order, not enforced on the gallows or at the bayonet's end, but proceeding from the heart of an harmonious people, shall secure in the enjoyment of these rights, and the control of this republic, the homogeneous people that established and has maintained it. The next step will be taken when some brave statesman, looking Demagogy in the face, shall move to call to the stranger at our gates, "Who comes here?" admitting every man who seeks a home, or honors our institutions, and whose habit and blood will run with the native current; but excluding, all who seek to plant anarchy or to establish alien men or measures on our soil; and will then demand that the standard of our citizenship be lifted and the right of acquiring our suffrage be abridged. When that day comes, and God speed its coming, the position of the South will be fully understood, and everywhere approved. Until then, let us— giving the negro every right, civil and political, measured in that fullness the strong should always accord the weak—holding him in closer friendship and sympathy than he is held by those who would crucify us for his sake—realizing that on his prosperity ours depends—let us resolve that never by external pressure, or internal division, shall he establish domination, directly or indirectly, over that race that everywhere has maintained its supremacy. Let this resolution be cast on the lines of equity and justice. Let it be the pledge of honest, safe and impartial administration, and we shall command the support of the colored race itself, more dependent than any other on the bounty and protection of government. Let us be wise and patient, and we shall secure through its acquiescence what otherwise we should win through conflict, and hold in insecurity.

All this is no unkindness to the negro—but rather that he may be led in equal rights and in peace to his uttermost good. Not in sectionalism—for my heart beats true to the Union, to the glory of which your life and heart is pledged. Not in disregard of the world's opinion—for to render back this problem in the world's approval is the sum of my ambition, and the height of human achievement. Not in reactionary spirit—but rather to make clear that new and grander way up which the South is marching to higher destiny, and on which I would not halt her for all the spoils that have been gathered unto parties since Catiline conspired, and Caesar fought. Not in passion, my countrymen, but in reason—not in narrowness, but in breadth—that we may solve this problem in calmness and in truth, and lifting its shadows let perpetual sunshine pour down on two races, walking together in peace and contentment. Then shall this problem have proved our blessing, and the race that threatened our ruin work our salvation as it fills our fields with the best peasantry the world has ever seen. Then the South—putting behind her all the achievements of her past—and in war and in peace they beggar eulogy—may stand upright among the nations and challenge the judgment of man and the approval of God, in having worked out in their sympathy, and in His guidance, this last and surpassing miracle of human government.

The South, under the rapid diversification of crops and diversification of industries, is thrilling with new life. As this new prosperity comes to us, it will bring no sweeter thought to me, and to you, my countrymen, I am sure, than that it adds not only to the comfort and happiness of our neighbors, but that it makes broader the glory and deeper the majesty, and more enduring the strength, of the Union which reigns supreme in our hearts. In this republic of ours is lodged the hope of free government on earth. Here God has rested the ark of his covenant with the sons of men. Let us—once estranged and thereby closer bound,—let us soar above all provincial pride and find our deeper inspirations in gathering the fullest sheaves into the harvest and standing the staunchest and most devoted of its sons as it lights the path and makes clear the way through which all the people of this earth shall come in God's appointed time.

The world is a battle-field strewn with the wrecks of government and institutions, of theories and of faiths that have gone down in the ravage of years. On this field lies the South, sown with her problems. Upon the field swings the lanterns of God. Amid the carnage walks the Great Physician. Over the South he bends. "If ye but live until to-morrow's sundown ye shall endure, my countrymen." Let us for her sake turn our faces to the east and watch as the soldier watched for the coming sun. Let us staunch her wounds and hold steadfast. The sun mounts the skies. As it descends to us, minister to her and stand constant at her side for the sake of our children, and of generations unborn that shall suffer if she fails. And when the sun has gone down and the day of her probation has ended, and the stars have rallied her heart, the lanterns shall be swung over the field and the Great Physician shall lead her up, from trouble into content, from suffering into peace, from death to life. Let every man here pledge himself in this high and ardent hour, as I pledge myself and the boy that shall follow me; every man himself and his son, hand to hand and heart to heart, that in death and earnest loyalty, in patient painstaking and care, he shall watch her interest, advance her fortune, defend her fame and guard her honor as long as life shall last. Every man in the sound of my voice, under the deeper consecration he offers to the Union, will, consecrate himself to the South. Have no ambition but to be first at her feet and last at her service. No hope but, after a long life of devotion, to sink to sleep in her bosom, and as a little child sleeps at his mother's breast and rests untroubled in the light of her smile.

With such consecrated service, what could we not accomplish; what riches we should gather for her; what glory and prosperity we should render to the Union; what blessings we should gather unto the universal harvest of humanity. As I think of it, a vision of surpassing beauty unfolds to my eyes. I see a South, the home of fifty millions of people, who rise up every day to call from blessed cities, vast hives of industry and of thrift; her country-sides the treasures from which their resources are drawn; her streams vocal with whirring spindles; her valleys tranquil in the white and gold of the harvest; her mountains showering down the music of bells, as her slow-moving flocks and herds go forth from their folds; her rulers honest and her people loving, and her homes happy and their hearthstones bright, and their waters still, and their pastures green, and her conscience clear; her wealth diffused and poor-houses empty, her churches earnest and all creeds lost in the gospel. Peace and sobriety walking hand in hand through her borders; honor in her homes; uprightness in her midst; plenty in her fields; straight and simple faith in the hearts of her sons and daughters; her two races walking together in peace and contentment; sunshine everywhere and all the time, and night falling on her generally as from the wings of the unseen dove.

DOCUMENT 17.6

Testimony of Benjamin Singleton

Washington, D. C., April 17, 1880 before the Senate Select Committee Investigating the "Negro Exodus from the Southern States"

Q. You have brought out 7,432 people from the South to Kansas?
A. Yes, sir; brought and sent.

* * *

Q. Yes; What was the cause of your going out, and in the first place how did you happen to go there, or to send these people there?
A. Well, my people, for the want of land—we needed land for our children— and their disadvantages—that caused my heart to grieve and sorrow; pity for my race, sir, that was coming down, instead of going up—that caused me to go to work for them. I sent out there perhaps in '66—perhaps so; or in '65, any way—my memory don't recollect which; and they brought back tolerable favorable reports; then I jacked up three or four hundred, and went into Southern Kansas, and found it was a good country, and I thought Southern Kansas was

Source: Found at http://kck.kancrn.org/immigration/single.htm.

congenial to our nature, sir; and I formed a colony there, and bought about a thousand acres of ground—the colony did—my people.

* * *

Q. Tell us how these people are getting on in Kansas?
A. I am glad to tell you, sir.
Q. Have they any property now?
A. Yes; I have carried some people in there that when they got there they didn't have fifty cents left, and now they have got in my colony—Singleton colony—a house, nice cabins, their milch cows, and pigs, and sheep, perhaps a span of horses, and trees before their yards, and some three or four or ten acres broken up, and all of them has got little houses that I carried there. They didn't go under no relief assistance; they went on their own resources; and when they went in there first the country was not overrun with them; you see they could get good wages; the country was not overstocked with people; they went to work, and I never helped them as soon as I put them on the land.

* * *

There is good white men in the Southern country, but it ain't the minority (majority); they can't do nothing; the bulldozers has got possession of the country, and they have got to go in there and stop them; if they don't the last colored man will leave them. I see colored men testifying to a positive lie, for they told me out there all their interests were in Louisiana and Mississippi. Said I, "You are right to protect your own country," and they would tell me, "I am obliged to do what I am doing." Of course I have done the same, but I am clear footed.
Q. Now you say that during these years you have been getting up this colony you have spent, yourself, some six hundred dollars in circulars, and in sending them out; where did you send them, Mr. Singleton?
A. Into Mississippi, Alabama, South Carolina, Georgia, Kentucky, Virginia, North Carolina, Texas, Tennessee, and all those countries.

* * *

Q. And you attribute this movement to the information you gave in your circulars?
A. Yes, sir; I am the whole cause of the Kansas immigration!
Q. You take all that responsibility on yourself?
A. I do, and I can prove it; and I think I have done a good deal of good, and I feel relieved!
Q. You are proud of your work?
A. Yes, sir; I am! (Uttered emphatically.)